Roddy Martine lives in Edinburgh and covering subjects ranging from Scottisl to the history of the Edinburgh Military *Scotland* magazine, and is editor of *The Keeper,* the house magazine of the Keepers of the Quaich, the exclusive international society formed within the Scotch Whisky industry. In addition, he contributes to a wide range of magazines and newspapers throughout the United Kingdom.

Published by

Librario Publishing Ltd.

ISBN: 1-904440-57-6

Copies can be ordered via the Internet
www.librario.com

or from:

Brough House, Milton Brodie, Kinloss
Moray IV36 2UA
Tel/Fax No 00 44 (0)1343 850 617

Printed and bound by
DigiSource GB Ltd, Livingston

SCORPION ON THE CEILING

A Scottish colonial family's adventures
in South East Asia

RODDY MARTINE

With best wishes

Roddy Martine

2005.

Librario

In Memory of Charles and Pat

Contents

Acknowledgements

The author would like to thank the following for their invaluable help and encouragement:

R. M. Arblaster, Dr Bernice Archer, John Baxter, John Beaton, Gerald Chan of the Sarawak Turf Club, Gillian Compton, Alison Edgley, Donald Fergusson, Sir Ewen Fergusson, Virginia Fitzwilliams, Vincent H. K. Foo, Stephen Freeth of The Guildhall Library, Simon Goh of the Changi Museum, John Hembry, Jenny Hjul, Hock Aun Teh, Heather Holden Brown, Margaret Hopkins, Pat Howgill, Brian Kitching, Lucy McCann of the Bodleian Libary of Commonwealth & African Studies at Rhodes House, Dorothy McLellan, Neil McLellan, Stuart Macleod, Patricia Martine, the National Library of Scotland, Jeremy C. G. Ramsay, Derek Robinson, Harold N. Smyth, Jenny Spurway, Dr Nigel Stanley, Rod Suddaby of the Imperial War Museum, Susan Sym, Lord Tanlaw, Commander Michael Wall, Jennifer Watson of the University of Ohio, Alan J. Wood.

The author would especially like to thank Miranda Grant and the Grant Family, Mary Wilkinson and the Hannay Family (Kirsty Johns and Patricia Percival) for permission to quote extracts from family letters, and the papers of Edward Campbell Hannay (for which Kirsty Johns and Patricia Percival hold the copyright).

The author is grateful to A. J. Stewart for generously contributing her editing skills, and to John Caithness for so meticulously overseeing the style and accuracy of the finished product.

Scorpion on the Ceiling follows the lives of a European civilian family caught up in the collapse of British colonial rule in South East Asia. The storyline focuses on the author's parents, Charles and Pat Martine, his two elder sisters Virginia and Patricia, his cousins, the Hannay Family, and on the friendships that his family formed in Singapore, Penang, mainland Malaya, Sarawak and Australia.

Key Characters

Charles and Pat Martine – the author's parents.

Virginia and Patricia Martine – daughters of Charles and Pat.

Harry Hannay Snr – mining consultant based in Ipoh, married to Charles's Aunt Kate.

Kate Hannay – younger sister of Charles's mother, Dora Martine.

Ted, Harry Jnr, and Mary Hannay – Charles's cousins; children of Harry and Kate Hannay.

Boris Hembry – rubber planter at Ipoh, mainland Malaya.

Jean Hembry – wife of Boris and life-long friend of Pat Martine.

Neville G. ('Red') Reddish – manager of Borneo Motors, initially based in Ipoh and Penang.

W. 'Joe' Penrice – manager of Mansfield & Co, Singapore.

(Sir) John Bagnall – chairman of the Straits Trading Company, Singapore; brother of Bobbie Fergusson (below).

(Sir) Ewen ('Fergie') and Winifred ('Bobbie') Fergusson – sister and brother-in-law of John Bagnall.

Archibald 'Mac' McLellan – manager of Mansfield & Co in Penang.

Dorothy McLellan – wife of 'Mac' and Pat's friend in Penang.

Kilner Black – Manager of the Sarawak Steamship Company in Kuching, Sarawak.

Joan Black – wife of Kilner.

Sir Charles Vyner Brooke – 3rd Rajah of Sarawak.

Gerard MacBryan – volatile sometime Secretary to Sir Charles Vyner Brooke.

Kenneth Simpson – colleague of Charles in the Borneo Company Ltd. Charles's best man and the author's godfather.

John Augustus Grant – colleague of Charles in the Borneo Company Ltd, Singapore.

Ong Tiang Swee – Teochiew Kapitan China, based in Kuching, Sarawak.

Temenggong Koh (Penghulu) – Paramount Iban Chief.

Wee Kheng Chiang (Dato) – Ong Tian Swee's son-in-law and close friend of Charles.

John Stuart Wink ('Winky') – Assistant Commissioner in the Sarawak Constabulary.

Introduction

EVERY Thursday they met for lunch in Edinburgh. All were born and brought up in this austere northern city, the Capital of Scotland, and yet, returning in the twilight of their lives, found little in common with the companions of their youth, smug in careers of law, finance and academia. There were those, indeed, who had never known another country and never wished to.

So the old men sought solace in each other's company: the army doctor from the Sudan, the colonial administrator with no longer a colony to administer, the one-time Chindit colonel, the High Court judge from Kuala Lumpur, and my father.

Then, as the years hurried past, the group grew smaller until, one day, it was no more.

Shortly before my mother died, ten years after my father, she turned to me and asked, 'Did we do the right thing? Bringing you home to Scotland?'

Only then did it strike me how hard it must have been for them. There had been other options – Australia and England, for a start. But as was the case with so many of their Eastern counterparts, the big colonial adventure was over. It was time for them to return to their roots.

How easily taken for granted was the priority they shared, which was to provide their children, notably myself, with a background and a sense of belonging to somewhere. And in doing so, how disappointingly small did their own world become.

Yet I was never conscious of this up until that moment. Small towns are ruthlessly unforgiving of sons and daughters who depart then choose to return. Little common ground was to be found with old acquaintances, only the shared privilege of occupying the same grey town, with its bitter winters and soggy summers. Although undeniably beautiful, Edinburgh, at least during the 1960s, was a village trapped in its own perceived self-importance.

For my parents, returning to Scotland after a decade in England, the Far East seemed a lifetime away. But it would always be there for them, a lingering reflection, out-of-sight but never out of mind. They bought a house on the west side of the city and, like my father, uncles and cousins before me, I was sent to school at Edinburgh Academy, arriving there in the winter of 1961. I remember the freezing rain of that first winter; the driving wind that swept across the rooftops and spires of the city. In the years that followed, I came to embrace that rain, that wind, and those rooftops and spires, but I suspect – in fact, I know – that my parents did not.

They hibernated against the chill, finding it as relentless as the Malayan sun. In the frugal stubbornness of their generation, they shunned the extravagance of central heating and simply wore more clothes.

Those weekly lunches, tickets for rugby internationals at the Murrayfield Stadium, antiquarian excursions into the East Lothian countryside of his childhood, such diversions preoccupied my father's retirement. As for my mother, there was the family, and that was enough. There were holidays in France and Switzerland, but increasingly ill-health made her reclusive. Neither she nor my father showed much of an interest in gardening, but on every wedding anniversary – and they celebrated twenty-two of them in Edinburgh – a bouquet of specially imported spider orchids from Singapore would appear.

Occasionally we did discuss my writing this book, but only in the vaguest terms. For me, the little that I knew of their story then was simply too fascinating to be allowed to be lost. My mother, an intensely private individual, insisted that I should only dip into it after their deaths. There were too many demons to overcome.

And it would have been too intrusive to attempt to persuade her otherwise, although latterly my father, aware of the advance of mortality, did begin to make notes of a kind, tapping with two fingers on the keys of an ancient manual typewriter I had given him. Whether those notes were for me, or for someone else, I shall never know. Others came to interview him on the subject, but while prepared to open doors he remained largely silent on personal involvement. It was not his way. He disliked vainglory.

However, he had, by then, already written the official history of the trading enterprise to which he had dedicated the greater part of his life, but it was never intended for publication. Writing was not his forte, but it was important to him that a record be kept. I doubt he ever seriously believed that I would be the one to take it up where he left off.

Two decades later, it was a faded copy of the *Borneo Times* tucked away in an old folder and gathering dust in a filing cabinet that triggered my conscience. Up until that moment I had not known how or where to begin. Moreover, I had no idea how my sisters would react. My family's emotions surrounding the loss of our parents were too personal and mixed up to make sense.

The discovery of that magazine published in 1952 provided me with the impetus. The reason it had been kept was that it contained a tribute to my father written at the time of his departure from Sarawak.

It referred to his courage under adversity, to my mother's resilience, and rather too effusively applauded my father's contribution to the emergent nation state of Malaysia through Sarawak's Negri Council, as 'spokesman of the unofficial members, in some degree, of the people of the country.' My father, a modest man, would have shunned such words, but would not have been entirely unhappy that his participation was noted.

In the preface to his collected short stories, W. Somerset Maughan observed that the vast majority of the Europeans in Malaya during the 1920s and 1930s, government servants, planters and traders, were 'good, decent, normal people.'

Good, decent and normal. That was their tragedy. They were rather too good, too decent, too normal. Confronted by circumstances far beyond their control, ordinary people became extraordinary people.

In researching this book I have uncovered at least two of those people whom I thought I had known well – Charles and Pat Martine – my parents. Against the great backdrop of iconoclastic events which engulfed them, I am seeing them as if for the first time. In consideration of what they found themselves up against, and how their world was blown apart, it actually amazes me that they stayed together. Inevitably, and with some humility, it draws me to the conclusion that, put to the test, genuine love endures everything.

I was born in late December 1946 in a large colonial house overlooking a muddy river in Sarawak, land of the White Rajahs, Orang Utan and Dyak headhunters. By then the Japanese war was over, and Sarawak, in company with its host island Borneo, and the Far East as a whole, was facing an uncertain future. In 1952, the date of the copy of the *Borneo Times* in the folder, there was talk of 'politics in their infancy.' Sarawak, together with Sabah, formerly known as British North Borneo, had joined with the Malay Federation to form Malaysia.

In the recently formed Indonesia, President Sukarno opposed the move,

The *SS Amarapura* on which Charles Martine sailed from Liverpool via
Rangoon to Singapore in 1922
(*Martine Family Collection*)

and a guerilla war known as the Confrontation commenced, lasting until
1965. That same year, Singapore, in deference to its ethnic Chinese, the
island's largest population, and the Malays who dominated Malaysia's
Government, chose independence.

All of this was a world apart from the vivid colonial waterfront which
awaited my father when, the same age as the century, he stepped ashore
from the *SS Amarapura* when it berthed in Singapore's Keppel Harbour
in the early spring of 1922.

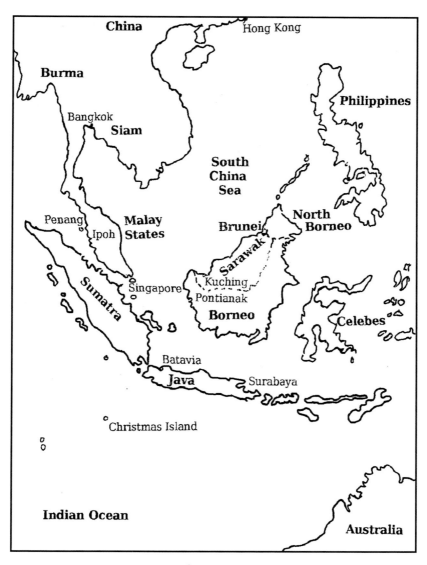

China

Hong Kong

Burma

Bangkok

Siam

South
China
Sea

Philippines

Penang

Ipoh

Malay
States

Brunei

North
Borneo

Sarawak

Sumatra

Singapore

Kuching

Pontianak

Borneo

Celebes

Batavia

Java

Surabaya

Christmas Island

Indian Ocean

Australia

Map of South East Asia

CHAPTER ONE

The Straits Settlement

He peered into the Chinese shops in Victoria Road where so many strange things were being sold. Bombay merchants, fat and exuberant, stood at their shop doors and sought to sell him silks and tinsel jewellery. He watched the Tamils, pensive and forlorn, who walked with a sinister grace, and the bearded Arabs, in white skullcaps, who bore themselves with scornful dignity. The sun shone upon the varied scene with a hard, acrid brilliance. He was confused. He thought it would take him years to find his bearings in this multicoloured and excessive world.

W. Somerset Maughan, *Neil MacAdam.*

FOR the young, male employees of UK trading and shipping interests, the Straits Settlement colony of Singapore in the early 20th century was the stepping-stone to a prosperity and lifestyle many of them would have found unimaginable back home.

My father had never been destined for a merchant trading career, but events have a way of orchestrating life. Born in Edinburgh on the Ides of March 1900, he was brought up in the East Lothian county town of Haddington and sent to school at Edinburgh Academy, where he lodged in town during the week with his widowed maternal grandmother and unmarried aunts. Indulging in the usual rituals of his background and generation, he played rugby with enthusiasm and gained a limited academic distinction. The second of three sons, with a younger sister, it was a comfortable, secure existence, mixing effortlessly in the social life of Scotland's Capital, a society in which it was more or less accepted that unless you were a professional in the fields of law, medicine or education, your future prospects were limited; unless there was a family business to join or land to nurture, you looked elsewhere.

As the First World War drew towards its climax, Charles was commissioned into the Guards Machine Gun Regiment and, on 1st July 1918, left for Wellington Barracks to enlist in the Scots Guards, thereafter joining the Guards Officer Cadet Battalion at Bushey in Hertfordshire. Shortly before Armistice was declared in November came the news that his elder brother Will, serving in France, was missing in action, believed dead.

For the Martine family, it was a devastating shock. There was a further implication. Coming from a dynasty of three generations belonging to an established Haddington medical practice, Will, having qualified in medicine prior to the war, had been named his father's successor. My father, being the second son, was immediately designated to replace him and, as soon as he was released from his regiment, dutifully enrolled to study medicine at Edinburgh University so as to be able to follow in his brother's footsteps. He was neither asked if he wanted to do so, nor did he question the decision. He knew that it was expected of him.

Fortunately, it proved a brief diversion. He had been a medical student for only a matter of months when Will miraculously emerged through the

Harbour view, Singapore

fog of war, thus removing the obligation. No longer was it necessary for him to pursue his medical studies, unless he was inclined.

He was not. Urged on by his father, who no longer needed a successor for his medical practice, he set his sights on other very distant horizons.

Moving to London towards the end of 1919, he was provided with a letter of introduction to the Borneo Company by his uncle's brother-in-law, a Liverpool shipping agent. For the two and a half years that followed, he worked out of offices in Fenchurch Street and shared a flat with Alec Macquisten, a friend from his school days in Edinburgh. Aged 22, he was posted to Singapore. It was the beginning of a great voyage of discovery.

* * *

On a windless, humid morning before the monsoon season, the sight awaiting the passengers as their ship glided past the many kelong, or fish traps, was of motionless Chinese junks and slim Malay boats. On the shore, low lying hills of lush green grass and tropical trees gave way to elegant residential mansions with clean cut lawns and flowering shrubberies, splashed with colour.

From a Malay village built out over the water, brown-skinned diving

(Martine Family Collection)

boys plunged and splashed perilously close to the prow of the boat, all the time calling out for coins until, suddenly ahead, the terracotta corrugated roofs of godowns and the Singapore Harbour Board wharf slid slowly into sight, shimmering in the heat.

On the quayside, an expectant crowd was assembled in a variety of tropical costume. Almost everybody sheltered under a topee, as did the ship's passengers who, having been told that such head wear was de rigueur to prevent the horrible effects of the sun on their heads, had made purchases from Simon Artz at Port Said.

When the liner berthed at the old P&O timber wharf, there was a ripple of excitement. First on board, once the immigration formalities were completed, came the company's agent, a peon, or office boy, with the mail, the man from Thomas Cook, and uniformed representatives from Raffles Hotel, the Adelphi Hotel, and the Sea View Hotel.

On average, it took a ship six weeks to reach Keppel Harbour from Tilbury. There were various options. Travellers could board a K Class P&O boat, not calling at Marseilles, or depart a week later on a train to Marseilles to join an N Class boat bound for Australia. They would then disembark at Colombo to join the K boat bound for Singapore.

The majority preferred to travel P&O, which carried numbers of up to 300 passengers. The wealthier among them booked cabins *Port Out – Starboard Home* since these remained cool throughout the journey both ways, and thus the word 'Posh' entered the English language.

Other options were the Blue Funnel Line from Liverpool, or the Glen Line (with red funnels) from London. Both companies had accommodation on their cargo ships for between eight and twenty passengers, the former with European crews, the latter with Asian. It was commonly observed that no matter how many passengers were on board, travelling P&O or Blue Funnel, they invariably ran out conversation before Suez. But at least it gave them the opportunity to become acclimatised between drizzly England and the relentless heat of the Indian Ocean.

Initially, it was the smells of the river and Kallang basin, of copra and the spices of the East, that saturated the senses. It was something my father said he would never forget as he was carried off into this exotic theatre, a world where the shopkeepers of Change Alley, the bazaar passageway of doorless shops which cut across the waterfront, spoke pidgin-English and French to welcome passers-by, or conversed with each other in Malay, Tamil and a variety of Chinese dialects.

In curious juxtaposition was Singapore's commercial centre, situated on adjacent Raffles Place, between Chinatown with its markets, temples, shops and dwellings, and the sea. Chinatown was once criss-crossed with a network of little canals which over the years had been filled in to make streets, five feet wide, to house the constant proliferation of pavement vendors, cobblers, letter writers, florists, locksmiths, sew-sew women, medicine men, barbers, and fortune-tellers.

Charles's arrival was a full year before the Ocean Building, the Singapore headquarters of W. Mansfield & Company,* was opened on Collyer Quay, marking the first breakaway from the business district's uniformly Victorian style of architecture. This was the first big building to go up after World War One and the rubber slump that followed it. Mansfield, founded in 1871 by Walter Mansfield, a ship-chandler, was a subsidiary of the Ocean Steamship Company managed by Alfred Holt & Co of

Charles Martine, 1925
(Martine Family Collection)

Liverpool. In tandem with the China Mutual Steam Navigation Company, it traded under the logo of the Blue Funnel Line.

Also in the Mansfield portfolio was a shareholding in the Straits Steamship Company which provided feeder ships, affectionately known as the Little White Fleet, or the 'Mosquito Boats,' delivering cargoes to the Dutch East Indies, North Borneo, Brunei and Sarawak. Prior to the First World War, services from Singapore to Borneo and Singapore to Bangkok had been German-run, but with the outbreak of hostilities the German ships were withdrawn, and the Straits Steamship Company received three ships from the Ocean Steamship Company in return for shares which gave its parent company, Mansfield, a third ownership of the Straits Steamship Company. In 1922, the Straits Steamship fleet had 24 vessels with a total tonnage of 25,446.[1]

---

* Mansfield's Ocean Building was a landmark for 50 years until it was demolished to make way for a new Ocean Building in 1971.

The Ocean Building on Collyer Quay, 1922
(Martine Family Collection)

Although the immediate First World War tin and rubber restriction schemes acted as a serious damper on trade, by the mid-1920s Singapore was annually exporting tin and rubber to the value of $350 million. Throughout the first four decades of the 20th century, the island population grew steadily to its pre-war peak of three quarters of a million. Today, well over a century later, it stands at 2.8 million, 76.4 per cent of which are ethnic Chinese, the remainder Malay and Indian.

The British Raj may now be only a distant memory, but in the second and third decades of 20th century Singapore, it dominated everything, creating a tableau of contrasts, extraordinary and exotic.

In the Singapore of 1922, while Chinese clerks and many Europeans continued to wear the high-necked white tunic uniform of the East India Company, there was everywhere an air of change and prosperity. There had begun an exciting commercial era.

And it was the great UK-financed trading enterprises which provided the life-blood of not just the Straits Settlement of Singapore, but of the surrounding region. The Shell Group had opened its first Singapore office on Collyer Quay in 1914. Concerns such as Boustead & Company, Mansfield & Company, Guthrie & Company, Dunlops, Harrison & Crossfield, William Jacks, McAlister & Company, Eastern Smelting, the Borneo Company, and the Straits Trading Company were jostling for their share of the action.

Working alongside these Far Eastern household names were three major banks: the Mercantile Bank, covering the east coast south from Kota Bahru, Malaya's most northerly port; the Chartered Bank of India, Australia and China, serving Kuala Lumpur, with branches in the main cities, and the Hong Kong & Shanghai Bank, mainly west coast covering Penang, Malacca, Sungi Plata, and Ipoh.

Furthermore, the tuans of Britain's most influential outpost on the trade routes of Asia, this tight-knit community of companies, largely dominated by Scots, formed a formidable unit, They all knew each other, and they worked and played together. In their heyday, the enterprises that they presided over provided the import/export fulcrum for every kind of commodity, from motor cars to Tiger Balm, from Rolex watches to Scotch whisky. Moreover, they formed an unexpectedly interdependent and co-operative community. Along the greater part of Collyer Quay, an outside veranda on the upper floor enabled access from one firm to another, except for the break at Change Alley. This was a throw-back to the days when the entire maritime trade of Singapore was conducted in the Roads and in the Singapore River, and British import and export houses kept long telescopes on their verandas to inspect incoming ships.

Across the way from the Hong Kong Bank corner of Collyer Quay stood the old General Post Office building housing the Singapore Club where 'tuan besars' cooled off of an evening to discuss the Colony's trade and politics over stengas (Scotch whisky with soda water). Towards the end of the 1920s, this moved into the newly built Fullerton Building. In the open space between the General Post Office and Battery Road were gharries for hire, their Boyanese syces waiting patiently in the shade of a cluster of dusty old trees.

On the streets, amid the gharries, was a constant stream of rickshaws, and 'mosquito' buses, old Model-T Fords, carrying the bulk of the travelling public. On the water, every two-seater sampan was propelled by oars, the sampan wallah facing forward, while every twakow was propelled by coolies who plunged long poles into the river mud and then ran back along the gunwale to repeat the process.*

My father, like every young man of his generation introduced to the Orient for the first time, was impressed by all of this. Everything was so very different from that to which he was accustomed, yet office working life in Singapore was ordered strictly on the patterns of England. The premises opened at 9am and stopped for tiffin between one and two. Unlike other eastern cities, there was no siesta time. Offices closed between five and six, which enabled employees to rush home to change clothes and set off to the various clubs to play cricket or tennis or rugby, or simply to drink. For the European community, it was a structured, well-ordered, well-mannered existence based on solid homeland values.

Each new arrival was branded a 'griffin' by the old guard, but in due course progressed towards becoming a 'tuan' on merit. Everything was fetched and carried for them; clothes were pressed, shoes polished, drinks served. My father felt as if he had been catapulted into an indulgent, promised land, where every demand was satisfied by simply shouting

---

* Another decade was to pass before the outboard motor took over.

'boy,' but that was the way it worked and everybody, European and Asian alike, took it for granted.

The disadvantages were the oppressive heat, the lack of air-conditioning, the monotony of jungle surrounds, the abundant insect life and, in particular, the prejudices and codes of conduct of disparate communities transplanted from a hundred environs to the static uniformity of this tropic colony.

The spacious accommodation made available to newcomers was not quite as wondrous as it at first appeared, although vastly different from Chinatown, where the inhabitants were often obliged to sleep ten to a room the size of a cupboard; for westerners there was no shortage of space, especially if they were signed up on a contract.

For Borneo Company employees there was a compound of several houses centred on Orange Grove Road, it being the practice of the more substantial companies to provide quarters for all of their employees. The senior men – managing directors, general managers and chief accountants – were allocated houses of their own. Unmarried staff shared a company-owned mess. There was little private ownership among the European merchant community; only the professional classes – lawyers, doctors and dentists – owned their own homes.

Although in the beginning, my father was quartered in the Borneo Company's Mess at No. 19, he soon found himself sharing quarters with two other young hopefuls, John McNeil, another Scot, and Kenneth Simpson from England. The two senior Borneo Company

Jimmy Kemp, Kenneth Simpson and John McNeil at Kroh in Perak
(Martine Family Collection)

houses were Belvedere and Neidpath, next door to each other, and both typical of European residences of that time.

Belvedere, the house in which Charles, John and Kenneth were quartered, was a large, rambling mansion set in substantial parkland.* Almost the entire ground level was one room, floored with old red Malacca tiles, and there was a high ceiling to keep it cool. There were no fans, but

Belvedere, Singapore, 1925

Indian punkahs, sheets of canvas hanging from the ceiling, swung overhead at meal-times. Like all similar households, it had a native staff of at least five or six.

On the floor above was another large room, employed as a lounge area, and off this were located the bedroom quarters, where each employee had his own flat. There were no fans, and at first it was hard to sleep under the mosquito nets at night. All of the houses had colonies of geckos or chickchacks, small opal lizards, which were encouraged to feed on the insect life. Traditionally, every bed featured a long bolster known as a 'Dutch Wife,' a comfort accessory which allowed air to circulate under the sheets. It was customary for a case of bottled water to be stored in every bedroom, the assumption being that it was not safe to drink Singapore water.

Refrigerators were not then widely available, although there were

---

* Today Belvedere is no more, and the site on which it was built is occupied by the Shangri-La Hotel.

iceboxes, and the cook brought back ice from the market on a daily basis. Every night, smudge sticks were placed on the floor during dinner to ward off mosquitos, and if a light was required in a bedroom for late-night reading, the sticks would be required here too.

Surrounding the houses were verandas, and there were big bamboo screens known as 'chicks' to let down when a 'sumatra' blew up from the

(Martine Family Collection)

sea. In the humid afternoons, the 'chicks' would be lowered and the gardeners would splash water onto them to cool the house inside.

To the rear was another veranda which accommodated the showers and toilet facilities. On the floor here were duck-boards made of teak which acted as an open drain. If anybody wanted a bath, they called for the tukanayer to bring buckets of hot water from the kitchen. In every room was a large earthenware Shanghai jar or 'Tong' for washing purposes, with dippers provided for hot and cold water.

One apocryphal tale has a portly guest at Raffles Hotel becoming stuck in the 'tong' because he thought that he could use it as a bathtub. His room boy was obliged to rescue him using a hammer.[2] It was also usual to wear Chinese wooden sandals in the bathroom to avoid the infection known as Singapore foot,* but everybody suffered from it sooner or later because

---

* Known as athlete's foot in the UK.

29

everybody sweated. Sweating was the reason why it became common practice for men attending formal dances to carry a bag containing six stiff white collars. During intervals in the dancing, it was customary to retire and put on a fresh one.

Wondrously, at least for those of the European community used to the confinements of English towns, there was no shortage of outdoor facilities. Some gardens featured large terraced compounds with tennis courts and often a mangosteen orchard. At night, the creaking sound of the cicadas was perpetual.

For the better-off colonials, Tanglin was considered the fashionable suburb, but the majority of Europeans preferred to live closer to town. Some business and professional men lived in Cavanagh Road, a quiet, pleasant suburban backwater only two miles from their offices. Here, the bungalows and compounds were large and well kept.

The recognised boarding-house district was on the other side of Orchard Road, where a European could live for as little as $90 a month, although most preferred to part with more for a somewhat higher standard of rental property. "I paid $150 a month out of my starting salary of $300, plus extras for room-boy and laundry," recalled one junior manager. "That did not leave much of a margin for other expenses, to say nothing of the bill I incurred for a dozen white suits at Wing Loong's in the High Street. I was always hard up."

Salaries for juniors were low, even if the standard of living, with household staff provided, was high by standards elsewhere. Only the senior individuals, and this included employees of the Malayan Civil Service, were able to accumulate significant savings.

Despite this, as one newcomer noted, the affordability, efficiency and speed of tailors was amazing. "I was taken to Wing Loong's shop at ten o'clock in the morning where I was measured for six pairs of shorts, six shirts and four white drill suits. We asked, 'When will they be ready?' and the man said, 'They can't be ready before two o'clock.'[3] In the afternoon, all of his clothes were ready for collection, and the tailor apologised for not having been able to send them to the dhobi." *

As late as 1935, certain formalities needed to be upheld before any newcomer was accepted into Singapore's disparate European community.

---

* Dhobi is the Indian word for "laundry."

First-time employees arriving off a boat from Europe were discreetly advised to have visiting cards printed if they wished to be invited to the houses of senior members of the firm that employed them. Such rituals were considered an important part of colonial life because, to its credit, the British community did go out of its way to look after its own. All of the more affluent European houses had a little card box at the entrance to the drive and a griffin was expected to drop a calling card into it before he could be formally summoned for a drink, or to dine.[4]

In commerce, and in local politics, Asians played their part with vigour and without prejudice. Representatives of the Asian communities were invited to official celebrations at Government House, but in their private and domestic lives kept to their own company. The two cultures – East and West – were different and did not mix socially. It was the way the majority on both sides preferred it, and any suggestion that the Chinese merchant or banker might have in any way been considered inferior to the European trader is simply not true. A good example of how the races worked together was the Straits Steamship Company. Managed by Mansfield & Co, there were a large number of local shareholders, and both Chinese and Malayan directors sat on its board.

Through associations with an array of Chinese and Malayan entrepreneurs, my father soon established a mutual respect which would endure, not least when relationships between East and West were at their lowest ebb during the Japanese occupation. That he took the trouble to learn Malay and Tamil, with a modest command of a couple of Chinese dialects, gave him not only access to the peoples of the Orient, but a profound sympathy towards them.

He soon discovered that the Malays were a gentle race whose interests were predominantly agrarian, when living in the interior, or maritime, when located on the coast. Of the Muslim faith, which had been introduced by Indian traders as far back as the 13th century, they were inclined to take the line of least resistance when challenged. Preferring the simple, village life, their inland houses were in the majority built on river banks with floors raised above the ground and surrounded by paddy-fields, allotments of sugar-cane, tapioca, and maize. Along the coastal waters, their fishing skills were unsurpassed, but again this was all part of their wider subsistence culture.

In contrast, it was the clever, hardworking, and predominantly urban based Chinese, who, with the assistance of the British, transformed Malaya. It may come as a surprise to discover that of the total population of the peninsula pre-war, only half were Malay, and of the Chinese inhabitants, only about a third had actually been born in Malaya. Yet it was the Chinese, professional men, money-lenders and shopkeepers, supported by a ubiquitous coolie population, who along with European rubber planters and tin miners, created Malaya's economic base.

In Singapore, it was Arabs, headed by the newspaper and property owning Hadhrami Family, who formed the wealthiest community. A few educated Indians from Ceylon*, clerks in government and commercial offices, formed another influential group, with Pathans and Sikhs found as policemen and watchmen. Tamil-speaking Indians from Madras, employed as labourers on the rubber estates, and in public works, completed the racial mix. Throughout all of this glittering diversity it was the Malay language that remained the lingua franca. All European newcomers were expected to master it within the first term of their contract.

One sociological anomaly in particular took some getting used to. With a marked absence of unmarried western women, it was inevitable that sexual tensions would sooner or later arise among the more hot-blooded of the European single men employed in the colony. A bachelor existence spent in an almost exclusively male society with the occasional invitation to dinner from a manager's wife was not unlike living in a single-sex English boarding school.

There were rarely more than a few dozen unmarried girls at one time in Singapore's early 20th century European community, and the majority of these had few illusions about the young men on a first company agreement. Some companies even went so far as to insert a clause forbidding those on their first five to six-year contract to marry. Not until the end of a second agreement, when employees were aged 26 or over were they considered capable of keeping a wife in the manner befitting a European.

In pre-1930 Singapore, however, a liaison between a European and a Malay or Chinese girl was not considered an option, with Malayan and Chinese families more often than not taking the stronger stance against

---

* Ceylon became the Republic of Sri Lanka in 1972.

it. A few Eurasian girls worked away from home in hospitals and offices, but young European men were, when it was thought necessary, politely warned to keep their distance.[5] It was not at all unknown for an employee to be packed off home on the next boat.*

Thus it became standard procedure for tuans to acquire their mems when on leave, or when the occasional European unattached girl turned up in Singapore to visit relatives. Not surprisingly, a lot of the European men married late in life. An equal number chose to remain celibate, whereas up-country it was common practice for native girls to move in with lonely, single bachelors. Sometimes cohabitation was even actively encouraged in order to learn the language.**

One fact in particular needs to be understood. Malaya was never conquered by the British. Their presence on the peninsula was by invitation and treaty. There was no occupying army. There never had been. The entirety of Malaya was ruled by a colonial police force answerable through the State Government to a colonial office in London and a Governor in Singapore. In their heyday, the Straits Settlements, the Federated Malay States Protectorate and the Unfederated Malay States made up one of the most successful multi-racial co-operatives that has ever been known.

Consequently, colonial Singapore had a great deal to offer everyone who found themselves there, whatever their race, but especially those Europeans who made the most of the Orient's cultural opportunities. There was luxury and full employment, although admittedly more profitable for some than for others. In addition, Singapore supported an active, healthy lifestyle in a climate that was never cold.

---

* In 1907, the writer and novelist Sir Robert Bruce Lockhart, working in Malaya as a young man, took a beautiful Amai as his mistress. He incurred such disapproval that he was immediately sent home to England.

** Asian girls who agreed to such liaisons were affectionately known as 'planters' dictionaries.'

CHAPTER TWO

The Borneo Company

I do not claim to understand the East; I merely scratched the surface for a few years. Only a person who has lived there all his life and knows the languages can hope to speak with authority, but even he must carry his studies further. To understand the Oriental you must be more than a fluent linguist, you must think as an Oriental.

R.C.H. McKie, *This Was Singapore.*

ON March 31st 1922, the Prince of Wales, later to become briefly King Edward VIII, arrived in Keppel Harbour on *HMS Renown.* His visit coincided with the Malaya-Borneo Exhibition, seen as an immensely important event planned to stimulate trade and bring the products of the two territories to world attention. The Prince struck a golden padlock and, having declared the exhibition open, toured it briefly.[1] With him was his cousin Lord Louis Mountbatten who, as Commander-in-Chief, South East Asia, was to return to Singapore twenty-three years later under very different circumstances.

Malay music and dance, agile fencing displays, and top-spinning demonstrations enthralled the visitors. Evening diversions ranged from Malay Shadow Puppetry and European plays to a torch-lit tattoo organised by the Chinese community. Hollywood films were screened, including Charlie Chaplin's *The Kid.*

When the gates closed on 17th April, more than 300,000 people of many nationalities had passed through them. Just over 100 years old, Singapore, which had been created as a halfway house between India and China, was no longer to be regarded merely as an 'Exchange Port.' It had become one of the greatest trading points in the world, with resources and capabilities to match any competitor.

The colony's first administrator, Sir Stamford Raffles, would have been delighted. When the island was reluctantly ceded to him by the all powerful East India Company, he wrote: "Our object is not territory, but trade: a great commercial emporium, and a fulcrum, whence we may extend our influence politically as circumstances may hereafter require."

His vision became a reality, but it took 100 years in the making; the great trading firms he envisaged were formed from small syndicates of merchant adventurers, the majority of whom were Scots.

One such firm was W.R. Paterson and Company of Glasgow. In 1846, there were two partners, Paterson and William Morgan, and they employed managers in Manila, Batavia and Singapore. The company's manager in Singapore was Robert McEwen from the west coast of Scotland, and one of the clerks was John Harvey, from Renfrewshire. When Paterson retired three years later, the firm was re-named McEwen & Company, with Morgan and McEwen based in Glasgow, and Harvey elevated to managerial status in Singapore.[2]

Across the South China Sea, an Englishman, James Brooke, traveller and adventurer, had succeeded in the remarkable achievement of becoming Rajah of Sarawak. In the beginning, however, the monopoly rights for trade between Sarawak and Britain were vested by the British Government in a short-lived trading company called the Eastern Archipelago Company.

This did not entirely suit Brooke who felt that his interests would be best served by operating independently from London politics. He therefore looked around for other options, and was naturally receptive when a Danish merchant called Ludwig Helms, who had been operating out of Singapore, offered him an alternative arrangement. Helms and John Harvey knew each other well, and before long MacEwen's office in Singapore, with Helms based in the free port of Kuching, began to act as Brooke's agent. For the purposes of conducting the Borneo trade, Harvey registered a firm with the Singapore Chamber of Commerce and called it the Borneo Company.

By then, as it soon became obvious, the conditions could not have been better. Brooke was presiding over a settled government and, more importantly, Sarawak was rich in antimony, iron, gold, copper, cinnabar, pepper, gutta percha,* and coal. The potential for development and export was immeasurable.

So Harvey made his move to 'take over and work Mines, Ores, Veins or Seams of all descriptions of Minerals in the island of Borneo, and to barter or sell the produce of such workings.' Granted development rights

---

* Gutta percha is the latex juice from a tree found exclusively in Malaya. It is used for electrical insulation.

by Rajah James under a Royalty agreement with the Sarawak Treasury, the Borneo Company was registered in London in June 1856,* and John Harvey, based in Singapore, became its first Managing Director.

The authorised capital at the time of its formation was £250,000, of which £60,000 was issued in 600 shares of £100. Robert Henderson was appointed the company's first chairman. The deputy chairman was Charles Templer, nominated by the Rajah, and the remainder of the board was made up of James Dyce Nicol, a British member of parliament, and two other directors from McEwen & Co.

By the 1920s, the Borneo Company had extended its interests to Siam, the Malayan Peninsula, and the Dutch East Indies, today known as Indonesia. With its head office in London, it now operated through general managers in Kuching, covering Sarawak, Brunei and British North Borneo; Singapore, covering Singapore and Malaya, and Bangkok, covering Thailand, who in turn reported back to managing directors and general managers in London.

Commercial activities encompassed the export of rice, rubber, tea, copra, tin, and timber. Agency work in the course of time included Black & White whisky, Gordon's gin, Nestlé's chocolate, Rolex watches, and the selling of motor cars through Borneo Motors, a subsidiary company created in 1925. As a publicity stunt, Pat Atkins, a First World War pilot, drove a Chevrolet up a 2,000 foot bridle path on Kladang mountain, near Ipoh, levering it and manhandling it around the corners. He cabled the manager in Penang saying, "Chevrolet climbs 2,000 foot peak," and received the answer, "Why?"

Atkins replied, "To get to the top."

The following year, two Borneo Motors employees, Neville Reddish and A.O. Marshall, sealed a Chevrolet in top gear and drove it, complete with a reporter from the *Penang Gazette*,[3] 500 miles over the passes from Penang to Singapore, where it was duly exhibited. Ten years later Reddish, who was called 'Red' by his friends, drove another Chevrolet over the same road in just ten hours, at an average of fifty miles an hour, including stops at interstate customs. This record was afterwards challenged many times, but it was nearly 20 years before it was broken.

---

* Not to be confused with the Chartered North Borneo Company launched in 1881.

The Borneo Company's Singapore offices (centre), 1922

(Martine Family Collection)

Accompanying Red had been his driver Mat Itam, and when they arrived in Singapore, Red took much pleasure in introducing him as Mat 'Puteh.' For those unfamiliar with bahasa, 'hitam' means 'black', and 'puteh' means 'white.' Such stunts might appear frivolous in hindsight, but they were to lead to Borneo Motors ultimately dominating over a third of Malaya's entire motor trade.

As a junior employee, Red certainly earned his reputation as a wild card. One Christmas Eve, he drove an Austin Seven onto the ballroom floor of the E&O (Eastern & Oriental) Hotel in Penang. The manager was furious and wrote to Red's superiors demanding that this irresponsible young man be repatriated. Red was too good a salesman to lose, and was sent to make his peace with the manager, which he did somewhere around 3am on New Year's morning armed with a bottle of Scotch. Thereafter, they became the best of friends.

During the 1920s and 1930s, British colonial power in South East Asia was at its summit. Singapore, Penang, Malacca and Labuan, had collectively come together to form the Straits Settlements, with a British Governor based in Singapore. The remaining Malay States – Perak, Pahang, Selangor, Negri Sembilan, Kedah, Perlis, Kelantan, Trengganu and Johore were ruled by Sultans, but came under the umbrella of the Federated Malay States Protectorate administered from Kuala Lumpur. The possibility of a future independent pan-Malayan federation of States was not even considered.

Against this background, the timing of my father's arrival at the Borneo Company's wharf side Singapore headquarters in 1922 could not have been more advantageous for a young man with ambition. So far as the expanding mercantile enterprise that he worked for was concerned, the second decade of the 20th century was seen as the turning point in its affairs, launching it forward as an influential force in the market place.

Since the 1890s, the Borneo Company had been growing tea in Sumatra through its subsidiary, the Haboko Tea Company, with varying success. There was a fall in tea prices immediately after the First World War, but suddenly, in the early 1920s, the tea industry took a notable turn for the better.

That was not all. Extensive rubber estates were in the process of being opened up and by 1924 every department in the Borneo Company was covering expenses and making a profit. An office was established in Bangkok, shares were taken in the Sungei Kinta Tin Dredging Company, and the

Fenchurch Street building in London was sold with the company becoming tenants, releasing tied-up capital to be employed elsewhere.

For all of the young men who arrived during the early 1920s to work for one or other of the trading companies, Singapore was the island of opportunities and inevitably a large number of them were Scots, a race renowned for its pioneering spirit, and there is nobody more clannish than the Scots when far from home.

Three years older than my father was Ewen Fergusson from Coatbridge in Lanarkshire, always known to his friends as 'Fergie,' who had answered an advertisement in the Straits Times for a job with the Straits Trading Company. Among their contemporaries were Archie 'Mac' McLellan, who worked for Mansfield & Company, and Dr 'Commie' Bain, who arrived in 1924, and was to practise medicine in Singapore for the next fifty-six years.

A couple of years younger was John Augustus Grant from Glemoriston in Inverness-shire, who came to work for the Borneo Company in the mid-1920s, as did Alec Fairlie from Edinburgh. Younger sons, like Charles, each of them had independently come to the conclusion that there was no future for them at home in Scotland.

But there was so much more to it than that. Through their work and their shared recreational pastimes, a camaraderie was struck up which was to last throughout their lives. The work was demanding, but not without interest, and pretty soon all of them succumbed to the Eastern way of life.

For the young tuans, with virtually no single young European women to be found in Singapore in those days, recreation on weekdays was limited to the Cricket Club, where they went for games on the Padang. Every new arrival was encouraged to join either the Singapore Volunteer Corps, the local Territorial Army, or the Straits Settlements Volunteer Royal Navy Reserve.* My father, being a former Scots Guards officer, was commissioned into the Scots Platoon in 1925.

On Sundays, there was golf at Sepoy Lines and Keppel Harbour, and for the more rarefied tuans, at the Royal Singapore Golf Club at Bukit Timah. If there was a high tide at the Singapore Swimming Club, a rickshaw was taken to the old Johnston's Pier, followed by a trip across the bay in a

---

* This had to be approved by employers since there was a requirement that, if necessary, volunteers could be called up for service.

The Singapore Volunteers on parade, 1930. Charles Martine is on the right-hand side, wearing a kilt and carrying his great grandfather's sword. The sword was originally owned by Peter Martine (1775-1865), who served with the Haddington Militia at the time of Battle of Waterloo. It disappeared during the Japanese occupation of Sarawak

(Martine Family Collection)

launch provided by the club management. Members swam in the open sea, protected by a pagar (enclosure), erected during the 1920s after an unfortunate lady was carried off by a shark. At midday, they ate a curry tiffin topped with slices of banana and pineapple, shredded cucumber, grated coconut and spoonfuls of chutney and chilli.

Afterwards, they lounged in the old clubhouse behind the ketapang trees growing in the sand. Chits were signed for drinks and settled at the end of each month when the club tamby called on the offices for payment. On Sundays, ladies and children were not permitted entry until after 4pm.

At the Sea View Hotel, some two miles from the town centre on the east coast road, there were gin slings and curry to be swallowed to the sounds of an orchestra in the heat of noon. On Sunday evenings, when dining on the lawn at Raffles Hotel, or dancing in the nearby ballroom, gentlemen wore white shark-skin dinner jackets, their ladies, evening gowns. Another band played at the exclusive Tanglin Club in Draycott Drive.

On week-day nights, sticky and still, there were trips through coconut groves to the Gap, one of the highest points on the island, to drink a beer, a stengha or a pink gin,* and enjoy the view across Keppel Harbour towards distant islands and the tip of Johore. Or there might be an excursion to one of the amusement parks for a Chinese opera. From a stall in Beach Road, there was late-night satay – spicy skewered meat cooked over charcoal.

Scotch and gin were cheap, and it was in Singapore that my father first acquired the habit of swallowing a prairie oyster, a raw egg topped with Worcester sauce, for breakfast.

Sometimes there was a show or film at the Capitol on Stamford Road, the Pavilion in Orchard Road or at the Alhambra in Beach Road where, if anyone tired of looking at black and white on the flickering silent screen, they could watch the masts of the junks rocking against the stars in the harbour outside. Prices were $1 or $2 for the better seats. For $3 an hour, a car could be hired for an excursion into the country. The roads were narrow, badly surfaced, and, at night, before the Causeway was completed, entirely deserted.

---

* A drop of Angostura was put into a glass first and swilled around. Drinkers were then asked if they wanted the Angostura 'in' or 'out'? If 'out', it was thrown out. If 'in', it was left in. Cold gin was then dropped on top and the liquid turned a light or darker shade of pink depending upon the quantity of Angostura in the glass.

The completion of the Causeway in September 1923 dramatically opened up the island to the mainland. Prior to that Singaporeans going 'up-country' left their cars, the few that had them, behind, to travel the 14 miles to the Woodlands ferry by train and cross the Johore Straits by ferry to the terminus at Johore Bahru. Planters coming in the other direction reversed the process.

Previously the Capital of the Straits Settlements had fronted onto the world with its waterfront, its back door detached from its Malayan horizons. The Causeway changed all that. It was astonishing just what a difference this mile long, 60 foot deep granite bank crossing made in opening up Malaya's economic potential. Before it was built, rubber and other produce from the mainland, and imported goods from Singapore, were carried by coastal steamer. Afterwards, almost everything was transported by road and rail, while an ever increasing number of privately owned cars transformed the landscape. Now the region's full potential could be realised from all sides and in all directions.

Despite competition from road and rail, however, the Straits Steamship Company continued its services from Singapore to Malacca, Port Swettenham, and Penang on the east coast; to Kuantan, Trengganu and Kota Bahru on the west. The Island of Opportunities had become the Land of Opportunities, and in the commercial arena of the 1920s and 1930s there were notable success stories – Willie Watt, the head of McAlister & Co, and J.I. 'Jiddy' Dawson, the Aberdeen-born managing director of Guthrie & Co.[4] Another Tuan Besar was John Bagnall, who had joined Alfred Holt & Company in Liverpool in 1911, and worked his way out to Singapore as a purser on a Blue Funnel Line ship. In 1912 he joined the Straits Trading Company and eleven years later became Chairman and Managing Director of Singapore's first public company.

In 1929, John Bagnall was made Chairman of the Singapore Chamber of Commerce, and since he was still a bachelor, his younger sister 'Bobbie' arrived from England to help him entertain.[*] It was not long after her arrival that she met and married Fergie Fergusson.[5]

In March 1930, Mac McLellan of Mansfield's, married Dorothy Turner, who two years earlier had also come out to Singapore from

---

[*] John Bagnall married in 1934.

John Bagnall
(Photo: Elizabeth Lochhead)

Liverpool to act as governess to the two daughters of an army family. After the ceremony held at St George's Church in Penang, Joe Penrice, Mansfield's Penang manager, held a wedding reception for them at Alden, his house on the island. Alden was later to become the McLellan's home when Joe was promoted to Singapore, and they were posted to Penang.

Mac and Dorothy McLellan. 1930
(Photo: Neil McLellan)

There is no denying that it was an incestuous society. The McLellan's married life had begun in a company-owned bungalow at Pasir Panjang, ten miles from the centre of Singapore. Sharing a Borneo Company house across the road were John Grant and Alec Fairlie. Both John and Mac kept mongrel dogs, Ben and Jerry, and there were endless parties and much to-ing and fro-ing between the two houses until she and Mac moved to live in Penang.

In 1937, John Grant too became engaged. His bride was Gwendoline Knight, the Dean of Durham's daughter who had come to Malaya to visit her brother Leonard, a police commissioner in Kuala Lumpur. John and Wendy's first home together was a Borneo Company house in Orange Grove Road.

In his book *Rickshaw Reporter*, published sixty-two years after he joined the staff of the *Straits Times* in 1923, the journalist George Peet[6] observed that 'these expatriates believed that an Eastern career was not incompatible with being a good citizen of the colony in the civic and moral sense. In the changing circumstances of their time, with wider horizons and a more varied and interesting life, Singapore no longer meant to this later generation what the early Settlement meant to the old times.'

In other words, they were becoming Singaporeans, working towards a better life for European and Asian alike. Nobody would have believed how soon their world, and all of the values that sustained and encouraged it, would disappear beyond recall.

CHAPTER THREE

Island of the Betelnut

There was no question of any resentment. The superior station of the British in Government and society was simply a fact of life. After all they were the greatest people in the world. They had the biggest empire that history had ever known, stretching over all time zones, across all four oceans and five continents. We learnt that in history lessons at school.

Lee Kwan Yew, *The Singapore Story.*

P AT Macquisten, my mother, was 11 years old when my father first set off for Singapore, and they had met one another only occasionally when he returned home on leave and called in to pay his respects to the parents of his old school friend Alec Macquisten. By then Frederick Macquisten, Alec and Pat's father, had been elected member of parliament for Argyll, and the family had moved to live at Beckenham in Kent, a comfortable commuter distance from the House of Commons.

Peggy, Fred and Pat Macquisten in Singapore, 1932
(Martine Family Collection)

In 1932, my mother's elder sister Riona married Freddie Armstrong, an Irishman employed on the Kinta Kellas rubber plantation, near Batu Gajah, just south of Ipoh, in Perak. When Riona announced that she was expecting her first child, her parents made the journey across the Indian Ocean to be with her for the birth, and a sophisticated, 21-year-old Pat accompanied them. No longer was she considered the baby of the family.

As a member of the British parliament, Frederick Macquisten was invited to inspect Singapore's defences, a massive strategical investment on the part of the British Government. With an eye on Japan's 1915 invasion of China, it had been decided to create a strong naval base in South East Asia. The site chosen to protect British interests in the South China Seas was a mixture of swamp and agricultural land on the south-east coast of Singapore island. Over almost two decades, the entire area had been cleared, drained and, in part, reclaimed, but not without controversy.

It was a vastly expensive project. Roads had to be built; barracks, storehouses and workshops erected. A floating dock was towed out and moored mid-channel. On land, the latest type of graving-dock was excavated, capable of servicing the largest warships. Powerful modern batteries of heavy guns were mounted to command all of the sea approaches to Singapore Island and the Johore Strait.[1]

Between 1924 and 1937, a huge sum of money, in excess of £12½ million, was allocated to make Singapore impregnable, and Fred Macquisten, with a group of other British politicians, was invited to see how the money was being spent. It would have been hard not to be impressed.

At Batu Gajah, the Kinta Kelas estate also held a special fascination for the Macquistens since William Kelly Smith, the previous owner, by then deceased, had owned a home in Argyll and become a close family friend.

If there was ever a classic example of a Scotsman on the make, it was Kelly Smith – plain Smith, or 'Toothy Bill' as he was known when he first appeared in Malaya aged 20. Working as a 'ganger' on the Seramban to Port Dickson branch railway, Toothy Bill saved his wages and, for a dollar an acre, bought land adjacent to the track being cleared. He soon owned hundreds of acres, and the rubber boom of 1912 made him rich. Never one to stand still, he set up the Kinta Kellas Tin Dredging Company.

In Scotland, he built a spectacular home at the head of Loch Melfort in Argyll. At Kinta Kellas, he created a mansion incorporating a bizarre and

William Kelly Smith of Kinta
Kellas, 1922. Photograph taken at
Loch Melfort in Argyll

(Martine Family Collection)

extravagant mausoleum, modelled on an Indian palace. Bricks were imported from India, and it was the first building in Malaya to have an elevator installed. With an incomplete tennis court on the second floor, a rooftop for parties, and two tunnels leading under the nearby river, one of them connecting with a Hindu Temple, Kelly Castle at Batu Gajah, survives to this day as an exotic reminder of the vast wealth accumulated by one of the more colourful and enterprising tuans of rubber and tin.

By the time of the Macquistens' visit to Malaya, Toothy Bill was long dead. The Kinta Kellas estate had been sold to Harrison & Crosfield, and it was only coincidence that Freddie and Riona were living there. It was no coincidence that Fred and Peggy Macquisten should attend a St Andrew's Night Dinner in Singapore, taking with them their youngest daughter Pat, and their eldest son's old school friend, Charles Martine, as her escort.

My father was entranced with what he saw. In the intervening years since he had seen her, my mother had grown into a spirited young woman, independent-minded and talented. Having been sent to a school in Switzerland at the age of 14, she spoke French as a second language. In her teenage years she could not only boast of having played the fiddle for the veteran Scottish music hall entertainer Harry Lauder, but the violin for Sir Henry Wood, father of the London Proms. Both Lauder and Wood were family friends. In her early twenties she accompanied her parents on trips to Africa and Australia, where Fred Macquisten had business interests. Back in London, she had enrolled for flying lessons at Brooklands, an airfield in West Surrey.

Pat Macquisten at Batu Gajah 1932
(Martine Family Collection)

At this stage, my father's career was progressing rapidly. In January 1932, he had become the Borneo Company's acting manager for Malaya; the following year his promotion was confirmed. Good-looking, established, much liked and well-respected, he was considered a catch for the right girl.

From the moment they were reintroduced, my mother knew that she was that girl. Although eleven years younger, neither saw the age difference between them as an obstacle. For my father, tall and dark haired, with his twinkling smile, and my mother, with her brown eyes and trim figure, the attraction was mutual. In London on leave the following year, Charles called in at the Macquistens' home in Beckenham to propose and was accepted. Despite the prospect of losing another daughter to the other side of the world, my grandparents were delighted.

Some may wonder why the 'confirmed bachelor' waited so long to marry. It was not so much through a lack of interest in the opposite sex, but the reality of his occupation. Most of my father's male friends married late rather than early. Large numbers did not marry at all. Marriage into the Far East was asking a lot of a white woman. Ignoring the illusion of servants and elegant houses, the isolation, the heat, and the snobberies took a lot of getting used to. My father was certainly not indifferent to this.

He had worked hard to provide for his bride. There had been flirtations with others, passing through Singapore, and when home on leave, but nothing that in any way could be considered serious. He was deeply conventional, well-mannered, and certainly not one for overt displays of capricious affection. With my mother it was a love match. He too had made up his mind. There was never any doubt about it.

Although she would often freely admit that she had had no idea what she was letting herself in for, my mother fully subscribed to the concept that when a girl from her background married, it was into her husband's life in totality. She became not only the mistress of his home and the mother of his children, she shared the social obligations of his colonial status.

As the daughter of a relatively well-known public figure, she had early on been exposed to the mainstream of British public life. But it had been a safe and often privileged existence, protected by the long shadow of her father. The rituals and expectations of the colonial community in South East Asia, as she was soon to discover, were full of pretensions and pitfalls for an unsuspecting bride. In the meantime, it was Charles's charm, his good looks and, above all, his considerate good manners, that reassured her. She would soon learn to cope with the rest of it.

The wedding took place at the old St Columba's Church in Pont Street, London,* on 6th September 1934, and shortly afterwards they embarked upon the long sea cruise that eventually delivered them to their first marital home, Goodwood, in Penang, where my father was now installed as the Borneo Company's manager covering mainland Malaya.

By the time of their marriage he had become an old Far East hand which, despite the euphoria of their being newly-weds, made it not entirely easy for my mother to tune into his accustomed way of life, especially given the complex social network which surrounded him. Initial misgivings aside, if there was anywhere in Malaya best suited for colonial newcomers to begin their apprenticeship, Penang, Pulau Pinang, the 'Island of the Betelnut', was the place.

Travelling north by train from Singapore, departing at 8pm and arriving at the Federal Capital of Kuala Lumpur at 8am, the view from the carriage windows while it remained daylight, was of endless padi-fields interspersed between coconut palms, as in a picture postcard. At Kuala Lumpur, passengers had the choice of either embarking to Penang from Port Swettenham to Georgetown on a steamship, or continuing their journey by rail, through Ipoh to Butterworth, where they might board the Penang Ferry and arrive on the island in the afternoon.

Europeans always travelled First Class; the Chinese, Second Class; the Tamils, Third Class, and the Malays, on whichever they could afford. After 1927, the fastest route from Singapore up the West Coast of the Peninsula, the Malaya which the Europeans had developed, and where they mostly lived, was definitely by sea on *HMS Kedah*,** the Straits Steamship Company's pride and joy. Embarking from Singapore on Thursdays at 11.30am, the *Kedah* arrived in Penang on Friday mornings at 8am.

Centuries before, the British, Portuguese and Dutch traders were lured here by trade and they brought in their wake settlements of Hokkien, and

---

* St Columba's Church was destroyed by bombing on 10th May 1941. Through the generosity of parishioners it was rebuilt in 1955.

** In 1940, the *Kedah* was requisitioned by the British Navy and fitted out as a headquarters ship for the planned invasion of Malaya. It was the leading ship into Singapore when the Japanese surrendered.

lesser numbers of Hakka, Chinese. From northern India came the Hindu culture followed by Islam from southern India. Islam remains the official religion, but peaceably has no quarrel with the numerous Christian churches, Buddhist, Hindu, or Chinese temples.

The rose-coloured roofs of the town below the heights of Penang Hill, 3000 feet above sea level, were situated next to wide expanses of white sand, and the nearby green of the Botanical Gardens. Few places have such an abundance of amenities combining hill, sea and land, all in such a compact presentation. Only five acres smaller than Singapore island, turtle-shaped Penang provided then, as it does to this day, a rich tropical paradise of contrasts, unspoiled and seductive.[2]

It was the rubber boom of the 1920s which brought vast and wondrous palaces and other buildings to Georgetown, founded on behalf of the East India Company in 1876 by Captain Francis Light, a merchant venturer. Light had the choice of the entire island for his Capital, but selected Tanjong Penaga, the sandy promontory which juts out towards the mainland, because it provided shelter for shipping. So it was this shipping, and the trade it generated, which made Georgetown prosper. Between 1911 and 1920, sugar, coffee, coconut oil, and tin in abundance, created fortunes for the already rich towkays who built princely mansions to accommodate themselves amid Penang's conglomeration of buildings and styles. And it was rubber, before the devastating slump of 1929,* that principally swept Malayan export firms to dizzy heights previously unimaginable.

From the prosperity that this created just around the time of my father's apprenticeship, emerged Georgetown with its stucco-fronted Chinese dwellings, and a proliferation of English homesteads spaced out in the adjacent countryside. Formal shapes and elegant porches dominated. Up on the hill, colonial residences were kissed by cool breezes among the flowers and the trees. On the flat lands sprang up the colonnaded mansions. Such a house was Goodwood.

A dwelling on three floors, which overlooked open fields, Goodwood, in McAlister Road, was yet another joy in the Borneo Company's residential portfolio. It had no refrigerator nor washing machine, deep freeze or

---

* Between 1925 and 1932, the price of rubber fell from 5 shillings to 5 cents a pound. It began to pick up again in 1933.

Goodwood, McAlister Road, Penang
(Martine Family Collection)

vacuum cleaner. In fact, it lacked all of the luxuries of modern times, but there was no need for them because there were servants. Instead, my mother found herself presiding over a household consisting of a cuki (cook), two houseboys, a tukang ayer (water carrier), a syce (chauffeur), and when the children came, an amah.

At meal-times, a servant arrived to operate the large canvas sail that hung over the dining table and acted as a fan. In the garden were three kabuns (gardeners), employed to cut the grass and keep the flowers watered: clumps of magenta bougainvillaea, peach and crimson hibiscus, the jacaranda, frangipani trees and hanging orchids.*

For somebody who was not unused to the presence of servants in her parental home, but who valued her independence, Pat found the expected

---

* On one of his leaves home, my father presented a dazzling collection of orchid cuttings to the Royal Botanic Gardens of Edinburgh.

over-dependency upon others hard to get used to. The syce, for example, was notoriously indolent. On one occasion when he failed to turn up on time to drive her to an appointment, she climbed into the driving seat of the car and drove it herself. The man was horrified; until then he had had no idea that mems could drive. He was never late again.

When on view, the uniform of the household staff was immaculate, but less so in the kitchen quarters, where the boys relaxed. In attendance, the uniform was starched tutup jackets and white Chinese trousers, while amah wore a long white blouse with short sleeves called a basu, over loose black trousers.

Although they for the most part understood English, it was customary for the servants to be addressed in Malay. My mother spoke fluent French and was soon able to pick up the necessary Malay expressions and command words with relative ease, but sometimes, if her mind was elsewhere, became confused and, much to her dismay, muddled up the languages. In later life, the face of a bemused porter at the Gare du Nord in Paris comes to mind when she shouted at him in Malay for failing to pick up one of her bags.

For most newcomers to the Far East, their most unpleasant experiences involved insects. Ants were everywhere, and mosquitoes never left anyone alone. In all of the houses, there burned coils of smudge sticks, giving off a spicy smell which to some extent acted as a deterrent.

Everyone was warned of malaria, the great killer. Once somebody succumbed to the fever, their temperature could rise to 105 degrees, and their bed sheets required to be changed constantly. Quinine treatment was the best known antidote, but in reality was far from being reliable. The fever was carried by the anopheline mosquito, and life became a constant challenge not to be bitten, which was not that simple since mosquitoes, particularly on the mainland Malaya, were ubiquitous.

CHAPTER FOUR

Rubber, Tin and Tiffin

The jungle still waited and, in the wood and thatch kampongs, the easy languid rhythms of planting and gathering still went on, not many miles from the clubhouse verandah.

Pat Barr, *Taming the Jungle – The Men who made British Malaya.*

FOR my mother, the social rituals of colonial life took time to get used to and although she always put on a good show, she never did entirely come to terms with them. In common with most mems, her biggest problem, certainly to begin with, was how to occupy her time. Once visited, the novelty of Kek Lok Si, the Monastery of Supreme Bliss, Fort Cornwallis, or the reclining Buddha at Wat Chayamangkalaram, soon wore off. Newly-wed couples from their background were enthusiastically welcomed into a social whirl, but it was a tight circle limited to those belonging to a similar commercial status, and exclusively white. For an intelligent, well-read woman, it was not always easy to conform. Kindred spirits could be hard to find.

With husbands largely preoccupied with business, everything for the mems of South East Asia centred around their families, that is until the children were of an age to be sent off to boarding schools. Children were the great catalyst, but in the narrow confines of colonial society there were formalities to be observed.

For the men it was customary to address each other only by their surnames, with individuals often identified by initials. In the European commercial world it was thought inappropriate for wives to become too chummy with each other unless their husbands were of an equal management status. Christian names were used only when people were related or became close friends. Thus it was considered perfectly normal for wives to address one another as Mrs Martine, Mrs Smith or Mrs Jones. There was a certain logic in this. Such designations provided status without unnecessary familiarity.

On Saturdays, there were formal dinner dances at the Runnymede

Kek Lok Si Temple, Penang
(Martine Family Collection)

Hotel, Pat's favourite, and the E&O Hotel. The Golf Course at the all-male Penang Club was a great distraction for the senior men and its doyen Grant Mackie. Mackie was yet another of those who had come to Malaya at the turn of the century to build the railway and, because of his great age, became the only club member allowed to wear his cap indoors to shield him from the draft of the fans.

Sports were seasonal. There was cricket and football from March until August; rugby and hockey between September and February. Every three months there would be a horse-racing week, working in rotation with Ipoh, Kuala Lumpur and Singapore. Charles was an enthusiastic race-goer, and with James Dickson Kemp, a miner from Kroh in Upper Perak, as president of the Penang Turf Club, great plans were put in place for a new club premises and course on a 230 acre site at Batu Gantong.

The Penang Swimming Club, with its rambling wooden clubhouse and nets cordoning off an area in the sea, was situated a few miles along the coast at Tanjong Bungah. On an evening when nothing else was planned, friends got together there to play bridge or Mah Jong. "Some played for fun, some seriously," recalled Dorothy McLellan, who had befriended my mother when she first arrived in Penang.

On the circuit of company business, there were regular house guests to be entertained. On such occasions, men talked shop while the women discussed servants, clothes, children and who was pregnant. When the children were born, there were excursions up Penang Hill on the funicular railway, but there was little or nothing in the way of any kind of intellectual distraction. Books were devoured the moment they were acquired. When particularly frustrated by boredom, Pat would resort to playing the piano she had brought over from England.

Under such conditions, moments of despair were predictable, and always, always, there was the shadow of homesickness to be overcome. To help mitigate the symptoms, she had taken most of their wedding presents with her from England, but nothing compensated for the lack of news from home. Letters took up to six weeks to arrive, and the only instant form of communication was a cable used only for emergencies.

Writing letters became therefore not just a duty, but a pastime, if only to ensure a regular response. As a result, the arrival and departure of the mail boats on a Thursday and Saturday became great occasions. "You have no idea just how important receiving a letter from home was for us," she would reminisce. "Sometimes it was the only thing that kept us sane."

There were times when the working life of the men was equally tedious. The money was good, as was the lifestyle it made possible for them and their families, but a removal of the restrictions on rubber exports, variable markets, and political instability inevitably effected them.

During the early 1930s, it became almost impossible for any of the companies to make profits and all Borneo Company employees agreed to take a pay cut[1] – unthinkable today. By 1933, the year of my father's promotion, the price of rubber had sunk to an all-time low, and there was no alternative but to close down the company's import activities in Java and Sumatra.

At this time, the Borneo Company had branches in Thailand, and was active in the northern teak forests. It had branches in Penang, Kuala Lumpur, Ipoh and Malacca. There were two associate companies – the Alexandra Brickworks in Penang, and Borneo Motors. In addition to general trading, the parent company acted as insurance and shipping agents, but it was always tin and rubber which dominated.

In his twelve years based in Singapore, and the six years that followed in Penang, Charles Martine had travelled extensively throughout mainland Malaya, gaining a detailed knowledge of the company's rubber estates and tin mining interests. In his bachelor days, he, Kenneth Simpson and John McNeil spent many a weekend with Jimmy Kemp, a mining consultant who owned a bungalow at Kroh (now renamed Pengkalan Hulu) in Perak, and who entertained them sumptuously. Over twenty-two stone in weight, Kemp, who had been educated at Loretto School near Edinburgh, and who played the bagpipes, attained a legendary status among those who came under the spell of this down-to-earth Scot, a bachelor bon viveur of the most hospitable kind, despite the words of the embroidery which hung on the wall of one of his guest bedrooms: "How very nice it is to see, our dear relations come to tea. But it is nicer yet to know, when tea is over, they must go."

Another of my father's older friends in the tin mining business was Vincent Baker, tuan besar of Sungei Lembing. Owned by the Pahang Consolidated Corporation, for which the Borneo Company acted as agents, Sungei Lembing, lying in a comparatively small area of 700 square miles, was the largest tin lode mine in the world. When Charles was Vincent's guest for the Coronation of the Sultan Abu Bakar of Pahang in 1933, a glittering occasion (attended by both the Governor, Sir Cecil Clementi, and the Chief Secretary, Sir Andrew Caledecott), he was given an exclusive tour of the excavations which were then down to a level of 1,200 feet.

Judging from the photographs of the mines that he sent home, my father was far more impressed by them than the coronation with all of its silks and colour. As a merchant trader, he found the extraction of tin as fascinating as that of gold. Millenniums had contributed to the creation of these ore deposits, erosion by the weather displacing the ore, particle by particle, and washing the tin bearing sand down to the valley. Anchored by its weight, deposits were eventually formed and hidden for centuries by the enclosing mountains to the north, and the impenetrable swamps and forests of the south.[2]

In the early1930s there were virtually no roads on the eastern side of Malaya, and to reach Sungei Lembing one had to travel most of the distance by boat, passing through Kuantan, the nearest town. A few miles before reaching the mine, visitors transferred to the Pahang Consolidated's miniature railway which took them through the jungle, over flimsy bridges across deep ravines, and along a ledge above a muddy river.

Eight thousand people were employed – Scots engineers, Cornish miners, Chinese, and Malays – but like everything else in South East Asia, there was a hierarchical structure, and it was a difficult, lonely place for a tuan besar's wife. Vincent had worked for Pahang Consolidated since 1911, and when Charles first knew him, was married to an Australian girl. Sadly, the remoteness and boredom drove her back to Australia with their three children, leaving him with no-one to keep house for him or, more importantly, to act as a hostess when he entertained.

Vincent's two-storey house, raised on stone pillars, was perched on a hilltop overlooking the village, and when he entertained, it sometimes meant that up to forty people stayed overnight.[3] Entertaining guests on company business was part of the job, and it therefore came as no surprise when Vincent cabled Penang to say that his sister Nona was coming from England to help him out. Charles was asked to meet her off the boat from England, and to despatch her safely on her way to Sungei Lembing. Although my father and Nona were not to meet again for many years, her subsequent story, touched on later in this narrative,* was to become one of the more remarkable episodes in the havoc that would soon engulf them all.

Borneo Company managers, wherever they were stationed, were expected to fulfil a range of civic duties. Charles therefore became a member of the Penang Chamber of Commerce committee, and a Municipal Commissioner, which meant that even more of his free time was occupied away from the marital home. Fortunately, my mother was not slow in acclimatising herself.

Since their arrival, she had steadily cultivated a close-knit group of friends drawn from Penang Swimming Club and, being Scots, the Penang St Andrew's Society. To begin with, there was Joe Allen, who became the family's doctor, and his wife Jean, and the Reverend Rab Minto, Penang's Presbyterian Minister, and his wife Mary.

In the year that followed, Pat's sister Jess arrived from England when their sister Riona gave birth to her second child. Although Batu Gajah was a distance of several hours by car, the sisters kept in regular contact and enjoyed each other's company whenever possible.

In addition, there were excursions to Singapore, a trip of 520 miles, where my mother was taken under the wing of the vivacious Bobbie Fergusson, by then established as one of Singapore's leading socialites. On such visits, it soon became apparent that she was developing her own defining style. Attending a smart dinner party at Government House, she had reached the pudding course and was seen deep in conversation with the dinner companion on her left. With her right elbow on the table and her arm up, she was casually clutching a much treasured petit point evening purse in her hand. All of a sudden, the hand with the purse was brought crashing down onto the dinner table shocking the assembled guests into silence. They were even more shocked when they saw that the purse had been used to crush a very large scorpion which had detached itself from the ceiling above.

Living on mainland Malaya was Charles's uncle, Harry Hannay, a successful mining consultant in Ipoh. Aunt Kate, Dora Martine's younger sister, had remained in Scotland while their sons Ted and Harry Jnr, and

* See pages 129 and 193.

Bobbie and Fergie Fergusson
(Photo: Fergusson family)

daughter Mary attended schools in Edinburgh. That was the way it was done in those days. In contemporary terms, the Hannays' lives seem curiously disenfranchised, but in that generation it was not at all unusual for families to be separated for long periods of time, particularly in the Far East.[4]

Harry Hannay, irrespective of the name,* was a character straight out of a John Buchan novel. Born in Trinidad, he had been brought up in the south-west of Scotland, and in 1905 was employed by the Borneo Company as a mining engineer in Sarawak. He proposed to Kate by letter from China and in the decade that followed was to be found in Newfoundland and

---

* John Buchan and Harry Hannay were exact contemporaries and certainly encountered each other, first in Wigtownshire, where the Hannay family had a home, and later in South Africa, where Harry was involved in intelligence work. The character of Buchan's hero Richard Hannay is widely held to be based on Edmund Ironside, later Lord Ironside, but it does seem curious first that both Hannays should be mining engineers, and secondly that both should have been at one stage involved in counter-espionage.

South Africa. With the exception of a breathtaking journey across country on horse-back to Nigeria from South Africa, the enduring Kate was always left behind, either in England or Scotland.

When their eldest son, Ted Hannay, left school in Edinburgh in 1930, it was Charles who suggested he apply for a job with Borneo Motors in Singapore. Ted jumped at the opportunity and eventually managed the company's spare parts department. Five years later, 20-year-old Harry Hannay Jnr also set off for Malaya to join Patterson Simons, shipping agents in Penang, where he shared an old bungalow below the Penang Swimming Club with two other young men.

Virginia Margaret Martine, my eldest sister, was born on 7th November 1935 and christened by Rab Minto, after which event there took place a seemingly endless round of children's birthday parties with ice-cream, sweets, sandwiches, and tea. Dorothy McLellan, who soon became my mother's best friend on the island, often invited Virginia, Ira Bisseker (daughter of the general manager of Eastern Smelting (Tin) Co Ltd in Penang) and Sonia Martin (another manager's daughter) to play card games with her son Neil, all of an age. "Neil hated it, because he invariably lost," said his mother.

Jean and Boris Hembry
(Photo: John Hembry)

Another close friendship that was initiated through having children the same age was with Jean Hembry, wife of the assistant manager of the Kamuning Rubber Estate in Sungei Siput, near Kuala Kangsar, north of Ipoh. Jean was a sparkling, neat and pretty woman and, since Virginia was the same age as her son John, she and my mother had a lot in common. Although their children fought continuously, they regularly found themselves staying in each other's houses, with amah installed as the referee.

In the spring of 1937, Pat's sister Riona and her husband Freddie Armstrong departed for England with their two young sons Gwin and Harvey. Freddie had enrolled on a course at Kew Gardens, but as the war in Europe approached, accepted a job offer to grow quinine in Guatemala. Their departure was obviously a blow for my mother to have to say good-bye to her sister, but by then there were other family members on the move.

With her daughter Mary now aged 17, and having left school, Kate Hannay sold the family home in Newton Stewart, let the family flat in Edinburgh, and headed for Malaya to join her husband. Arriving in Penang, she and Mary stayed overnight at Goodwood before driving the 120 miles distance to join Harry Hannay Snr at Ipoh. Two months later they returned to help out when my mother was rushed into hospital for the

Kate Hannay
(Photo: Kirsty Johns)

birth of her second child, but soon discovered that there was little for them to do. Goodwood was run by the staff.

In Ipoh, the pattern was similar. Harry Hannay Snr preferred to employ a woman cook, and there were also two young Chinese girls working as 'boys', cleaning and serving meals and drinks. In the garden, an Indian kabun cut the

Harry Hannay Snr
(Photo: Kirsty Johns)

lawn with a scythe. Everything indoors and out-of-doors was immaculate. "Women – wives and daughters – were left very much to our own devices," recalled Mary. "Before dinner I used to frequent the Swimming Club, or accompany my mother to the Ipoh Club, where Dad was usually to be found playing billiards."[5]

Some evenings they played badminton until dark, with long lime drinks to follow. "I did learn Mah Jong, not taking it too seriously though. There were always dances at the Ipoh Club and at the Swimming Club – a St Andrew's Night Ball, a New Year's Eve Ball, and lesser celebrations. You invited friends to dinner and proceeded to the club in that group, but knowing the other people made it very informal."

On one occasion there was a fancy dress ball at the Ipoh Club, and Red Reddish, by then the Borneo Motors manager in Ipoh, decided to go as an Egyptian Mummy. He instructed his driver, Mat Itam, to drive him to the main entrance where he got himself out of the car and promptly lay down on the club doorstep while Mat Itam ran into the club screaming to attract attention.

There were a few people drinking in the bar that night and eventually somebody came to investigate. Finding a mummified corpse spread-eagled outside, the club secretary said, "Good heavens, Red. What on earth are you doing?"

"I'm here for the fancy dress ball," he answered.

"Well, your costume is fine. But you're a week early," came the reply.

Patricia Ann Martine, my second sister, was born at Penang General Hospital on 23rd December with Cuthbert Stanley, the resident doctor, in attendance. On Christmas Day her delighted father dressed up as Santa Claus and went the rounds of the colony's children's parties, some held in company offices, others in private homes. The photographer employed to record the occasion, and who by then had acquired quite a reputation for himself for covering virtually all of the European community's social events, was H. Tokisatsu.

Many of his pictures survive, but what nobody even remotely suspected at the time was that Mr Tokisatsu was a Japanese agent sent under cover to take photographs of Penang's harbour and its defences.

CHAPTER FIVE

White Rajahs and Dyaks

Sarawak belongs to the Malays, Sea Dyaks, Land Dyaks, Kayans,
Kenyas, Milanos, Muruts, Kadayans, Birayahs and other tribes, not
to us. It is for them we labour, not ourselves.

James Brooke, 1st White Rajah of Sarawak.

WHEN in 1939 my father was posted to Sarawak, on the island of Borneo, he had already lived in the Far East for eighteen years, twelve in Singapore as a bachelor and six in Penang as a married man. As a career challenge, it was irresistible.

Sarawak, of which Kuching, twenty miles inland on a river, is the capital town, comprises a large chunk of the coastal territory on the north-west coast of Borneo, and occupies 48,250 square miles (124,485 square kilometres). The country is divided into three regions; a swampy coastal plain, a broad sweep of undulating hills, and a mountainous interior rising 4,000 feet (1,200 metres) above sea level. Rivers and streams provide the only natural communication links, and three quarters of the region is covered by dense tropical rain forest.

Borneo, next to Australia and New Guinea, is the third largest island in the world, and lies across the equator, directly in the path of the seasonal rain-bringing winds. All of the countries within – Brunei, Sarawak, British North Borneo, and Dutch Borneo in the 19th and first half of the 20th century; today, Brunei, Sarawak, Sabah, and Kalimantan – share the same climate. Blowing up from the south between April and September, and from the north-west between October and March, two monsoons pour their rain over the island.

Seen from an aeroplane, the tropical jungle of Borneo extends like a brilliant carpet of every shade of green. From the central highlands, through hilly lowlands downwards and onwards towards the coastal areas, a multiplicity of rivers drain away the raging torrents like one enormous sluice system.

In the absence of roads such waterways form the only practical means of human transportation inland, but the terrain is irregular, swampy, unpredictable and overgrown. River edges are straddled by the roots of nika trees hanging in mid-air. Access from the sea is restricted by sand-bars, sometimes too shallow to be crossed by anything larger than a canoe. Further to complicate ease of passage, there runs a daily bore* which causes sudden and often fatal, tidal aberrations.

Added to the obvious drawbacks brought about through the remoteness of this terrain, the indigenous inhabitants of Sarawak in the mid-19th century comprised numerous native tribes of different origin, not to mention immigrant Chinese and Malays.

This was the diverse community upon which James Brooke, the 30-year-old son of an East India Company employee, first came in 1838. Having invested his inheritance in a schooner, which he named *The Royalist,* Brooke sailed up the Kuching River to quell a native rebellion on behalf of the Sultan of Brunei's representative, Pangiran Muda Hasim. In return for his services, Brooke was offered the country, along with its government and trade. In 1841, he accepted and became the first White Rajah of Sarawak.[1]

The British Government was piqued; why had he not accepted the Sultan's gift on behalf of Her Britannic Majesty? To answer this charge, he was summoned to an official inquiry in London which, after much deliberation, vindicated him of any wrong-doing; the British Colonial Office had no idea what to do about him.

James Brooke had his own ideas about governing Sarawak, and six years later, Lord John Russell's administration in London swallowed their reservations and appointed him not only British Governor of Labuan, but Consul General to the island of Borneo. The following year he was knighted.

Ultimately, it was his management of the ethnic make-up of Sarawak that proved the key to his success. Malays were the fishermen and rice farmers, content with their lot when left to their own devices. Although the Dyak tribes liked to exchange jungle produce for basic goods, it was the productivity of the Chinese, the entrepreneurs, traders, miners, and coolies, which fuelled Sarawak's economy. The financial support of the Borneo Company helped, of course.

James Brooke proved an astute organiser. He suppressed slavery and

---

* A bore is a tidal wave created when the flow from a river hits the incoming tide of the sea.

piracy. By a series of annexations and cessions, large areas such as the Rejang and Barang river regions were added to his domain. By the following century, his nephew, followed by his great-nephew, were firmly entrenched as oriental rulers, ranking in Imperial Precedence before the rulers of Malaya. Whenever their yacht entered Singapore Harbour, they were honoured with a twenty-one gun salute.

Within their own territory, the Brookes were among the last autocratic rulers with absolute power of life and death over their subjects. But this was a benevolent rule; power was exercised with wisdom and restraint. The British Government had the right to appoint a Consul to Sarawak, but not an Advisor or Resident. Only the word of the Rajah was Law, and on matters of humanity, it was never abused.

From every aspect, it was a model and benign dictatorship. At all times was the Rajah informally accessible to his people, regardless of gender or creed; subjects, rich and poor alike, had their grievances heard personally. Every day the Rajah would be rowed in the State Barge from the Astana across the Sarawak River to the Court House. Sheltered from the sun by a symbolic yellow silk umbrella, he carried a spear, a gift from the Sultan of Brunei. In the Court House he sat, as had his predecessors before him,

The Astana, Kuching, 1939
(Martine Family Collection)

at a table placed in the centre of a small office with an open door on each wall. No guards were necessary to restrain the silent litigants who sat cross-legged or squatting, chewing betel as they patiently waited their turn to be seen. None departed unheard.

Genuinely loved and respected for three generations, the rajahs Brooke wisely recognised the State religion as Islam, to the extent that when ceremonies, such as the blessing of the Sarawak Rangers' colours, were performed, it was the Muslim Imam who took precedence over the Anglican Bishop of Sarawak during the consecration.[2]

From its beginning, the Brooke tradition was to hold Sarawak rigidly in trust for its people, no matter how loudly progress came knocking at the door, and to administer it on their behalf along feudal lines under their own tribal chiefs, the Malay ministers, known as Datus, the Iban Penghulu Temenggong, and the leaders of the Sarawak Chinese, in co-operation with five European officers, known as Residents, who presided over specific divisions.

Encompassing western Sarawak, from the Border with Dutch Borneo, the First Division had Kuching as its Capital. Simanggang was Capital of the Second Division which incorporated the tributaries of the rivers Lupar and Kalaka, stretching to Betong and beyond to Enkilili and Lubok Antu. The Third, and largest Division, with Sibu as its Capital, embraced the Rejang, with outposts on the coast at Igan, Mukah and Bintulu, and inland, before the vast hinterland begins, at Kanowit, Kapit, and Belaga. Miri was the Capital of the Fourth Division, fed by the rivers Niah, Tinjar and Baram, stretching deep into the jungle to Long Akar and beyond. In the north, the smaller Fifth Division, with Trusam and Limbang, enclosed Brunei from the land on three sides.

Supporting the Residents in their complex responsibilities were District Officers, but because of the disparate terrain in which they too operated, they were almost always left to their own devices. Letters were exchanged once a month; similarly regular reports were forwarded to the Rajah,[3] but there was little interference without cause.

The Rajahs implicitly trusted their Residents and District Officers who were, for the most part, recruited among the Brooke family's circle of friends in England and expected to remain in their posts without leave for between seven and ten years, to identify themselves with the native outlook and to refrain from marital commitment. The marriage clause was amended during the 1920s, when only marriage during a first turn of duty was unacceptable. All the same, some recruits never married at all. They had no need to. An abundance of local women was available in the uncomplicated world in which they found themselves. It was a challenging, often lonely way of life, but one that suited a certain type of British temperament.

Responsible for putting this structure into place in the 19th century was the Rajah Charles Johnson Brooke, James Brooke's nephew, and although latterly dismissed as a humourless tyrant, there is no doubt that he was, in many ways, a visionary. Charles was 23 when he arrived in Kuching in 1852, and the heir presumptive to his uncle's realm – the Tuan Muda, as he was called – was his elder brother Brooke Brooke. Ten years posted to a remote out-station, during which time his uncle gradually fell out with Brooke, stood him in ideal stead for the role which James, in the course of time, was to bestow upon him. Certainly, when James Brooke died in 1868, his successor could not have been better prepared.

It is hard to empathise kindly with Rajah Charles, living at the Astana in what were described as "spartan" conditions,[4] but one should never under-estimate the benefits of such a regime. His relationship with the remarkable Ranee Margaret, from whom he remained separate for twenty years, is equally complex, but by then she had born him seven children, one of them still-born, three others dying of cholera on a sea voyage to England.

Exasperated as she undoubtedly must have felt at times, she went along with his intransigent ways and never let him down. She too came to love Sarawak and, in an age of prejudice, made an invaluable contribution towards the stability of Brooke government by forging close friendships with wives of the native hierarchy.

It was not at all easy for her. Sarawak was seen as a man's world in which her husband imposed an often ruthless regime of rigorous discipline not unbecoming to an old-style public school headmaster. Next to radically upgrading the country he had inherited, and paying off its debts, he succeeded in abolishing the widespread slavery that had existed among the native tribes for generations. He also managed to clamp down on the Dyak's widely indulged ritual of headhunting, not an easy victory since it was largely associated with their religious beliefs.

The name Dyak is used collectively to describe the indigenous people living in the north of the Borneo watershed, but this can cause confusion since it implies that all of them share a common origin. That is simply not the case. In the 20th century, there were at least twenty racial groupings involved, the more remote designated the Orang Ulu, the up-river people. Only a few remain of the primitive Penans or Punans, light skinned and mongoloid in feature. Long ago they roamed the entire island, but by the 19th century their habitat had become restricted to the forests encroaching upon the waters of the Baram and Limbang rivers in the Fifth Division.

Nearby, inhabiting the inland hills, were the Kelabit ('people of the River Libid') and in the valley of Trusan, lived the Lun Bawang, also known as Murut, planters of padi and cattle farmers. Occupying the nearby Lawas District, with an overlap into North Borneo, were the Tagal, best known for the sprung dance floors in their long-houses.

Largely confined to the Fourth and Fifth Divisions were the Kedayan and Bisaya, the former occupying small farming communities and prevalent in Brunei, the latter in the Limbang Valley, where they farmed buffalo. Concentrated in the Baram Valley in the Fourth Division, were the warlike Kayans, small and stocky in stature, but physically well-suited for travel by canoe. Their neighbours, the Kenyahs, were aristocratic, with hereditary chiefs, but less forceful, although equally famed for their singing and dancing, carving and bead work.

In the swamplands of the Third Division, north of the Rejang, were found the Melanau, related to the Kayan and Kenyah of the interior. A hundred years ago they planted sago palms to make starch, but as the demand dried up, timber, padi and fishing took over.

Mainly occupying dry ground on the Sarawak and upper Sadong rivers in the First Division were the smaller and darker Bidayuh, or Land-Dyaks, the second largest racial grouping with long-houses at Kampung Anna Rais and Kampung Gayu. In the valleys of the Second Division, travelling almost everywhere by canoe, were Sea-Dyaks. These people, taller and fairer, became known as Ibans, in many ways a more appropriate name since Iban means 'wanderer' in the Kayan language. By 1939, with long-houses on the Skrang, Lemanak, Batang Ai and Rejang river systems they were by far the largest group.

Nothing ever dies in Borneo; everything mortal is spiritual. Collective Dyak belief makes certain of that. The vague concept of an all-powerful being exists, but it is the spirits who control the earth, sky and water. There

Dyak ceremonial costumes
(Martine Family Collection)

Dyak women in ceremonial costume
(Martine Family Collection)

is an after-life, not dissimilar to earthly existence, but there are various levels at which it can be entered, depending upon your status in life. Preferably the dead should accompany the dead, and the taking of a human head in honour of somebody who has already deceased ensures prosperity for the departed in the after-life.

Fundamentally, the taking of a human head was seen as a rite of passage. If a young man wished to be accepted as a grown-up, or to take a wife, it was customary for him to first bring home a trophy. Most Iban brides insisted upon it. More importantly, the ownership of heads brought status to a long-house. When a parent died it was seen as a family's duty to acquire a head before a funeral could take place. In such circumstances, families were expected to remain in mourning until the spirit of a servant could be found to accompany the deceased into Sembayan (the shades).

Finally, following a successful decapitation, the achievement was advertised by the tattooing of one joint of one finger on one hand with blue dye. A second score earned a further tattoo on a second joint, and so on. As late as the 1970s, there were Ibans alive who could boast not only handfuls, but armfuls of tattoos.

During the rule of Rajahs Charles and Vyner, the practice of head-hunting was rigidly outlawed, and perpetrators of such acts were treated as criminals. Among those recruited to enforce the law was a reluctant and already much tattooed Iban chief, Temenggong Koh, in whose long-house Charles Martine and many of his European colleagues often stayed overnight on their excursions up-river.

When the Japanese invaded, however, headhunting became open season again, and it is approximated that over 400 Japanese heads were collected between 1942 and 1945 to decorate up-river long-houses. Among them was that of the Japanese Army's Director of Education, whose gold-rimmed spectacles were replaced on his skull, and respectfully polished each morning by the chief of the house.[5]

Under such circumstances, the great Rajah Charles would certainly have approved, but he had gone to great lengths to stamp out this practice. To control the indigenous population, he built a series of forts, notably Margherita at Kuching, affectionately named after his wife. Others were given acronyms after the Brooke family and their friends. Fort Alice was raised at Simanggang, Fort Burdett at Muda, Fort Charles at Kabong, Fort

The Borneo Company launch on the Sarawak River in front of Fort Margherita
(Martine Family Collection)

Emma at Kanowit, Fort Florence at Trusan, Fort Keppel at Bintulu, Fort Lili at Netong, Fort Rose at Baram, and Fort Vyner at Valaga. Rajah Charles would appear at these outstations annually, always welcomed by a 21-gun salute. Usually he would stay for several days, hearing court cases and renewing the friendships he had cultivated as a young man with the local people.

Before his death in 1917, Kuching was transformed into a model town with improved roads, such as existed. He built offices and churches, turned the Sarawak police into a competent force, upgraded the hospital, and introduced a waterworks, a railway (although the track ran only ten miles into the interior), and the wireless.

Writing about Charles Brooke at the time of the Centenary celebrations in 1941, Ong Tiang Swee, head of Sarawak's Chinese community, had this to say: "Even today the memory of his impressive personality remains vividly in my mind. He looked very stern, but withal was really quite human and I shall always remember his many kindnesses. He was a good friend to my people, and adopted a policy of general tolerance and respect for our ancient customs – a policy which has been followed by his successor, our present Rajah."

Ong Tiang Swee was sent for when Rajah Charles took his final leave of Sarawak in 1917. "I shall not see Sarawak again," he told him. "My time is up. Whatever happens I want you to serve and advise my successor as you have so well served me. We are in the same boat, Tiang Swee, we float or sink together."[6]

CHAPTER SIX

Gossip and Rumour

After all, the East has been the foundation of all that is best in Europe.

Ranee Margaret Brooke, *Good Morning and Goodnight*

V YNER Brooke succeeded his father as Rajah of Sarawak in May 1917, although such was the changeable nature of affection within the Brooke family that at one stage it looked as if he too would be passed over in favour of his brother, in his case his younger brother Bertram. As it was, their father's will stipulated that the Tuan Muda Bertram must always stand in for his brother on all occasions when Vyner was absent from Sarawak. Over the years Betram was to do so with great dedication. Uncomplaining, he became the workhorse of the family, but harboured no ambition to supplant his brother. The love that they shared for Sarawak was sufficient incentive.

Yet Vyner Brooke remains a puzzle to many of his biographers, not least when trying to make sense of his erratic relationship with his volatile, sometime Private Secretary, Gerard MacBryan, a curiously charismatic, Machiavellian figure who joined the Sarawak Civil Service in 1920.

In 1937, MacBryan was the subject of a book, *Triumphant Pilgrimage*, written by the journalist Owen Rutter.[1] It tells of how, after witnessing the execution of a Malay murderer at Limbang, MacBryan (referred to by Rutter throughout the text as 'David Chale') was so overcome by the condemned man's calm in the

Sa'erah MacBryan, 1941
(Martine Family Collection)

face of death, that he converted to Islam. This also inspired him subsequently to embark upon a pilgrimage to Mecca taking with him Sa'erah, a beautiful divorcee of mixed Bidayuh and Melanau parentage whom he had come across by accident while walking in the Rajah's garden at The Astana.

In the Borneo Company archives is a confidential report on MacBryan prepared shortly after my father took charge of the Kuching office. Handsome and clever, Gerard MacBryan was the son of a respected neurologist, and brought up near Bath in a house which his father ran as a mental asylum. Given a post in the Third Division, it appears that he was directly responsible for a feud between certain leading Malay chieftains. As a result, he resigned in 1924, being re-appointed three years later. In 1931, he was once again permitted to resign.

In 1935 MacBryan re-applied to join the service, but his request was rejected and he set off to Arabia on his voyage of self-discovery. When he returned to Sarawak the following year, he was refused entry and when he made an attempt to do so, was immediately deported to Singapore where he threatened to give "sensational disclosures to the press." The threats were soon afterwards withdrawn, and he wrote to the Rajah promising "never to attempt to return to Sarawak as long as you live."

Aged 38, and back in England accompanied by Sa'erah, he discovered that he was eligible for National Service. With war in Europe looming, he therefore petitioned Rajah for his wife to be allowed to return to her people, and to be allowed to accompany her on the understanding that he "would not interfere with public life or participate in State politics."

When Vyner agreed to this, the MacBryans were allowed to leave England on condition that Gerard return within six months to enlist. On arrival in Sarawak, however, he inadvertently dropped his passport in the river and succeeded in acquiring a new one without the British Government endorsement. Much to everyone's amazement, Vyner then appointed him his political secretary, with a place on the Supreme Council.

Throughout every account written on the end of Brooke rule in Sarawak, Gerard MacBryan's name features as the bogey-man.* Even the Ranee Sylvia, who admitted to plotting with him herself, claimed to be baffled by why her husband should have been so clearly mesmerized by this devious and, towards the end of his life, openly mad individual.[2] But there is another possibility.

MacBryan, it has to be said, was clever, decisive, and regardless of his personal motives, not afraid to act on his employer's behalf. The inevitable

---

* The Ranee Sylvia called him 'The Baron'.

conclusion has to be that Rajah used him as his agent provocateur,[3] which of course suggests that there was very much more to Vyner Brooke's instinct for survival than is generally acknowledged.

The Ranee Sylvia, whom Vyner married in 1911, was also not averse to playing politics. Youngest daughter of the 2nd Viscount Esher, she and her sister Dorothy shared a rarefied childhood, which might to some extent explain why they so boldly championed the unorthodox. Both were star struck. Three years older than the Ranee, Dorothy Brett became a painter of note and lived with the novelist D.H. Lawrence and his wife Freda in New Mexico. For her part, Sylvia was early on lured into the fantastical world of J.M. Barrie and George Bernard Shaw.[4] A proposal from the Rajah Mudah of Sarawak must have been irresistible.

In London, she often wore Malay dress, especially the yellow sarong which was her Sarawak royal prerogative.[5] Coupled with her gossipy books and forays into popular journalism, she soon acquired a certain celebrity which did little to enhance the image of Sarawak in the English home counties.

After 1930, her visits to Sarawak became less frequent, and critics began to suggest that she had become bored with the place. When my parents arrived in Kuching, she had not been there for three years and was off in Hollywood trying to interest the actor Errol Flynn in a film script.

Vyner Brooke's principal difficulty, which increased with the advancement of his years, was that he had no immediate male heir, only three glamorous daughters whose social antics were the talk of 1930s London. In its inimitable way, the British media[6] tagged them Princess Gold, Princess Pearl and Princess Baba, which was entirely inaccurate since their native prefix was the rather more modest 'Datang,' an honorific title bestowed upon them by their father.

Leonora, the eldest daughter, known as Noni, made a happy marriage to the 2nd Earl of Inchcape, chairman of P&O. Elizabeth, 'Didi,' married Harry Roy, 'King of the Hot-Cha Orchestra,' and Valerie, 'Vava,' wed Bob Gregory, an amateur all-in wrestler. However, it was Didi's first husband, Harry Roy, who came up with Sarawak's best known publicity stunt, the foxtrot song *Sarawaki*. An instant popular hit tune, it was played all over the world.[7]

What added to Vyner Brooke's difficulties when it came to the succession was that his younger brother Bertram had produced a son, Anthony, known to his family and friends as Peter. In addition there were other claimants such as Hope Brooke, son of the second Rajah's disinherited elder brother. In 1927, Isaka (Esca) Brooke, the English-educated illegitimate son of Rajah Charles by a native woman, instigated a lawsuit to achieve recognition of his status.* [8] And so it went on.

At one stage, a rumour was even put about that Gerard MacBryan, having converted to Islam, was hoping to succeed Vyner, and before long the Ranee was pressing for her daughter Leonora to be recognised as heir. As late as1940, she was still proposing that Leonora's son, Simon Mackay, be named Vyner's successor. ** [9]

All of this behind-the-scenes gossip was around when my parents set off to live in Sarawak, but my father undoubtedly had other things on his mind. With the ups and downs of the rubber market, the dispersal of its mineral interests, and a general sense of malaise throughout its agency activities, the Sarawak branch of the Borneo Company required a major shake-up. His immediate preoccupation therefore was to reorganize the branch offices in Salim, Sibu, Miri and Kapit.

His European team was already in situ.*** In each location, were company offices and employee bungalows complementing the five in the compound in Kuching – BMK, Aneberg, Snipe Cottage, Ivy Lodge, and Batek.

Next to the Rajah and Ranee, in the Sarawak society which awaited my parents in 1939, were several men of extreme importance who had to be acknowledged. Foremost among them was Penghulu Temenggong Koh, the much revered Iban chief from the Balleh region of the Upper Rejang, whose headquarters were at Kapit, 200 miles up river. Old and muscular, his everyday dress was a loin-cloth and a jacket of goatskins. His hair was styled in a labong (turban); his earlobes stretched with traditional boar

---

*   Esca renewed his claim when cession was announced in 1946.

**   Following a distinguished career in commerce and politics, the Hon. Simon Mackay was created Baron Tanlaw in 1971.

***   It consisted of Richard Sagar and Patrick Merrells in Kuching. Charles Horn was based at Salim, with William McKerracher in charge of the sawmill; Peter Cobbold, at Sibu, and Kenneth Cargill, at Miri. Connup 'Batty' Miles was forestry manager at Kapit.

The waterfront at Kuching showing the Borneo Company offices, 1939. To the left are the steps up Bukit Mata Hill leading to BMK

(Martine Family Collection)

tusks, which he alternated with heavy brass rings. Koh unashamedly revelled in the inheritance of his ancestors and his tribe, staunchly believing in the countless good and evil spirits which inhabited the rivers, forests and hills of his territory and presided over human destiny.[10]

My father was spellbound by the Dyaks, and by their childlike joys, loves and habits, not least the pagan ceremonies in which they expected all others to take part. Going among them, he was captivated by the shy gentleness they displayed towards strangers, equally aware that, less than two decades earlier, his welcome might have been entirely different.

Having in 1938 helped to launch the Borneo Company's timber activities on the Rejang, in which the Ibans played a significant role, he became a frequent visitor to the bazaar township of Kapit, where Koh and his lesser chiefs and followers had their headquarters. A few miles up river was Seputin, where Connup Llewellyn Miles, the forestry manager, known to his friends as 'Batty,' employed an Iban workforce in the felling and cutting of logs which, having been assembled, were floated down river to the company's sawmill. Extraordinarily energetic, and a genuine eccentric, Batty integrated effortlessly into the native community where stories about him abound to this day.

When one of his sawmill elephants took ill and the visiting vet prescribed a course of tablets, Batty decided that the only way to persuade the beast to co-operate with the treatment was to position a Dyak blowpipe in the elephant's mouth, insert the pill, and blow. Unfortunately, the elephant burped first and it was Batty who swallowed the pill. He felt unwell for a month. One lonely Christmas, he prepared a roast turkey with all of the trimmings and sat down to dine alone by candlelight in the heart of the jungle wearing his white dinner jacket. Quite what the Ibans must have thought of this is anyone's guess, but they certainly revered him.

Before western customs encroached upon them, all of the Iban men retained the traditional slim loin-cloth; the women, their skin only a little darker than that of a European, wore sarongs and went about their chores bare breasted. Their custom of wrapping coils of brass wire around arms and legs, with arms held away from the body, had resulted in a strangely graceful swinging walk, yet the young men, who wore similar body adornments, remained upright and strong. All chewed the ubiquitous betel nut, staining their mouths bright red.

There was nothing patronizing in my father's insight into this other world. His view was that the Dyaks of Sarawak, in their uncomplicated way, were in far closer touch with the important realities of the universe – death and survival – than many a philosopher from our western civilisation.

After the Iban, the largest native grouping in Sarawak was that of the Malays, many of whom were settlers from Sumatra, but others had come from Brunei at a time when the Sultanate had held dominion over the entire northern coastal region as far east as Kuching. By the end of the 19th century there were Malay kampongs established in every town and, being staunch supporters of three generations of White Rajah, a number of their representatives by then held significant posts in the Brooke administration.[11]

Representing the Malay community in Sarawak therefore was the ageing Abang Haji Abdillah, the former Datu Bandar and now Datu Patinggi, Sarawak's principal hereditary Malay chief. There was some discrepancy over whether he was the 14th or 17th Datu Patinggi, but that hardly mattered. He was the senior non-royal Malay chieftain, and the Malays, retaining the example of their homeland, maintained a healthy respect for royal and noble birth. For some years, the Datu Patinggi and his fellow Datu Amar* were preoccupied with a feud over which one of them should receive the profits from the sale of turtle eggs from Talang Talang and Satang, Sarawak's Turtle Islands to the west of Santubong. In 1941, the feud was finally settled with the establishment of a Turtle Trust accompanied by a cash concession to both claimants.[12]

Sarawak's most recent immigrants were Chinese, although by 1939 most of their families had been resident there for at least two generations. The earliest arrivals were Hokkien and Teochew, traders from the sea, and Hakka gold-miners, who travelled overland from Dutch Borneo. Soon Cantonese arrived to plant pepper, followed by padi and rubber planters from Foochow.

Still presiding over Sarawak's Chinese community in 1939 was the venerable Ong Tiang Swee, Teochew Kapitan China, to whom my father had an early introduction. It was an initiation into an extraordinary dynasty founded by Tiang Swee's father, the Singapore-born Ong Ewe Hai who

---

* Abang Suleimanbin Haji Taha, assistant Lands Officer, was appointed Datu Amar in 1928.

Ong Tiang Swee
(Martine Family Collection)

had come to Sarawak at the age of 16 and made a fortune through barter trading.

Ong Tiang Swee himself was born in Kuching in 1864 and joined his father's firm Ong Ewe Hai & Co in 1882. By the age of 22, he had become a director of the Sarawak & Singapore Steamship Company, in which the Borneo Company had a major interest. From 1914 onwards, he ran the Sarawak Farms Syndicate which held the monopoly of opium and gambling in the region. Having bought over the Borneo Company's steamship interests in 1919, he remained chairman of the renamed Sarawak Steamship Company until its controlling interest was in turn taken over in 1931 by the Straits Steamship Company.

Tiang Swee was also chairman of the Sarawak Chinese Banking Company and owned the Kuching Sawmill Company with its office in front of the Tua Pek Kong temple.* When the bank closed and the sawmill company was sold, he formed Chop Hiap Soon Hin, general merchants. Tiang Swee and Vyner Brooke were firm friends for many years, and Vyner, who enjoyed roast sucking-pig and snipe, was a regular luncheon visitor to the Ong farm at Batu Kinyang.

The Ong Family's town house, dating from 1886, stood on a hill behind Ewe Hai Street, in central Kuching. But Tiang Swee was more likely to be found at his farmhouse on the Batu Kinyang estate, at 2nd Mile Rock Road, a model agricultural enterprise incorporating cattle, pigs, poultry, deer, orchards and a coconut-oil factory. In addition, he owned sago and jelutong factories and several hundred acres of rubber plantation at Temelan and Batu.

---

* The century old Temple of Tua Pek Kong in Kuching is located at Jalan Tunkul Abdul Rahman.

Second of Tiang Swee's seven sons* (and three daughters), was Ong Kwan Hin, born in Kuching in 1896 and who, during the Japanese occupation, took on his 78-year-old father's responsibilities as Kapitan China. He was a founder-member of both the Sarawak Rotary Club and Sarawak Turf Club, and Chairman of the United Merchants' Association. His younger brother, Ong Eng Hin, was a gifted musician and a founder of the Sarawak Musical Society, and Tiang Swee's fourth son, Ong Hap Leong, a gold-miner by profession, sat on the Negri Council.

Ong Kwan Hin himself had ten sons and four daughters. His eldest son, Datuk Ong Kee Hui was to become Chairman of the Sarawak United People's Party and hold posts in the future Malaysian Government.

Another family member who through business contact, then social interaction became one of my fathers's earliest friends, was Wee Kheng Chiang. A Hokkien banker in both Singapore and Kuching, Kheng Chiang was married to Tiang Swee's second daughter. Fast talking, with a wrinkled face and an engaging giggle, he stood over six feet tall, which is unusual for a Chinese. The Ranee Sylvia described him as 'The Uncrowned King of Sarawak,'[13] and as founder of the United Chinese Bank (UCB),** Wee Kheng Chiang did, in fact, become an enormously rich man.

The Chinese, when they befriend you, are thoughtful and loyal, and Kheng Chiang was to prove the full measure of this on more than one occasion. In his retirement, my father's greatest treasure was a lacquered Chinese stoneware statue of Tua Pek Kong, the Hokkien God of Prosperity, a gift from Ong Tiang Swee. In the years that followed his appointment as manager of the Borneo Company's Kuching office, he was to become deeply proud of, and grateful for, the close relationships which developed between himself and the Ong and Wee families.

---

*   Ong Hap Hin, Tiang Swee's eldest son died of an illness when young. Two other sons, Ong Yam Hin and Ong Han Hok, died in an accident at sea in 1923.

** With Wee Kheng Chiang's son, Wee Cho Yaw, as chairman and chief executive officer, the United Chinese Bank changed its name in 1965 to become the United Overseas Bank (UOB).

CHAPTER SEVEN

Kuching

People speak of the silence of the East. Sarawak had no such silence.
All day, hawkers plied their wares in the bazaar, gongs beat in the
mosque and, now and again, one heard the wailing of a one-stringed
instrument lingering on the air.

Sylvia Brooke, Ranee of Sarawak, *Queen of The Headhunters.*

CHARLES and Pat Martine arrived in Kuching towards the end of
February 1939. Traditionally, Borneo Company managers occupied
a bungalow on Bukit Mata hill named 'Aneberg' after the first manager's
wife, but at the time of their arrival this was still occupied by my father's

BMK, Kuching, 1939
(Martine Family Collection)

predecessor. Instead, they were allocated, on the far side of the hill, a commodious, but gloomy mansion called Bukit Mata Kuching, always known simply as 'BMK.' Striped canvas blinds drooped over the windows of the upstairs verandah, and the first impression on entering through the front door was of a vast decayed museum filled to capacity with quite the filthiest furnishings my mother had ever seen.

Aneberg and BMK were situated, to the right and left respectively, above the Borneo Company's offices on the northern bank of the Sarawak River as it enters into a long and broad reach with small hills rising on either side. Across the river from the sweeping lawns which overlooked the water's edge, could be seen Fort Margherita, rebuilt in the 1870s and named for the bride of the second Rajah Brooke.

Around the river bend lay the main town of Kuching. Here were Malay kampongs dotted against a distant backdrop of the jungle-clad Matang mountain range, rising to its peak of Serapi. On the right bank, situated amid tall palms in a parklike garden, was the Astana, the palace of the Rajah Brookes. Built for the 2nd Rajah in 1870, a Gothic tower formed the entrance, with wings on either side. Reception rooms and bedrooms were all on the first floor, and the roof was high pitched, with wooden shingles which resembled slates.

Approaching Kuching up-river to take up residence at the Astana after an unpleasant voyage, the Ranee Margaret had expressed her pleasure at seeing a good sized, whitewashed bungalow. This was the first Aneberg, erected in 1874 and reassuring her that she was not destined to live in a jungle hut. Below was a picturesque street of shops which comprised the Chinese bazaar. This was the principal thoroughfare of the town. Moored close to the shore were all sorts of odd craft – Chinese junks, Malay schooners, barges and canoes.[1]

Seventy years later, when my mother caught her first glimpse of her new home, the scene had hardly altered. There was little time to spend enjoying the view, however, because her first day in Kuching, from ten in the morning until dusk, was spent disposing of rotten and bug infested furniture with Ah Cheow, the houseboy. Virginia soon became a mass of mosquito bites and dirt, and Patricia was nearly suffocated in her pram by the mosquito net installed to protect her from the many and varied insects which had made BMK their ancestral home.

Scorpions and large black spiders tumbled out of dark recesses. When opening an old cupboard door, Pat at first imagined that it must be lined with tortoise-shell. Then the tortoise-shell moved, revealing itself to be wall-to-wall cockroach.

The former occupant, it transpired, had moved out to live with a native woman having hardly used the place. Even if he had, it seems unlikely it would have made a difference because it was obvious he was not the house-proud type. There was not a chair or cushion that did not smell of something unpleasant.

That first night Pat paced the floor of the bedroom. Unable to sleep, her mind was filled with nightmare images of the enormous array of Dyak spears hanging on the walls. The first sight to greet her on the staircase was of a Dyak headhunter's shield with the scalp hairs of his victims waving in the breeze from an open front door.

Joan and Kilner Black with baby
Margaret
(Photo: Margaret Hopkins)

The blessing was that they had brought their own mattresses and pillows with them and were at least able to sleep on clean bedding. The first thing to be scoured and disinfected was the only possible looking bed, a lumpy, creaking contraption.

The following afternoon, Kilner Black, manager of the Sarawak Steamship Company arrived to welcome them with his wife Joan, a friend of Dorothy McLellan. Joan took one look around the entrance hall and said, "God, I had no idea it was so awful in daylight. You can't possibly stay here until it has been cleaned up."

So the Blacks packed up the household, including the amah and Ah Cheow, and installed them in their house on Reservoir Road which, having been built for the managing directors of the Sarawak Steamship Company, was generally considered to be the most modern and comfortable residence in Kuching. My mother was put to bed and thoroughly spoiled with dinner sent to her room and, in the days that followed, my father must have employed all of the coolie labour in Kuching to have BMK scoured from end to end.

It was not the best of beginnings, but soon put to rights. Afterwards, Pat's only complaint was that BMK's former occupant, whom they encountered from time to time, never even had the decency to apologise. But then, of course, he was soured, having apparently hoped to stay on with the company. Instead, he had been 'allowed' to retire.

That was part of the problem. The affairs of the Borneo Company in Sarawak had fallen into considerable disarray, and my father found himself in charge of an office with far-flung responsibilities, often involving days of travel by motor launch. Aside from the agency work, which had been disintegrating for some time, the company was primarily concerned with rubber, pepper and timber, the much exaggerated mining concessions having by then been discarded.

Everything about Kuching in comparison to well-ordered, civilised Penang, was such a contrast. Humid days when it was impossible to remain dry out-of-doors for a second were followed by a sudden plunge of darkness and the exhilarating cool of evening. The nights that followed were soot dark and filled with noise: the chorus of beetles and tree-frogs was carried on the air. Then there was the bubet bird with its full-throated call; trees were hung with flying foxes coming to life as evening fell. Bats flapped in through windows, and enormous atlas moths fluttered across the balconies that encircled BMK.

All around, the jungle approaches were alive and crawling. My father's job often required him to visit remote mines and plantations, and when the servants retired to their quarters at the foot of the garden, my mother was left alone in the house with the children. Although the natives were a gentle, considerate people, it was lonely for a woman to be left for days on end. For her protection, a Dayak called Hantu was employed to walk the grounds at night. In effect this alarmed her all the more, especially as he would sit on the verandah until dawn and was so dark skinned that in the shadows of night it was impossible to see him.

Daytime could be equally hazardous. One morning she had been into the kitchen to collect a hot baked potato for her lunch. She was on her way to the nursery when she saw coming towards her a huge python slithering down the passageway. Without a moment's hesitation, she hurled the potato at its snout, scoring a bullseye.

The snake came to an abrupt halt, turned around and shot across the hall, through a door, and onto the verandah, out of sight. Afterwards my mother said she could not make up her mind whether she had "been more shocked at the sight of a snake in the house, or proud of having such a straight aim."

The colonial community in Kuching was tight, its administration and focus centred on the Astana, with social life, for the most part, revolving around the small hand-picked band of Rajah's expatriate administrative staff. Although the Tuan Besar of the Borneo Company occupied an important station in the community, the company's importance to the well-being of the country was not considered to be as great as it had been under the Rajah Charles. In the final decade of Brooke rule, there were those among the Sarawak Civil Service who looked down their noses on 'traders,' a throwback to the snobberies of the small, self-important European community encountered by the Ranee Margaret the century before.

"It is rather amusing, but somewhat disconcerting," she wrote in her biography, "to realise how the members of almost any community of English men and women settled in out-of-the-way places take pleasure in having rows with one another, especially those who are ignorant of the world, who know nothing of society with a big S, and who, suddenly finding themselves in a remote land, imagine that they are Somebody."[2]

With few roads, since the official line was that the country was to be kept as a reserve for the Dyaks, there was a strikingly mediaeval feel about the place. Each morning at 5am, a gun fired from Fort Margherita sounded the wake-up call, and a similar shot fired at 8pm announced the end of day. So far as my mother was concerned, the most welcome gunshot was the one that announced the arrival of the Mail Ship.

Every ten days the *Vyner Brooke* sailed back and forth from Singapore. The voyage took two days and three nights. Sailings were geared to the tides so as to navigate the sand bar at the mouth of the Sarawak River and allow travel up the 20 miles up river to Kuching town on the flood tide.[3]

In addition to the post, the *Vyner Brooke* brought over films which were projected in The Sylvia, a small cinema built by the Rajah, usually one of the *King Kong* series because the Malays in particular adored them. The boat also brought satchels of books for library subscribers. On seeing the vessel approach up river, my mother's heart soared rapidly and sank when she watched it depart.

Between 4.30pm and 6pm, there were games of tennis, or a round of golf in the cool of the evening before darkness fell. After that the men played snooker or bowls, and the women, either bridge or Mah Jong. Once a month, on a Saturday night, there was a dance.

In an almost exclusively all-male environment, informal social life centred on the Aurora Hotel, the only hotel patronised by Europeans. Many of the same people assembled at the Resthouse Bar or at the "men only" Sarawak Club, a dingy place, where Tiger beer was drunk over curry tiffin on Sundays.

It did not take long for my parents to discover that among the European community, despite their snobberies, the lines of moral approbation were distinctly more liberal than in Singapore. Extraordinarily outspoken and far-sighted for a Victorian Englishman, Rajah Charles had once written that the most suitable population for developing a tropical country was one derived from intermarriage between European and native races.

On this basis, he had no objection to his officers keeping a native mistress providing that no preferential treatment was given to her family. Children of such unions, although sometimes resentful of their parentage, were regularly found minor posts in the Brooke administration.

In some ways, therefore, pre-war Sarawak was very definitely ahead of the times. In other ways it was not dissimilar to an oriental/ex-patriate adaptation of Jane Austen's *Pride & Prejudice.*

As a consequence, you chose your companions carefully in Kuching. For my parents there were return dinner parties at the homes of Kilner and Joan Black, and Sandy Trail, Manager of the Chartered Bank, and his wife Armey. Every month, there were visitors from Singapore and mainland Malaya, sometimes on business, sometimes friends on holiday. It was Charles's initiative to introduce curry tiffins (lunches) on Sundays for Borneo Company employees and their friends, a tradition that was maintained until the company's Kuching office finally disbanded.

Slowly, the young family settled into their new routine. It was not at all the same as Penang, but they knew that they had to make it work.

Besides, the household staff were infinitely more entertaining than at

Goodwood. One day, hearing a racket coming from the kitchen, my mother went to investigate and found Ah Cheow and Cookie having a 'humdinger of a row' and throwing pots and pans at one another. Storming in, she informed them in Malay that if they wanted to kill each other, they should go outside into the garden. Startled by her sudden appearance, all three of them fell about laughing.

Then she contracted her first dose of dysentery, a tropical infection to which everybody sooner or later succumbed. What with that and one thing and another, the house being clean and fit to live in, it was decided that she should return to Britain with Virginia and Patricia and stay for a spell with her parents in Kent. The change in climate worked like a tonic. The long sea voyage forced total relaxation, and my sisters had the opportunity to meet both sets of grandparents for the first time.

The war in Europe had been postponed in 1938, but in August 1939 Nazi Germany invaded Poland and although this theoretically obliged France and Britain to honour their guarantees to safeguard Poland's interests, there followed a winter of inactivity known as a 'phoney war.' There was still hope that the crisis could be resolved.

But it soon became obvious that the peace in Europe was not going to hold and Pat, convinced that if they did not get away from England soon they might not get another chance, made arrangements to return to the Far East in January. Then her mother took ill and, just as she was showing signs of recovery, her father fell victim to influenza followed by pneumonia. After everything the family and doctors could do for him, with night and day nursing, Fred Macquisten died from a cerebral haemorrhage on 29th February 1940.

On 10th March, my mother embarked for Malaya with her daughters. Having crossed from Folkestone to Paris, they caught up in Marseilles with a Blue Funnel ship from Liverpool, and sailed via Suez to Port Dickson.

Despite repeated warning of German submarines in the vicinity, the journey through the Mediterranean and the Suez Canal proved uneventful. Passengers were not allowed lights on deck and they were told to remain in their cabins at night. This turned out to be a blessing as, with over 150 children on board, coughs, colds and influenza were everywhere. Both Virginia and Patricia easily succumbed and just as they were on the road to recovery, my mother went down with the infection.

So when they eventually reached Penang, she was grateful to find Joe and Jean Allen waiting to welcome her. My father met them at Port Swettenham and after a short break staying at Woodside, the Bagnall's large Singapore house, the family returned to Kuching.[4] Shortly after their return, Jean Hembry, and her son John, joined them. Boris Hembry, by now planting rubber near Kuala Lumpur, had originally intended to come too, but the Colonial Government had issued a request for Volunteer Officers not to travel too far afield. Boris had therefore remained behind in Malaya.

In the event, the Hembry's visit was a success despite the running fight between John and Virginia which continued as ever. At one stage they were made to take their meals at separate ends of BMK's large nursery, with Virginia's amah, Ah See, stationed in between to keep the peace. Fortunately, Patricia was too small to join in the conflict.

Some mornings they went to the Astana to swim in the Rajah's pool. Occasionally Vyner would appear in person to invite them for a drink or a coffee while Amah looked after the children, but mostly they were left on their own to swim and relax. Some days, when he had to travel down river on business, my father took them with him on the *Batek*, the company's launch, and dropped them off on one or other of Sarawak's beaches. Equipped with a picnic, they lazed about until he arrived to collect them in the evening. Another time they visited the famous bat guano caves.

Out of the jungle, beside the Niah River in the Fourth Division, is a range of limestone hills rising 1,000 feet and punctured with caves. In the depths of the largest of these caves live millions of bats, and swifts, or male swallow, whose nests of glutinous saliva form the basis for the much coveted bird's-nest soup.

Bird's-nest soup is a Chinese delicacy with 'rejuvenating effects.' As a health-giving tonic, it is much in demand in the Far East, and has recently been shown to contain the epidermal growth factor and a water soluble glycoprotein which, it has been claimed, promotes cell-division, tissue repair and disease resistance.

In fact, the name is misleading. The nest itself is not eaten, only the flaky wall of saliva. In addition, it is both difficult and dangerous to collect, and has to be cleaned, making the end-product expensive.

Access to the caves of Niah is through a wide mouth in the mountain slope, made possible for human beings with ladders but totally inaccessible to jungle predators other than scorpion, snake and centipede. The species of bat and bird which live here are therefore safe from their enemies, but their excrement, a natural fertiliser, was once much in demand throughout the drained land of Sarawak. The foul-smelling guano deposits left by generations over the centuries once proved to be of infinite value to an island where no other form of compost was available, but in their own right, these cavernous vaults, today centred in a National Park, remain a marvel. Hung with seething, restless life, the caves of Niah are among the wonders of the world.

CHAPTER EIGHT

Cameron Highlands

*Strawberries and fresh roses arrived daily from the hills at up-country
Cameron Highlands, smoked and fresh salmon from Australia. In
those happy days Singapore was the last resort of yesterday in the
world of tomorrow.*

Noel Barber, *Sinister Twilight – The Fall of Singapore.*

THE news from Europe deteriorated rapidly over that summer of
1940. First, the Germans overran Denmark, Norway, the Netherlands,
and Belgium, and in June they invaded France. My father was scheduled
to take home leave in 1941, but under the circumstances decided it was
not such a good idea. Instead, he suggested they might all go to Australia
for a holiday, but in February a cable arrived from Dr Martine in Scotland
to say that my grandmother, Dora, had died.

There now seemed even less point in going home to Scotland, and
Australia somehow lost its appeal. In July, however, my parents decided to
take Virginia and Patricia on a trip to Cameron Highlands, a hill station
in central Malaya.

The underlying purpose of the Martine Family's visit was for my
mother to look at schools, having reached the conclusion that Virginia, with
no-one of her own age to play with in Kuching, was unhappy. She was
becoming visibly bored, and in the intense and relentless humidity of
Kuching had fallen victim to a mild form of diphtheria. Cameron
Highlands, 5,500 feet above sea level, was highly recommended for its clear
air and healthy outdoor activities. Not for nothing had Rajah Brooke chosen
it for his Malayan holiday home.

Set among the peaks of Banjaran Titiwangsa, Malaya's central mainland
mountain range, Cameron Highlands is the smallest district in the state of
Pahang and takes its name from William Cameron, a British government
surveyor who happened across the plateau in 1885. In 1925, Sir George
Maxwell, a senior civil servant, saw the potential of the cool peaks with their
tea plantations, waterfalls, terraces of vegetable, fruit and flower gardens,

Rajah Brooke and Ranee Sylvia with Sa'erah MacBryan in the garden of the
Astana, Kuching, 1941

(Martine Family Collection)

to be developed as a hill station. For colonials, it was to become a home
away from home, a 'little corner of England in Asia.'

Children from European families were often separated from their parents
and sent off to boarding schools at a young age, but in the Far East there was
no realistic alternative. In Singapore, Fergie and Bobbie Fergusson had
already sent their eldest son, aged five, to a boarding school in England.

That families should be divided in that way was inevitable, and parents
had at least the consolation of knowing that their children were being well
looked after. Moreover, most children, once they got used to their
surroundings, missed their parents far less than their parents missed them.

First they looked over the Convent School in the clean air of Cameron
Highlands. Leaving the girls with Boris and Jean Hembry, they made a quick
trip across to Sumatra to inspect the Kaben Djahe School at Brastagi, where
Kilner and Joan Black had sent their daughters Barbara, aged 7, and
Margaret, aged 3. Run by a Miss Griffiths Jones, they liked what they saw,
but concluded that if troubled times did indeed lie ahead, British soil was
a safer bet than Dutch.

The family returned to Sarawak on the 7th August, and my mother settled down to preparing Virginia's clothes for September when her first term at the Convent School began. However, the storm clouds of South East Asia were already gathering.

Japan had been at war with China since July 1937, and for some considerable time there had been speculation over Japan's long-term colonial ambitions, fuelled by a widely held suspicion that the unravelling situation in Europe would provide just the opportunity for whatever Japan's leaders had in mind.

In the summer of 1940, a new cabinet in Tokyo, under the leadership of Prince Konoye, but dominated by Japan's war minister Hideki Tojo, took office, and soon made its ambitions abundantly clear: to free Japan from economic dependence upon the United States and the countries of the British Empire.[1] Their ultimate goal was 'Asia for the Asiatics,' but under Japanese control. That September two major developments gave forewarning.

First, when France fell to the Germans, Japanese troops moved in to occupy the northern part of French Indo-China. This provided Japan with a strategic base close to the Malayan peninsula, giving unchallenged control of airfields within 300 miles of Kota Bharu, Malaya's northernmost port. Second, Japan signed a Tripartite Pact with Germany and Italy.

Initially this treaty was explained as a political move to prevent the United States from rallying to Britain's aid, but what Japan clearly wanted in return for supporting the Third Reich was possession of all British and Dutch territory in the Far East when the war in Europe was over, and Germany had won.

To gauge the political climate with a view to making decisions, my father once again despatched Pat to Singapore with the girls, proposing that she remain there until it was time for Virginia to begin school at Cameron Highlands. In Kuching, he had more than enough to keep himself busy.

To fill in time, therefore, my mother took the girls to stay first with Kenneth Simpson, then to the Hembrys, going on to Pahang in mid-September, where she booked into an hotel while finding a bungalow to rent. Having delivered Virginia to her school, she waited on for a further ten days to see her settled in, then returned to Singapore where she and Patricia literally hung about, staying at the Sea View Hotel for a further fortnight, all the time attempting to reassure herself that they were doing the right thing.

24th September 1941. Celebrations to mark 100 years of Brooke rule in Sarawak, and Rajah Vyner Brooke's 67th birthday. *Above* – the Rajah and Ranee are seated in front of the Sarawak Government Offices.
Facing page, above – the Datu Patinggi Abang Haji Abdillah addresses the Rajah; *below* – the 2/15 Punjabi Regiment on Parade

(Martine Family Collection)

However, nobody she encountered appeared unduly pessimistic about the threat of war, and besides, should it happen, which was considered highly unlikely, Singapore was invincible. The schools were full of children, and there was no prevailing sense of alarm about what might or might not occur.

Meanwhile, back in Kuching, lavish celebrations took place to mark not only a hundred years of Brooke rule, but the present Rajah's 67th birthday. A guard of honour furnished by the Sarawak Constabulary was drawn up near Pengkalan Batu, whilst detachments of the Royal Navy, Indian Army, Sarawak Rangers, Sarawak Volunteer Force, and the Sarawak Coast Guard lined the streets and approaches to the business quarter.

Triumphal arches were erected, and the Datu Patinggi and Cyril Le Gros Clarke, Sarawak's Secretary for Chinese Affairs who had been appointed Chief Secretary on the sudden resignation of John Archer, were received by the Rajah and Ranee seated under a canopy of Royal Sarawak yellow. Acting as lady-in-waiting to the Ranee was Sa'erah MacBryan,[2] whose husband Gerard had been reinstated as Rajah's Private Secretary.

At night the town was lit up by fireworks, and the river was thronged with decorated boats. Of particular beauty was the torch and lantern procession. The lantern bearers assembled at dusk in St Thomas's School, and a few minutes before seven o'clock, the great playing field looked like an illuminated flowerbed. Ingenuity had been employed in the making of the lanterns – animals, fish, fabulous monsters and puppet figures alongside which were the more sinister representations of aeroplanes and tanks. Gongs, flutes, cymbals, drums and brass added to the gaiety.[3] Light rain fell throughout the evening, but failed to disrupt the spectacle. In the days that followed, there was horse-racing, and other amusements, to commemorate an historic occasion.

Simultaneously, another historic, and in many ways more significant, event took place – the Rajah's handing over of much of the responsibility of his government to a Council before setting off on a holiday to Australia. Nine months previously, he had announced his intention to surrender his absolute powers and introduce a written constitution to be presided over by a democratic Legislative Council. As he informed the President and Members of the Supreme Council and the Committee of Administration, he had for some time felt the need and desirability of ending autocratic rule in Sarawak by substituting a Liberal Constitution in its place.[4]

However, there were those, including John Archer, his Chief Secretary at the time, for whom the implications were unsettling. Archer had lived in Sarawak since 1913, had married into the country, and recognised the dangers of the Rajah relinquishing his responsibilities. Apart from Vyner, and presumably his close advisers such as Gerard MacBryan, nobody in Sarawak felt that it was necessary.

At some stage during Vyner's reign, a Governor of British North Borneo had written to him and introduced himself as 'an anomaly writing to an anachronism.'[5] It had obviously started Vyner thinking. For a new breed of liberal thinkers, particularly in Britain, who believed that the absolute rule of the White Rajahs of Sarawak *was* an anachronism, the initiative of devolving power was long overdue.

From now on, Sarawak would be self-governing under a Supreme State Council, consisting of not less than five members, a majority of whom should be members of the Sarawak Civil Service and members of the Negri Council. The Negri Council, ranking below the Supreme Council, was to be composed of fourteen members of the European Sarawak Civil Service and eleven representatives of the races which inhabited Sarawak. The Rajah would in future become just a figurehead.

It sounded straightforward enough, but meant little to the indigenous people of Sarawak who continued to assume that Rajah Vyner, despite his advancing years, would still hold onto the reins. In the past, particularly in the reign of Vyner's father, the Rajah was considered a wise and stabilising force. When it became apparent that it would no longer be necessary for him to be consulted on the running of his country, there was growing ill ease.

Since he was not involved in the politics of Sarawak, my father's reaction to this was ambivalent, albeit uneasy about the direction the country was taking. From the moment he had taken over control of the Sarawak office, he had found himself constantly at odds with the petty officialdom of certain Sarawak Government figures who seemed intent on blocking any form of progress. He complained bitterly to Sir Adam Ritchie, the Borneo Company's chairman in London, who brought it to the attention of Lord Moyne, Secretary of State for the Colonies.[6] What made the situation even more exasperating was that increasingly there appeared to be no redress. Vyner Brooke had intentionally distanced himself from any decision-making process and was relying more and more on Gerard MacBryan, whom most of his own government officers loathed.

Following a visit to Kuching and Sibu earlier that year, Kenneth Simpson, now in charge of the Borneo Company's Singapore office, also wrote angrily to Sir Adam, "I have heard it suggested that the Dyaks have no respect whatever for the Government officials, except as representatives of the Rajah, and that, if he leaves, trouble may be expected." [7] It was Simpson's considered opinion that the time had finally come for Malaya to intervene in the affairs of Sarawak.

Meanwhile, my mother returned to Kuching largely reassured. Six months earlier, Sir John Bagnall* had sent Fergie and Bobbie with their sons Ewen** and Donald to Australia, reasoning that if there was going to be trouble, the Straits Trading Company should have a senior executive established in a place of safety. It was also proposed that an emergency headquarters be set up should the company be obliged to move from Singapore. Sir John had now decided to recall them.

As the seventh child of a seventh child (two of her siblings miscarried), my mother was often jokingly accused by members of her family of having second-sight. All of her life she was to rely upon her instincts, but on this one occasion she convinced herself that she had been worrying unnecessarily. Instead, she tried hard to concentrate upon more immediate, domestic concerns, but when listening to the radio news, however, was forced to admit to herself that in her own words, her heart was still a bit 'queasy,' particularly in moments of guilt at having left Virginia behind at Cameron Highlands.

Her heart was to become even more queasy towards the end of November.

---

*   John Bagnall was knighted in 1938 for services to the Singapore Government as a member of the Legislative Council and the (inner core) Executive Council.

** Ewen Fergusson Junior (from 1987-92, UK Ambassador to France), returned from school in England to Singapore, aged 7, and was sent to Geelong Grammar School in Victoria. He vividly remembers the flight over from Singapore on a seaplane taking four days, stopping off at Batavia, Surabaya, Darwin, Townsville, and Brisbane on the way. As fate would have it, the Fergussons did not return to Singapore, their passage being cancelled following the Japanese attack on Pearl Harbor.

CHAPTER NINE

Denial

Christmas Day brought no joy in Malaya. Half the tin mines and one rubber tree in every six were in enemy hands. The big ships were at the bottom of the sea. The aircraft strength was halved. Dissension and squabbling rent the War Council, fussy protocol strangled civil and military co-operation.

Kate Caffrey, *Out in the Midday Sun.*

TOWARDS the end of November 1941, my father announced that he was going to Singapore on business, and that he would bring Virginia back with him. My mother's relief was transparent. All she had been able to think about was having Virginia safely returned to her. Then they could decide what to do next.

Things were looking pretty bleak on the day Charles departed on the *Vyner Brooke*, but he nevertheless felt confident that he could make it comfortably back without incident. It was the 2nd December.

Two days earlier it had been announced on the radio that all troops at places of entertainment at Singapore were to return to barracks immediately. From the War Office in London came unconfirmed reports that the diplomatic negotiations between the Americans and Admiral Nomura, Japan's Ambassador to Washington, were breaking down. All hopes were pinned on the intervention of Saburo Kurusu, Japanese Ambassador to Belgium and later to Nazi Germany, who was married to an American wife. Those moving in both British and American military circles were nevertheless warned to expect imminent offensive operations against Thailand, the Dutch East Indies, and the Philippines.[1]

Rumours apart, there was still a widespread belief that the Japanese, whatever their grand design, would never bother with Sarawak. With the exception of the oil-fields at Miri, there was nothing that would be of much use or interest to them. Of course, what nobody had fully considered was the island's immensely important strategic position in the Imperial Japanese plan.

To this end, the advance party was already in place. Similar to the Borneo Company, Mitsubishi Shoji Kaisha of Tokyo was actively engaged in a range of investments from rubber plantations to consumer goods. The headquarters of the Borneo Fishery Company, which had branches at Sandakan, Taiwau, and Banggi Island, was also Tokyo based.[2] There was a Japanese Consulate at Sandakan, and a flourishing Japanese colony in the Taiwau district which included a mix of professionals – doctors, dentists, and market traders. In Sarawak, Nissa Shokai owned a rubber plantation on the Samarahan River.

Borneo is huge, five times larger than the British Isles, with fine natural harbours. On one side it flanks the sea routes from Japan to Malaya and Sumatra, and on the other, to Java. What particularly struck Lt-General Arthur Percival, General Officer Commanding in Malaya, during a reconnaissance visit, was the vastness of the area to be defended, and the small resources he had at his disposal.

The State of Brunei was considered of some importance as it held the large Seria oil-field which, with those at Miri, supplied the refinery at Lutong. However, the Governor of North Borneo was informed that his territory was impossible to protect, and that such volunteers and police as he had should be employed on internal security, rather than defence.[3]

As for Sarawak, it was allocated one infantry battalion, the 2/15 Punjab Regiment, of which one company had already been despatched to the oil-fields in East Sarawak. That left the Sarawak Rangers, the Sarawak Volunteers, a mainly jungle-based force comprising Dyaks, and some administrative detachments. It was not at all a happy state of affairs.

Only the previous March, the Rajah had reminded the British Government of its responsibility to defend Sarawak under the treaty of 1888. He had confirmed that he would continue to contribute to the British War Fund to the limit of his country's resources, but he expected protection in return. His terms had been accepted, but as John Noakes, Sarawak's Secretary of Defence, Director of Air-Raid Precautions and Security Officer, was to point out in a report written post-war, such measures as the British Forces did introduce were entirely inadequate.[4]

The best that General Percival could promise when he attended a meeting of the Negri Council was that he would send a few anti-aircraft guns. He comforted the delegates with the news that the pride of the

British navy, the battleship *Prince of Wales* and battle-cruiser *Repulse,* were scheduled to arrive at Singapore within days.

It was widely accepted that if the Japanese were going to launch an attack on British interests, it would come from the sea. During a dinner at Government House, Sir John Bagnall had asked what plans were in place for an attack overland. The day following he received a call from the Colonial Secretary to say that such talk was alarmist. One might justifiably wonder how so many of the European community could have been so trusting, but what other option had they?

It was not as if returning to England or Scotland was even a consideration. Everyone had seen newsfilms of the evacuation of Dunkirk the previous June, and the subsequent bombing of London. In comparison, the Far East appeared an infinitely safer place to be.

My parents were not alone in such thinking. Everyone was in a state of disbelief. In Singapore, the Governor's advisors, notably Air Chief Marshal Sir Robert Brooke-Popham, Commander-in-Chief Far East, gave repeated assurances that there was no likelihood of a Japanese attack during the North-East Monsoon.[5] At night, the dance floors of the bars and restaurants were thronged with men in tuxedos and women in evening gowns. Only a couple of weeks earlier, Alfred Duff Cooper, Winston Churchill's personal envoy to the Far East, had confidently informed his audience at a Rotary lunch that the Japanese had definitely missed the bus by not attacking at the time of Dunkirk.[6]

So the plan at the beginning of December was for my father to stay on in Singapore after his business meetings and collect Virginia from Cameron Highlands when her Christmas holidays began on Saturday 6th. He would then bring her back with him to Kuching on the *Vyner Brooke* the following day. At Cameron Highlands, accompanied by Virginia's amah, he found a group of excited children. Virginia was overjoyed to see him and, before they set off, went to her room to collect her favourite Shirley Temple doll and a woolly lamb. But the nuns would not let her take the doll with her. "She'll be waiting for you when you come back next term," they told her.

On the following day the Japanese bombed the American Fleet in Pearl Harbor, Hawaii. In the early hours of the morning, they hit Singapore, the British naval base at Sembowang and the Tengah and Seletar airfields.

Almost as if to symbolise Japan's contempt for the island's trading stature, their first bomb landed on the headquarters of Guthrie & Company.[7]

On her way to collect her daughters from their school in Sumatra, Joan Black arrived in Singapore from Kuching on the following day. Galvanising herself into action, she stormed the Dutch Consulate for a visa and in fluent Dutch persuaded the captain of the *Op ten Noord,* the Sumatra ferry ship, to set sail at once. On reaching Kaben Djahe, she discovered that most of the staff and children had already been evacuated by air to Australia, but another mother was also stranded with two daughters of a similar age to Barbara and Margaret.

The two mothers agreed to move the four little girls into the Mansfield bungalow in Brastagi, where they spent Christmas together. As the situation worsened, Joan and her daughters made a dramatic escape across Sumatra by taxi and train, crossing by boat to Java where, at the end of January, they found Kilner Black anxiously waiting for them at the station in Batavia.

Needless to say, the *Vyner Brooke* did not sail from Singapore on the 7th December 1941, nor on next day. On Mainland China, the Japanese Army seized Shangahi, and in northern Malaya, they began their shelling of the beaches of Kelantan's Kota Bharu – Subak, Bachok and Pasir Puteh. Ironically Pasir Puteh translates into English as 'The Beach of Passionate Love.'

At Belvedere, three air-raid shelters, two rounded and one square, were hastily erected out of sandbags and corrugated iron. That same night Virginia was roused by her amah and rushed to safety as the sirens wailed all about them. Clutching her woolly lamb, she peeked out of the shelter doorway at the searchlights scanning the starlit sky. Then the explosions started. She was very frightened.

It was the speed at which everything took place that was so shocking. Kenneth Simpson had travelled to Bangkok with the food controller for Singapore to organise supplies of rice from Siam, and was captured when the Japanese arrived at almost the same time. The Borneo Company's Bangkok office was requisitioned as the Japanese transport headquarters, and Kenneth, along with other members of staff, were interned in a hastily set up compound in the grounds of the University of Moral and Political Sciences.[8]

Nor did the *Vyner Brooke* sail from Singapore in the weeks that followed. On the morning of the 10th December, the *Prince of Wales* and *Repulse,* having arrived in Keppel Harbour five days earlier, set sail northwards off the east coast of Malaya. They were attacked by Japanese strike aircraft approximately 60 miles off Kuanta and sunk.

It was a portent of the future. With the elimination of the American Pacific Fleet at Pearl Harbor, the Japanese now had almost unchallenged naval control of the entire south-west Pacific. On the morning of the 11th December, three formations of nine Japanese bombers appeared over Penang. They had been raiding the airports for days previous, but still there was not even one defensive anti-aircraft gun to challenge them. This time they targeted Georgetown.

European women and children were hurriedly ferried to the mainland and taken by train to Singapore. Among them were Dorothy McLellan and her son Neil. Mac had been on a visit to the Navy Office in Penang when somebody said to him, "If you've got a wife or a child here, get them out quick."

"As I'm representing Mansfields, we'll need to get *all* of our wives and children out quick!" he responded.

Dorothy remembered being given 20 minutes' notice. "Edna Starkey, the wife of Mansfield's accountant, and I reached Singapore with just the clothes we stood up in," she said. "It was only then that we began to realise what was happening to all of us."

In Singapore, they stayed with Joe Penrice at his house Creehall before boarding the Blue Funnel Line *SS Ulysses* to Perth in Australia. Unlike some of the companies, Mansfield & Company acted fast to evacuate their employees. The Borneo Company had no such plan but Wendy Grant, with her two sons Ian and Peter, also set off for Perth, where they remained for the following three years.

Mac meantime remained in Penang to help with sabotage activities such as pushing cars and vans into the sea to deny them to the invaders. When he and the remaining Penang Volunteers were ordered out, they commandeered the Penang to Butterworth Ferry, burning the ship's furniture on board as fuel. Having made it out to sea, it broke down, but just when it looked as if they were going to be stranded, out of the mist came a Straits Settlement steamship to transport them to Singapore.

From Singapore, Mac boarded a British India ship heading for Balawan in Sumatra. Although attacked by Japanese strike aircraft mid-ocean, with a bomb landing straight down the centre of a funnel, miraculously it reached its destination. From Balawan, he was sent to Ceylon and made contact with Charles Wurtzburg, his former boss at Mansfields, now running the Ministry of War Transport in London. Wurtzburg appointed him Deputy Minister of Transport under Sir John Masson to work with Sir Geoffrey Layton, Commander-in-Chief China Station. The only object Mac had taken with him was a silver cigarette box containing a $10 bill and his marriage lines. "I thought I'd better keep them so as to one day make an honest woman of you," he told his wife when they were eventually reunited.

In Singapore, the taking of the island of Penang by General Yamashita's soldiers was met with a mixture of disbelief and consternation by the European authorities. In the Asian community there was panic, heightened, were that possible, by a radio broadcast from Duff Cooper who announced that the "population of Penang had been evacuated."[9]

Of course, what he should have said was that the "Europeans" of Penang had been evacuated. Was it any wonder that the Malays, Chinese, Tamils and Eurasians felt slighted, left behind defenceless to face whatever fate the Japanese had in store for them? They had relied on Britain to defend them, and the British had run away.

For Nicholas Ponnudurai, the Borneo Company's Indian chief clerk in Penang, the reality of the situation was only too clear. On 20th December the Japanese came to look for him at Tanjong Bungah, where he had taken his family for safety. Having been marched under armed guard to the local gaol, a bayonet was pressed into his flesh and he was told that he was to become an announcer with the local radio station. The invaders had done their research as they knew that he had already considerable broadcasting experience with the Penang Wireless Society. If he refused them, he was told, his wife and children would suffer.[10]

"In any withdrawal or movement of population there will be no distinction of race," announced Singapore's Governor in a last minute attempt to mend bridges with the Asian communities.[11] He was, of course, referring to the unthinkable, the fall of Singapore, and he meant well. But his hindsight was simplistic, and the majority of Asians knew it.

If came the crunch and Singapore did fall, where was there for them to go? To Australia? Commonwealth countries had agreed to take 1,500 Chinese, but what about the remaining thousands?

The Asian communities' sense of betrayal over British withdrawal was profoundly to influence attitudes towards post-war colonial rule. Moreover, when the first Japanese troops arrived in Penang on 16th December it rapidly became clear what Japan's alternative colonial vision entailed; two Malay youths caught creating a minor disturbance in a coffee shop were publicly beheaded.[12]

Meanwhile, the propaganda war was hard at work. Singapore Malays tuning in to Japanese broadcast channels began to panic, departing en masse over the Causeway into Johore, while at the same time, the Europeans and various other refugees were pouring onto the island in droves from the north, convinced of the impregnability of the 'Fortress.'

At Orange Grove Road John Grant, still in situ with the Borneo Company, was joined by his brother-in-law and sister-in-law, Leonard and Nita Knight, who had arrived from Kuala Lumpur where Leonard was a police commissioner. John took them to the Tanglin Club for dinner, and while they were eating they could hear the guns pounding in the distance. Nobody paid any attention.[13]

The following day, Jack Bennett, the Borneo Company's Singapore Manager in Kenneth Simpson's absence, called in on Orange Grove Road to warn John of the likelihood of displaced employees being billeted upon him. Although in a curious way John welcomed the company, he heaved a heavy sigh of relief that Long Chaney, the houseboy, had loyally stayed on to look after him. The Grants' amah was still living in the house and although told that it would be safer for her to join her own family, had refused to move out until word came that Wendy and the children had arrived safely in Perth.

All of the houses occupied by Borneo Company employees were allocated refugees. John moved into the dressing room, giving up his bedroom to an up-country miner and his wife while next door, his colleague Ketchil* Ashworth and his wife Pat had several women to lodge with them. One, a Russian lady, became so agitated that they had to cable

---

* Loosely spelled, 'Ketchil' in Malay means 'small.' Ashworth stood well over 6 feet tall, and had enlisted as a Lieutenant-Commander in the Malayan Royal Navy Volunteer Reserve.

her husband to calm her down. While the woman was bending over a table to write the telegram, her small son slapped her on the behind, and she threw a fit, accusing her hosts of assault.

Ah Cheow, the houseboy at BMK, had accompanied my father from Kuching, pleading to be allowed to do so on the basis that he had not been to Singapore since the family had moved into BMK. He was longing to look up his old friends on the island, but left Ah Soh, his Kuching-born wife and little baby behind. It was the first time they had been parted since their marriage. She was very young and when the bad news started to filter through, Pat tried not to let her see how worried she was.

Meanwhile, my father sent a succession of wires to reassure them. They would try to get back to Kuching somehow, and meanwhile she should not worry. There was nothing anyone could do but wait and hope. Every day a cable arrived to reassure her, promising that he and Virginia would be home on the next available boat.

There was no next available boat. Nothing was moving, and before long, Kuching began to have problems of its own.

CHAPTER TEN

Exodus

For I am a Japanese, with all the contradictions that make my race: violence and kindness, reason and madness, love and hate, all on the edge of a sword. We are born on the edge of a sword, in a world of bamboo and paper, and that world is a place of violence, uncertainty, earthquake, upheaval, struggle.

R. Hugh Hickling, *Crimson Sun Over Borneo.*

INCREASINGLY cut off from the rest of South East Asia, the Sarawak Government started to introduce long overdue precautions to defend Kuching as best it could. The air-raid warning system was improved, and coastguards posted to out-stations to provide advance warning of Nipponese troop movements. The Sarawak Rangers and Sarawak Volunteers were allotted specific defence positions, and a variety of emergency evacuation plans were drawn up.

With no incoming vessels bringing food to the harbour, Kuching was becoming conspicuously vulnerable, and the occasional Japanese reconnaissance plane seen flying over prompted my mother to think about building some sort of air-raid shelter in the garden. With the aid of the Borneo Company's office carpenter, and two of the native gardeners, she gave instructions for holes to be dug in the gully at the side of the house, with sacking to line the earth floor.

In Kuching town, shopkeepers, normally open all hours, decided to close between 9am and 4pm, and it was announced that all of the colonial women and children who had not already left were to evacuate Kuching town.[1] That was all very well, but when pressed on the subject, officials freely admitted that they had no actual means of getting anyone off the island.

Nevertheless, there was a contingency plan and most of the women, with the exception of a few nurses, agreed to move inland. Here, where the great rivers divided into smaller streams winding like ribbons into the jungle, it was thought that they would be safe. But my mother refused to go with them on the grounds that if her husband and daughter could somehow get back to Kuching, she had to be nearby for Virginia's sake. She simply could not be expected to abandon her; moreover, she knew perfectly well that the Government would be highly unlikely to provide transport for one solitary child to be sent after her.

The Sarawak authorities did not like this very much. It was a male domain and women were expected to do as they were told, however, my mother, as was her nature, stuck to her guns. It was only after a great deal of coercion that she agreed to accompany the wife of Kenneth Cargill, a Borneo Company employee based at Miri, who had a six month old baby, to the Dahan Estate. Dahan was part of the Sarawak Rubber Estates in which the Borneo Company had an interest, located twenty miles south-west of Kuching town.

Then on the eve of their departure on the 19th December, fifteen Japanese planes flew over Sarawak, eight of them to strike at Pontianak in Dutch Borneo, and seven to attack Kuching. They dropped their bombs all over the Bukit Mata hilltop, one landing on the lawn only a yard from the house.

For no apparent reason my mother had been on edge all of that morning, feeling, as she said, jittery every time she heard the sound of a plane anywhere near. Time and again in the years that followed she would learn to act on such instincts.

Mostly Dutch, there had been aircraft flying over Bukit Mata all morning and she made intermittent exits through the veranda windows onto the lawn to watch them. To keep her company, Mrs Munro, whose husband was employed on the Sungei Tengah Rubber Estate, had moved in with her the night before with her two children. Around midday they were in the dining-room rolling bandages for the local hospital and listening to the wireless when they heard a very strange sound coming from very far away. Involuntarily, Pat rushed out to have a look.

It was a very clear day with a brilliant blue sky and little white clouds were floating around like balls of cotton wool. Then she saw them; thousands of feet up and so small that only her gut feeling warned her who they were. Without a moment's hesitation, she yelled out to the people in the house, and for Patricia, and grabbing the things she had been keeping handy for such an emergency, rushed for cover.

No sooner were they out of the house and running down the gully to the improvised mud and wood shelter, than the sirens sounded and the first bombs dropped. The line of bombing was from the Hindu Temple, Ban Hock Road to the Borneo Company office.[2] One hit the oil dump next to the Borneo Company, causing an enormous explosion. Another went through the office roof. Fortunately, nearly everyone had gone for lunch, but it immediately crossed my mother's mind that under normal circumstances Charles would have been there. He rarely left his desk before 1pm.

By now the bombs were falling all around them on their little mountain top, and one dropped just a few feet from the house. The mud trench soon filled up with two European men and women and three children, the remainder a mixture of terrified Chinese, Malays and others. For such a hastily erected shelter, it was not at all bad, my mother reflected, although it was open to the sky and the noise was dreadful.

The women plugged the children's ears with Vaseline and cotton-wool, and wee Patricia went to sleep, for which her mother was mightily grateful. The little group remained there nervously for about two hours until the All Clear sounded and they felt safe to emerge into the afternoon sun. Afterwards, they were driven to the Blacks' house in Reservoir Road where they had a much needed drink and changed the children's clothes which were wet with sweat and fouled with mud.

Later, after a rest, Pat returned to BMK with Kenneth Cargill to see what food they could forage. It was only then that she saw how seriously the poor old house had been hit. A bomb had landed right on the back doorstep which led into the garden.

The building itself was a shambles, but it had not fallen down anywhere, which proved that it had many years ahead of it yet. The damage inside was frightful. Locked cupboards had been blasted open, their contents spilt across the rooms. There was plaster everywhere, and interior doors were either jammed or had fallen off their hinges. My mother's beloved old piano was almost inside out, and there were chairs lying upside down and tables blown into corners.

She and Cargill collected all the tinned food they could find, some eggs and a few other basic necessities, and drove back to brief the others where they were told that there were 33 dead and 78 wounded in the air-raid, mostly Chinese who had failed to find cover. That night she and Patricia stayed at the Blacks' house, but sleep did not come easily. At 6am, she, Patricia, Joan Cargill, Rosemary, the Cargills' baby, and the Cargills' amah, were bundled into a car with their goods and chattels by Kilner Black, who had instructions to drive them as far as he could away from the town.

He saw them onto an army lorry, followed by another lorry to carry their belongings. For the next three hours, the two women and their children endured the most awful bumpy and hellish journey over muddy roads. It was only after they had travelled in a full circle, and back almost to where they had started, that my mother discovered that the Punjabi driver had no idea where he was going. To make it worse he had managed to lose the other lorry.

There were not that many diversionary roads to follow, so they just carried on, and when they did eventually catch up with the other lorry, they found it had become stuck while attempting to cross over a very fragile-looking bridge, certainly not designed for anything heavier than a Morris Eight. The lorry, in comparison, was a huge affair, but after a great deal of effort, with everybody pushing and shoving, and the amazement of all concerned, it did manage across.

Then the heavens opened with sheets of warm, soaking rain. But it was as nothing compared to what lay ahead.

At the Dahan Estate, A.R. Dee, the Manager, turned out to be a very kind and helpful man. In gratitude, the damp and dishevelled group tried not to be too much in his way though, as the house was small and they all slept in one room, it proved rather difficult, and all the more so as everybody was over-excited and it was hard to conceal their anxiety.

None of them had any idea what was happening in Kuching town or elsewhere, for that matter, although it was known that the majority of the remaining colonial women had already left by boat. Led by Father J. Paisley of the S.P.G. Mission,* Mrs Munro, her children, and Armie Trail, were on the *Margaret* bound for Simanggang, whence they planned to walk overland to Dutch Borneo which, for the time being, was considered safe.[3] Several planes were heard flying overhead, but the plantation house, being in the midst of a forest of rubber trees, was well hidden. At least, that is what they all hoped and prayed. Meanwhile, there was nothing to

---

* Society for the Propagation of the Gospel, London.

112

do but wait for further instructions, and my mother tried hard not to think about what might have become of Charles and Virginia. Patricia's birthday on the 23rd December provided a small diversion, and her mother did her very best to remain cheerful.

Fortunately, the child was far too young to understand why her life had been so suddenly and traumatically disrupted.

On the morning of Christmas Eve 1941, Sandy Trail arrived at Dahan, bringing with him valuable security documents from the Chartered Bank safe. Around midday he set off on foot for Pontianak in Dutch Borneo.[4] On Christmas Day, the women's kind host provided them with a glass of champagne, but once again my mother felt 'jittery.' There was no logical reason for it, but just in case, she told Joan Cargill to have her bag ready with essentials for the baby and herself. The two women decided to stay in slacks and blouses, even though their host had promised to lay on a sort of Christmas dinner to cheer them up. Within hours came reports that Japanese transports were anchored in Santubong Bay, and that landing-craft had been spotted on the Santubong River.

What they were not told was that Japanese soldiers had already penetrated as far as Kuching Town, many of them disguised in British and Sarawak police uniforms. This was a ruse which on more than one occasion deceived the Pubjabi soldiers. At 4pm, the Japanese flag was flying over the Astana.

With all of this taking place, Edgar Elam, Sarawak's Assistant Secretary, Naval Reporting Officer, Censor, and the Food Supply Officer for Miri, whose wife Lisa, baby Susan, with Ah Kit, the family cook, were among those on the *Margaret,* ordered that all remaining Europeans be evacuated, although senior government officers were expected to stay in place.[5]

Around 8.30pm, Mr Dee attempted to provide his guests at the Dahan Estate with a modicum of Christmas cheer by mixing White Lady cocktails which they had just finished when the telephone rang. It was the District Officer at Bau with anxious instructions for them to come to his house immediately, not to waste any time, and to bring with them as little as possible.

So the women gathered up their few belongings and made ready, thanking their stars that they did not have to change their clothes or pack anything. My mother was already wearing her DAKS slacks and one of her husband's shirts. Ever practical, she slipped her passport which included Patricia in its remit, some money, a few medical supplies, and a small purse containing her jewellery into an old vanity-case. This old carrier case was to take on magical proportions in the days that followed.

After a half-hour wait, they took leave of their host, who had decided to stay behind, and set off, this time in his tiny car, bumping over the most awful messed-up tracks imaginable.* The roads had not seemed nearly so bad the day before, but it later transpired that all of the approaches to Kuching town had been intentionally sabotaged by 'interested parties,' in other words, Japanese sympathisers.

---

*   Looters arrived at the Dahan Estate shortly after Pat and the Cargills departed. Five days later Mr Dee was collected by a local Japanese resident and taken to Kuching where he was handed over to the Japanese authorities. He was imprisoned at the Batu Lintang Camp.

CHAPTER ELEVEN

Jungle Tracks

The tree trunks, though similar in that they were all straining straight upwards towards the light, were of every colour and texture of bark – smooth and black like Purbeck marble, red and scaly as our own Scots pine, pale grey or ghostly green like the nightmare jungles in Snow White and the Seven Dwarfs, or beautifully marbled and dappled like a moth's wing.

F. Spencer Chapman, *The Jungle is Neutral.*

A T this stage, the women had no idea what was happening elsewhere or whither they were going, and as they left the Dahan Estate it even crossed my mother's mind that they were being taken to be handed over to the Japanese. Eventually, however, they came across a group of men who told them not to go to the District Officer's house, but to continue instead towards the Dutch frontier. Seeing their alarm, the native driver told them not to worry about their host and his car as, had he been asked, he would have certainly agreed to them being taken anywhere that was safe.

Their journey therefore continued until they came across a little police hut at Krokong, the road's end, where the jungle, in all its density, began. There they had an hour's rest before being joined by some of the Sarawak Volunteer Force who arrived directly from Kuching, and, much to his wife's delight, Kenneth Cargill. Apart from this, they brought little consolation; the Japanese were busy rounding up any potential prisoners of war.

In a letter written shortly after her arrival in Sydney, my mother makes it sound as if she had embarked upon a brisk walk across a Scottish moor. Anyone who has ever ventured into the Borneo jungle will know that it is a different place entirely.

On the forest floor, there is no grass and little undergrowth. Light is scarce, and in a world without seasons, trees shed their leaves all the year through, and this debris from a world above feeds the scavengers below, both plant and insect. In this way, thousands of species, animal and vegetable, are linked into a secretive and satisfactory web of life. Throughout the year, temperatures remain high and, while the sun covers the canopy of trees for a minimum of five hours every day, the forest air below is always saturated with moisture.

By the time the assembled small group of refugees were ready to make a move, it had been dark for some time. In fact, it was about 11.30pm, and they were told to start walking along a footpath which, under the circumstance, was not entirely sensible as they were very nearly shot.

The Dayak Bridge at Krokong. It was across this bridge that Pat and Patricia escaped in total darkness on Christmas Day 1941

(Martine Family Collection)

Mercifully, it was Pat who noticed the momentary flash of a light up in front and, once again responding to her instincts, shouted out who they were. There was a brief interchange of voices, and they were allowed to pass. Later they were told that when the guard ahead of them had seen the blue light from their torch, they were mistaken for Japanese soldiers, especially as they made no sound as they moved forward. Everyone was jumpy, and the pace quickened.

Having asked for help to strap Patricia onto her back with a blanket, and with her bag in front of her, Pat kept pace with the others, following the jungle track over native bridges and passes for about four hours, with a ten minute rest every fifty minutes. The guides went ahead carrying torches held low, and behind came some fifteen or twenty of the Sarawak Volunteers, mostly men from the Kuching offices, all of them loaded down with equipment. They were weary after what they had been through earlier in the day, not to mention over the previous week, and nobody spoke.

It seemed as if they walked for years that night. There was a faint moon, but mostly the forest closed in around them like a black silk glove, which was probably a blessing since none of them could see what faced them in the darkness. Mosquitoes buzzed about. A few bats windmilled into the bushes. Other night insects bumped into faces with their soft bodies. Native bridges which scarcely seemed strong enough to hold the weight of one child, let alone adults of heavy weight, spanned ravines with a drop of one hundred feet or more below. Most were just a log of wood thrown over a steep gully with nothing for anyone to hold on to but their breath. Others shook and swayed at every step, with bamboo rails thrown across which moved in the hands as the refugees tried to steady themselves.

Amazingly, no thought of snakes, or scorpions, or anything similar, entered their heads, not even when they stopped for five minute rests and an occasional sip of water from their bottles or flasks. At last, the pace became too much for some of the men who had not slept for nearly three days, and at around 3am, the group decided to stop at a Bidayuh jungle compound set back in the trees, walking through mud and slush to get to it.

It was the first time that my mother had ever been in one of these little houses slung up on high bamboo sticks, and she confessed later that "her nose seemed a little too long that night." The group was split up among the different habitations, and her heart was in her mouth as she climbed up the rickety step-ladder with my sister. She could not see how the weight of eight of them added to that of the five native Dyaks already in residence, could possible be sustained by the flooring, but it was.

Exhausted, they lay down on the floor as they were, and tried to wipe off some of the mud from their shoes and feet while they drank huge glasses of water from the house supply. Caution was thrown to the wind. Gone were the days when everything drunk had first to be boiled, then filtered, but they made sure that the bottled water was kept for Patricia and Rosemary.

At around 6am, they were off again. My small sister had slept, but my mother's imagination had been too busy for sleep, and she was glad of this as it was easier for her to start off than it was for some of the others. This time she tied Patricia to her front, and balanced the weight with the "handbag" on her back.

There is no dawn in the tropics. When night ends, the day arrives without warning.

They kicked off at a surprisingly good pace, despite having had nothing to eat, but soon the others got ahead of them as my sister's weight became unbearable and my mother had to keep putting her down. It soon began to irritate her that Joan Cargill and her baby were way ahead of them, as they had both the amah and Kenneth to help, and the Cargill baby was very small. In comparison, Patricia was older, therefore heavier, and Pat soon began to wonder if she would ever arrive.

She was angry and tears started; where was Charles? How the Hell had they got themselves into this mess?

She had just reached the point of not caring if the Japanese caught up with them or not, merely wondering what would become of Patricia if they did, when one of the Sarawak police officers arrived.

His name was John Stewart Wink, known as 'Winky', a Probationary Assistant Commissioner in the Sarawak Constabulary, who had served his apprenticeship with the Canadian North-West Mounted Police.[1] He was furious when he saw their plight, and immediately slung away his rifle and equipment to pick up little Patricia. From that moment onwards they strode along with ease.

In the hazy green light of the dense vegetation, it was difficult to know what was the time of day. All about them the jungle was full of sounds; monkey calls and shrieks from birds. Occasionally, a snake slithered across their path – they had been warned to look out for thin black and gold snakes called krauts, considered particularly lethal. From rotting logs sprouted a dazzling display of tropical fungi and the air was filled with the pungent jungle smell of decaying vegetation. All they knew was that they just had to keep moving.

About halfway to their destination, Winky told them he had to turn back to pick up stragglers and retrieve his equipment, but not before he had fixed Patricia up with a couple of the Punjabi soldiers who had also caught up with them. From then on, the two of them took turns in carrying her, which allowed my mother to follow on behind. Of course, Patricia bawled her head off. This was partly caused by fear, but also because the Punjabi soldiers carried her sitting on the backs of their necks as they would have done with their own children.

But children are nothing if not adaptable, and Patricia soon quietened down when one of them gave her a biscuit. Thereafter, they moved along at great speed, easily catching up with the others who, much to my mother's annoyance, expressed great surprise at seeing them.

"We thought you'd got lost," said Joan.

"Oh no!" responded Pat tartly. "Just taking my own time."

Since she had been carrying about three times the weight of each one of them (Rosemary had been carried by their amah the whole of that night and day), and there were three of them to take turns in carrying different weights, she felt entitled to feel slightly piqued.

It was at this point that Kilner Black and another friend, 'Shot' Spurway, both Sarawak Volunteers, joined them. As managing director of the Sarawak Steamship Company, Kilner had been obliged to see to his company's affairs before taking up his command of No 5, Sarawak Volunteer Company. With the invasion, secret records had to be destroyed and as many as possible of the company's ships immobilised. On Christmas Eve, with the Japanese already at Santubong Bay, he had gone down river by launch with Captain Gibson, the Superintendent of Shipping, pausing at each bend to see if they had left it too late. Firstly, they removed the fuel pumps from the *Margaret* and *Kim Chin Seng*. Before retreating, they had scuttled the *Gladys* by opening her sea-cocks.

Back in Kuching town, Kilner hastily dispersed the dock-workers and paid a month's wages to his coolies and office staff. He had finally left with his volunteer party on the morning of Christmas Day, catching up with the women to help them on their journey.

Shot Spurway was a forestry man employed by the Sarawak Government, and knew the hinterland inside out. He and Kilner soon decided that they were going to break away from the main body and go along under their own steam. My mother, with the Cargills, decided to go with them, and was glad she had done so when, moments later, Shot hacked his way through some undergrowth with his parang to uncover a small stream. Well hidden from the jungle path, he invited them all to bathe their aching feet.

The water, my mother was assured, was safe to drink and she set about making a mixture of Klim milk, adding some whisky from the mono-grammed pewter flask her father had given Charles, and which she was extremely glad to have brought with her. Everybody shared it, including Patricia, and afterwards felt disinclined to move again as it was heavenly to rest their feet in that cool water, though by green pastures – hardly! Even if no-one had pointed out the giant python coiled into a tree trunk on the opposite riverbank, or the seething swarms of ants, some an inch and a half long, nobody was in any doubt that they just had to keep going.

Pat was fixed up to start off in front this time, and while exploring a little further down river, around a corner, came across a Dyak fishing. He looked startled to see her, but in her best Malay she asked him if he could find someone to help carry their stuff. He replied, "Yes," but to make sure that he had understood, she led him back to the others, where Shot talked to him fluently.

As a result, within the next twenty minutes there were suddenly five bearers, and for a fleeting moment it seemed as if all their troubles were over. One carried my sister, another carried Rosemary, and the other three took the bags. Their group soon caught up with the others ahead and passed them, my mother leading, followed by my sister with her 'Horsey', the three baggage men, the Cargills' amah and baby with her 'Horsey', and the Cargills, husband and wife.

After that, they all got along quite well, each partially overtaking the other when it was their turn to stop. As their only food was Klim milk and a few biscuits, hunger became a problem. That night at 8.30pm they came upon a Dyak longhouse which was to be the stop for the night, and my mother admitted that she was agreeably surprised after what she had been told about them.

A Dyak village is a communal establishment. It does not consist of separate huts occupied by single families, but of a large common hall built on a platform, sometimes 800 feet long, abutted by the dwelling areas. The construction is of wood and supported upon poles, sometimes 20 to 40 feet above the ground. This varies depending upon the location and the particular tribe.

In most cases, the common habitation runs the entire length of the structure. The back part is divided by mat partitions into the private apartments of the various families, so there are dozens of separate doors leading from the public area. However, young unmarried men and widowers occupy the public room, as only those with wives are entitled to overall privacy. Here also live dogs, birds, monkeys, and chickens, and a sense of bustle and confusion reigns, especially when the Dyaks, the most hospitable of people, have guests.

Interior of Dyak Longhouse
(Martine Family Collection)

Small, brown-skinned natives with large eyes and betel-stained teeth watched their arrival with curiosity. The fugitives, all of them, were allocated the Headman's House, situated nearly in the centre of the building, and they slept on what appeared to be an enormous raised platform on mats. With the money she had with her, my mother bought a sarong and hung up their clothes around the household fire which was in a corner of the room. Fortunately, she had brought a pair of pyjamas with her for my sister.

They ate some rice and chicken, the latter a bit tough having been killed on the spot and being none too young, and my mother made some Klim milk again, this time with boiled water. It was a welcome relief, but the sanitary arrangements, she concluded, took a bit of courage. They were expected to go out onto the bamboo veranda in full view of the village and squat, while below them the pigs – there seemed to be dozens of them and they kept the night lively – did the rest. Providentially, by then the night had closed in on them.

The next morning, when they came to consciousness, there were frenzied attempts to scrape the mud off their trousers. In drying out, the congealed slush had become as hard as cement, and no-one had any spare clothes. Their shirts were nearly dry, which was a good thing, but nobody had any socks left.

All of the men in the party wore shorts, so it was not too big a problem for them. However, Joan and my mother had long trousers and eventually decided to cut them off above the knees with a pair of scissors found in my mother's magic bag. Of course, the drawback to this was that from then on they were as vulnerable as the men to the leeches that accompanied their progress.

Leeches, and there are two identified species in the Borneo jungle, one large and one small, are equipped with three circular teeth inside their anterior suckers. Having attached itself, each creature cuts a y-shaped hole in the skin, pumps anticoagulant into the wound, and feasts on the blood of its host. The entire process is so well lubricated that unless a nerve is cut, no pain is felt to draw the attention of the victim.

Around 8am, before starting off again with their five Dyaks, there was time for some hot tea and biscuits. The day that followed was much a repetition of the day before. The jungle track sloped ahead between enormous trees which soared into a roof of thick foliage hung with creeper. The small procession walked for as long as they were able, rested a little, and stopped at every stream, the streams becoming fewer as they approached Dutch territory. The jungle terrain towards that part of Kalimantan flattens out without mountain stream or gravel.

As before, it became a bit of a game to pass the time. The Cargills' party would catch up and overtake them. My mother, Patricia with her 'Horsey', and one bearer, did the same each time they stopped for a rest. For a short spell, they actually got far ahead of the main group, but thought that they had better slow down.

A couple of small snakes did slither into view, but my mother later claimed that she had not given them a moment's thought as by this time they had come across real mud and had great difficulty in making any progress at all.

Two steps and three skids, losing a shoe and, when going back to retrieve it, losing the other, they persevered. "I am still wearing those shoes," she later wrote to her mother in England. "They did me proud!"

Afterwards, she sat for a long spell at a stream, trying to pull off the leeches from her legs, and one of the Dyaks was just considering whether or not to light a fire in order to boil some water to fill up the bottles, when the others caught up. They wanted to keep going, but Pat decided to wait a little longer as she knew that without Patricia to carry she could walk faster than they and would soon catch them up. Then the rain came down with a vengeance . . .

With an old raincoat she had with her, Pat covered over Patricia and the Dyak so that they were in a sort of tent, and they moved on. The others had stopped under a tree for shelter, but as they had a ground sheet, an umbrella, and a few more clothes than she, my mother decided not to worry about them and to push on further since the Dyaks had told her that that night's stopping-place was not too far away.

It turned out to be a couple of hours' more walking, but by then everyone had been soaked to the skin and dried off again. One incident though was rather shameful. Wee Patricia got rather distressed. Whether it was the smell of the Dyak under her 'tent,' or because she felt hungry and miserable, she would not say, but she bit him on the back of his neck!

The poor man was horror-stricken. "I shall never forget his face," said her mother later. "I think he thought she'd turned cannibal!"

However, my sister burst into tears and said she was sorry, and they continued on their way, once again overtaking the others.

Very soon they were very grateful that they had pushed on as they were nearly the first to arrive at that night's destination and, since this was the Dutch Border, there were ample supplies of coffee and coconuts. " I can tell you, I had three of the latter to myself," she wrote to her mother. "The juice from them, that is, and some coffee also. Nothing ever tasted as good!"

At the Border, most of the natives belonging to the kampong had fled into the interior, and there was just a handful left. My mother soon made friends with the Headman who instructed his little boy to wash out some clothes for her and to help dry them, bring hot water for baths, and generally make himself useful. There was indeed light at the end of this tunnel, but nobody could tell her what was happening in Sarawak, behind them, or across the sea in Singapore.

Then the others arrived en masse, and from then on people kept turning up throughout the night. The plantation house they were allocated had two rooms and a veranda room, all very small. Six women and two children slept in one, and the men crowded into the others.

That night there was a feeling of having at least got somewhere, and everybody became a bit talkative. The mosquitoes were ubiquitous, but with clothes drying by the fire in the kitchen and some coffee to warm them up, the walkers all felt a bit cheered. It was all relative, but they genuinely began to feel that the worst was behind them.

The next morning Pat and Patricia with her 'Horsey' started off once more, again ahead of the others, but this time the Punjabi Commanding Officer, who had turned up with his men overnight, detailed someone to accompany them. Much to my mother's delight it was Winky, the Sarawak Constable, who having doubled back to look for stragglers, was now with them for the remainder of the trek.

Instead of a jungle track this time, there was a road of sorts, and although muddy in spots, the first part of it was easy going. Winky turned out to be a cheery person and much to my mother's relief somebody who walked at the same pace as herself. She even found herself laughing at his jokes.

Consequently, they strode ahead without losing sight of the others behind them, and on the way found the odd handful of fruit to eat. They covered twenty miles that day with one long rest of an hour at a Dutch camp where they were given hot tinned soup and some other produce. It was the first normal food she and Joan had had since Christmas Day.

After this, although pretty tired, they pushed on again. Joan's shoes had given out, so Winky, who by this time was wearing plimsolls, gave them to her and walked on in his bare feet. My mother, who needless to say had some bandages in her magic bag, bound his feet to begin with, but they soon unravelled. "He never complained," she said.

They had another short rest about 6pm at a Dyak compound, rather larger than the ones already visited, and there they ate more native fruit with coconut juice. My mother then had her first real fright. While walking down the middle of a path she was confronted by a large wild pig which stopped immediately in front of her and stared. It looked terrifying, but Winky roared with laughter at the look of horror on her face, forcing her to move forward, whereupon the brute ran away from them far more scared of her than she of him.

Well, that is how she told the story later, and there is no doubt that she believed him. However, while wild pigs have been hunted for centuries by the Ibans, Dusuns and Punans, and generally keep their distance from human beings, boars can inflict fearsome damage when cornered.

Again, it seemed that they walked for hours until it got dark, and my mother was having visions of sleeping by the roadside when suddenly, around 9pm, they came upon a huge river. It was a tributary of the River Kapuas, and scrambling down the muddy bank to get into a boat to take them across, she was nearly swept away.

On the far side, it was even worse. Because it was dark, it became impossible to see what was happening, and my mother's immediate concern was that her daughter's latest 'Horsey' was older than the previous ones, who had been replaced at each resting place. She was far from convinced that he could take the strain and, helpless to do anything about it, she had visions of them both being sucked into the river and devoured by crocodiles.

Fortunately, the 'old' Dyak was made of stronger stuff than my mother imagined, and he and my sister slithered and skidded up the embankment unharmed, then slithered and skidded about for another quarter of an hour up a road to the Dutch Commanding Officer's bungalow at Sanggau. There, a kindly soul brought hot water for them to bathe their feet and lent my mother a pair of pyjamas, doing the same for Joan and Rosemary when they arrived.

Soup and fried eggs and bacon were served for supper, and that night my mother and sister, the Cargills with their baby, and their amah, slept in real beds with mosquito nets for the first time in six days. They had travelled a distance of 140 miles.

CHAPTER TWELVE

Deliverance

Singapore was a town of bewildering contrasts. On the one hand, in the wealthy residential areas, bombing had destroyed the drains, and the stench was nauseating – the Government gave free anti-typhoid injections. On the other hand, the streets in the shopping and business areas were meticulously cleaned every day and were thronged with European men and women.

Charles McCormack, *You'll Die In Singapore.*

THE following morning, an old, rusty bus arrived to take the walkers to Benkajang and on to Pontianak where they remained for three weeks, accommodated part of the time in a convent school, then at a friend's house since my mother was unable to persuade my sister to eat or sleep for the noise and smell of food. In Pontianak, all of the Kuching women, including Mrs Munro,* Armie Trail, Lisa Elam, and Daphne Large, who had managed to escape from other directions, joined them, about twenty in all, with seven children.[1]

Bill Large, Commander of the Sarawak Volunteers, Teddy Edwards, Commander of the Sarawak Volunteers and Sarawak's Director of Public Works, and 'Shot' Spurway were immediately commissioned 2nd Lieutenants (Emergency Commissions), Indian Army, and sent off at once to join the 2nd/15th Punjabi Regiment on the Dutch Border with Sarawak.** Edgar Elam, Richard Sagar and Gordon Myles, the District Warden at Sarikei and Sarawak's Rubber Regulation Officer, elected to travel on to Batavia with the women.

It soon became evident that the majority of the European men stationed in Kuching had chosen to stay on to face whatever fate had in store for them. Among them were Cyril Le Gros Clark, the Chief Secretary,

---

* Her husband, T.J.C. Munro, was taken prisoner by the Japanese on 27th December 1941.

** All three were captured by the Japanese following the fall of Pontianak.

127

Gordon Aikman, Under-Secretary, and Dennis White, Sarawak's District Officer. With their hands tied behind their back they were taken to the Rest House where they were joined by John Noakes, Sarawak's Secretary of Defence, and John Archer, the former Chief Secretary. Charles Horn from the Borneo Company's Salim office had been put in charge of a lookout post at Tanjong Po, but decided to surrender when Kuching was taken. He and the others were locked up in the police station, but later transferred to Zaida, then Padungan and latterly the Batu Lintang Camp.

Colonised by the Dutch, Pontianak today is capital of the West Kalimantan province of West Borneo, and forms part of Indonesia. It sits at the mouth of a small stream in the Kapuas Delta on Borneo's western coast, and when Pat and Patricia arrived there on New Year's Day, 1942, it was garrisoned by 500 men. It also boasted a Dutch Naval Air Station with three flying boats, part of a string of auxiliary seaplane support bases operated by the Dutch Naval Aviation.

Since the Christmas Eve air-raids, Dutch territory throughout the region had come under heavy attack. All of the Dutch support bases were under pressure, and the word was out that the Tambelan Islands in the Karimata Strait were now occupied. It was common knowledge that Terempa Island in the Anambas Group had already been heavily bombed by Japanese aircraft. Among the casualties were 40 dead and 100 wounded, mainly Indonesian civilians, and there was a great deal of material damage inflicted.[2]

On the north-east coast of British North Borneo, the Japanese had taken the Island of Labuan and Jesselton. More disturbing still, came news from the British Crown Colony of Hong Kong, which had surrendered on Christmas Eve. British soldiers who had already laid down their arms, were bayoneted by the victorious Japanese. A Red Cross flag flew over the door of an emergency hospital packed with wounded, but this did not prevent the conquering army from swarming in to rape the nurses and murder both doctors and patients.[3]

For my mother, the realisation that the enemy she had escaped in Sarawak was daily closing in on them, was terrifying to contemplate. Furthermore, there was very little that she or anybody else could do about it except wait to see what would happen next.

On their arrival in Pontianak, she made desperate attempts to get in touch with my father in Singapore, but nothing was getting through. The enemy was advancing down the Malayan peninsula with virtually no air defences to stop it. Anti-aircraft fire proved ineffective, and such was their self-confidence in the skies that the Japanese had even begun to bomb Singapore's aerodromes in daylight.

Yet the island community still remained confident it would hold out, partly because there was no alternative. To leave would have meant abandoning everything they had, and since there was so little information available to the public most people were, or wanted to be, convinced that the danger would soon pass. When Sir Archibald Wavell of the newly created Allied South-West Pacific Command, chose to set up his headquarters in Java.[4] Singaporeans, in all their naivety, still clung to their faith in the ultimate might of the British Raj.

Writing to Wendy by now safely landed in Australia, John Grant was confident. "It infuriates me these people who panic about their own skins – we are all frightened at times with good reason, but with the enemy still hundreds of miles away, I can't see why we cannot carry on a normal existence."[5]

When the Battle of Slim River was lost and Kuala Lumpur fell on the 12th January, cars filled with European women and children, Chinese and Indians, followed by planters and civil servants, arrived on the island in droves. At Sungei Lembing, Vincent Baker and his sister Nona, having supervised the flooding of the Pahang Consolidated tin mines, decided to stay behind. Deep in the forest, near Kuala Jeng farm, they took refuge in a hideout stocked with provisions, and prepared to sit out the war. Their whereabouts were known only to a couple of loyal Chinese employees.

John Grant

(Photo: Grant Family)

The following day, Duff Cooper

and his wife, Lady Diana, departed from Singapore in a hurry. It was no secret that Churchill's envoy was seriously disliked by the Straits Settlement Governor, Sir Shenton Thomas; nor had Lady Diana, despite her reputation as a society beauty and her achievements in persuading people to give blood, won much favour.

Yet my father, who met her at a Government House reception, considered that she brought a welcome, if unreal, touch of glamour to a situation that was rapidly deteriorating. When they arrived in September, they had brought with them 100 suitcases of personal luggage.[6] The same number of cases accompanied them when they left on the private plane which Cooper commandeered to fly them to safety. This was particularly insensitive since there were many others desperate to leave, and only military transport was being allowed on and off the island.

From the beginning, the behind-the-scenes personality clash between the Governor and Duff Cooper had proved a disaster. On the one hand was Thomas, old-style colonial servant and former Governor of Nyasaland who, when he became Governor and Commander of the Straits Settlements in 1934, was aged 55. He was now 62.

On the other hand was Cooper, who had been appointed Resident Minister for Far Eastern Affairs with Cabinet rank; eleven years younger than Thomas, an author of considerable brilliance, a socialite and intellectual snob married to an English duke's daughter. The relationship between the two men reached breaking point when Cooper became responsible for the recall of Sir Robert Brooke-Popham, Commander-in-Chief Far East, and the Governor's personal friend. Cooper even plotted to have the Governor dismissed, but was warned off by the enormous popularity Thomas commanded among both the European and Asian communities.

There was another fundamental problem. For some years a widespread mistrust had been developing between the Malayan Civil Service, over which the Governor presided, and many of the European commercial interests, a not dissimilar bias from that which Charles had experienced in Kuching, but more personal. F.D. Bisseker of Eastern Smelting, Malaya's largest tin processing company, based in Penang, was one of the sternest critics of government apathy and was thoroughly disliked by the Malayan Civil Service. When Bisseker was selected by Cooper to set up a Civil Defence Organisation under Brigadier Ivan Simson without prior consultation with the Governor, Sir Shenton's entourage bitterly opposed him. When Bisseker rented and furnished an office in Tanglin Road and financed and staffed it at his own expense, the bureaucrats were even more outraged. Simson and Bisseker were ignored and left to their own devices.[7]

In Pontianak they knew nothing of this. For my mother and the other women refugees waiting to be evacuated time seemed an eternity until finally, on the 15th January, there arrived a large Dutch seaplane chartered by Cecil Pitt Hardacre, Sarawak Government Agent in Sydney, to take them, under cover of darkness, in relays to north-east Java. Two days before they were scheduled to depart, my mother was taken into hospital with suspected blood poisoning, but released just in time to take the plane.

It was a nerve-wracking flight. The plane had barely taken off before a radio message was received warning of Japanese aircraft. The pilot decided to land in a river until the danger passed and, my mother momentarily forgetting that they were in a flying boat, became convinced that that they were going to crash. After all they had been through it seemed so unfair. Then they were told not to talk until the all-clear was given.

At last they heard the sound of the Japanese fighters passing overhead. After a cautionary delay, the seaplane took off again and landed without further incident early in the morning.

In Batavia* my mother was taken directly to a hospital. Her face had swollen up like a balloon, and at first the doctors were unable to pinpoint the cause until it was diagnosed as poison from a tropical plant. While resting in the jungle, she had inadvertently sat down beneath a Bintangor tree,** which drips its toxins onto the earth beneath.

That night there were two air-raid warnings, so she and Patricia, who never left her side, slept beneath the hospital bed. On waking up the next morning, they found that Charles and Virginia had arrived. Patricia was the first to see them, and ran up the hospital ward shouting "Daddy! Daddy!" Overjoyed, my mother could scarcely believe it. He explained to her that Ah Cheow had gone to his relatives and Amah to her family in Singapore's Chinatown. The Sarawak authorities had notified him of their escape,

---

*   Batavia's name was changed to Djakarta following Indonesian independence in 1949.

** It has recently been discovered that certain properties from the Bintangor tree contain an antidote for HIV and AIDS.

and Pat McKerron, formerly Singapore's chief censor and now head of the island's Manpower Bureau, had given him permission to fly Virginia over from Singapore in a supply plane. My mother had almost begun to believe in miracles when Charles awkwardly confessed that he had promised to return within ten days.

It came to her as a bolt out of the blue. She would have given anything to prevent it, but she knew the nature of the man. There was no point in trying to make him change his mind. Back in Singapore, the Governor had called upon everybody – Europeans, Indians, Chinese and Malays – to stand shoulder to shoulder. So he would.

My father was convinced that he had no option but to return. The situation was critical. He had given his word. My mother was equally aware that it was her responsibility to take the children to safety and, under the circumstances, Australia seemed the best bet.

At least in Australia they had contacts and spoke the same language. My father had already transferred some money to the Bank of New South Wales in her name, and if it was insufficient, she was to get in touch with the Borneo Company in London. The war would soon be over and they would be together again.

Both of my parents came of a class and generation that would have expected nothing less of either of them. In later years, neither would discuss what must have been the most testing moment of their married life, and almost certainly the most difficult decision my father ever had to make. My mother accepted it.

Taking rooms in the Hotel de Nederlanden, at least they were able to spend a few days together as a family before their ways parted. On 25th January, Winky joined them for Sunday luncheon. He was on his way to General Wavell's headquarters in Bandoeng, and much to the delight of my sisters scribbled cartoons on the back of the menu card.

The following Wednesday, my father did return to Singapore, leaving on the last supply plane out of Batavia. He arrived just in time to witness the British and Australian forces make their final retreat over the Causeway on the nights of 30th and 31st January. From then on, Singapore was isolated.

Island propaganda, desperate to save face with the native populace, continued regardless. 'WORKERS, every hour counts in the battle of

The Singapore Causeway
(Martine Family Collection)

Singapore. Don't let the sirens stop your work. The enemy bombers may be miles away. . .'

To Wendy Grant in Perth, John sent confirmation of this. "Don't worry about wireless news regarding hundreds of Japanese machines over Singapore, etc. I know it sounds alarming on the news, but to be truthful we were surprised to hear that there were more than about twenty of them: the damage through bombs is to date negligible, and I can't see them doing much in air raids unless they take the risk and come over lower." [8]

Two days later he was equally optimistic. "Raffles Hotel looks rather like a theatrical scene from *Behind the Lines* – everyone in khaki, with people all shouting for drinks. I still wear mufti (he was a Singapore Volunteer) in the evenings as it is much more comfortable."

To keep himself busy, Charles threw himself headlong into any available work that needed to be done. When his plane had touched down in Singapore, he was unable to find a bus or taxi, so walked the distance to his old home Belvedere where, despite its being packed with up-country refugees, he was able to move into Kenneth Simpson's quarters. The following morning he walked over to Creehall to see Joe Penrice, who offered him a room when the Mansfield evacuees left. To my mother he wrote: "I will see what happens as at present, with the office in the house and no car, it is convenient to be where I am as I can use Kenneth's Austin sparingly.

"I am not going to say much more," he concluded, suppressing his emotions, as was his way. "What you have come through is so miraculous that we can only be thankful and pray that this next move will land you in safety until the tide had turned. God bless you my love and keep you safe and sound. Your loving Charles."

Before long, he was joined by Boris Hembry. Unknown to him, Boris had enrolled in Lt-Colonel Frederick Spencer Chapman's guerilla "left-behind" party. For the previous month he had been occupying a hideout 48 miles to the north of Kuala Lumpur, eventually joining forces with a group of young Chinese, mostly drawn from Singapore's illegal Communist Party. Also unknown to my father was that Red Reddish too had signed up to go behind the lines. Two years later Red was to parachute into Bidor as part of Force 136.

When the situation finally deteriorated, Boris had escaped from the occupied mainland in a sampan to Sumatra from where he hitched a lift back to Singapore in a Tiger Moth. Having reported to his superiors, he sought out my father at Belvedere and told him that Jean and John Hembry, who had driven south from Perak before Kuala Lumpur fell, were now also in Australia. In no uncertain terms he chided my father, saying that he must have been mad to have returned from Batavia. "All through some misplaced sense of honour," he told him.

By now everybody on Singapore island – European, Indian, Chinese and Malay – was pitching in to destroy anything that might conceivably be of use to the approaching enemy. One of my father's first assignments, accompanied by Chan Seng Ann, the Borneo Company's Singapore storekeeper, was to land and store a shipload of explosives under constant bombardment from Japanese aircraft.[9] When it became obvious that the cargo would be more valuable to the enemy than to anyone else, they blew up the warehouse.

The very last issue of the *Straits Times* to be published before Singapore fell, was just a single sheet carrying a defiant message from the Governor. 'Singapore Must Stand; it SHALL Stand.'[10] Despite such bravado, orchestrated by Robert Scott, head of the Far East Bureau of the British Ministry of Information, in order to prevent panic, the authorities had at long last woken up to the realities of an imminent catastrophe.

CHAPTER THIRTEEN

The Impending Catastrophe

The people in Malaya, especially in Singapore, both military and civil, lived in a fool's paradise. The policy of the government and the fighting services was 'Don't worry, it may never happen.'

Ivan Simson, *Singapore – Too Little, Too Late*

SINGAPORE had been the major centre for the storage and distribution of petroleum products in South East Asia since the early 1930s.* If captured, its off-shore depots on Pulau Bukom and Pulau Subarok would provide an invaluable asset to the invaders, and on the 13th February 1942 it was decided to turn upon them the guns at Siloso Point. With the help of a group of Royal Marines, survivors of *HMS Prince of Wales,* Donald Howgill, general manager of Shell Oil's Bukom depot, set fire to the stores and escaped in a tugboat to Java under the pall of smoke created by the explosions.

Watching from Ocean Building on the mainland, Sir John Bagnall thought that the burning storage vessels added their quota to the general eeriness which surrounded him. All of the glass doors and windows had been removed from his Board Room where he had taken up residence with a mattress, pillows, towels and a collection of cutlery, crockery and glassware. Before long he was joined by other Straits Trading Company employees.[1]

With the blackout, they were without light, except for torches, so from seven o'clock onwards retired to bed, some of them sleeping out on the veranda. All night long the guns on the neighbouring islands fired at short intervals, the burning oil tanks at Pulau Samboe and Pulau Bukom casting a sinister glour over the night sky.

It had been put about that the Japanese while insufferable when sober, would be infinitely worse when intoxicated. In the Borneo Company's godown in Magazine Road were 36,000 bottles of assorted brandy, whisky

---

* The oil refinery at Pulau Bukom was built post-war.

and gin, not to mention champagne, and it became the unwanted task of my father and Jack Bennett to destroy the entire stock.

Jack's wife Cecily and his two daughters had been safely evacuated to Britain on the somewhat inappropriately named *Empress of Japan*, so early in the morning he and my father began tipping the stock, case by case, through a hole in the floor of the warehouse. As the pile of 'empties' grew, they tried throwing individual bottles against a wall, which was effective, but time consuming. At least they could encourage each other that they must have been the only two men in history to destroy upwards of £30,000 worth of spirits single-handed.** [2]

The work went on throughout the day, and was all but finished when a Japanese shell pitched through the roof of the godown, forcing them to leave in a hurry. The whole bizarre scene was illuminated by a soap factory blazing nearby. They must have looked particularly scruffy because as they fell out into the street an old Chinese man stopped them and, opening a tin of cigarettes, offered them a smoke. He must have thought that they had come straight from the battle which, in a way they had. However, it had kept my father's mind off the fate of his family.

John Grant too was preoccupied with Volunteer duties and in a reflective mood. To Wendy he wrote: "I have dreamt several times that you are still here; very sweet dreams, but rather sad-making when I wake up to the grim realities. If I should be unlucky enough to meet my Waterloo, I would like you to PROMISE me My Dear that you will bring up Ian and Peter as Highlanders, even if you are not in the north of Scotland." [3]

On 12th February, Boris Hembry loaded up a lorry with stores – water cans and explosives – and drove to Belvedere where he found the water was still running from the taps. Seizing advantage of the opportunity, he filled up the cans and parked the lorry under the veranda while he joined Charles and the rest of the household who were enjoying the first of many stengahs. Despite the air-raids and the shells falling nearby, it was a cheery evening. It was only on the following morning when Boris noticed the shell craters in the garden, and the direct hit on a nearby house, that he remembered the explosives he had packed into his lorry, parked feet away from where they had been having their party.

---

*   Worth over £1 million today.

As Boris set off, he confided to Charles that his orders were to help prepare an escape route along the islands from Singapore to Sumatra.* Boris did his best to persuade Charles to join him, but my father would not be persuaded. Under no circumstances was he prepared to abandon his friends on the island.

At noon on Friday 13th February, F.D. Bisseker called on Sir John Bagnall with instructions for all technical and key men, and a limited number of heads of banks and mercantile firms, to call at the Union Building at 2pm to collect their passes to leave. Luggage was to be limited to that which could be carried in one hand, and those who had been selected were to meet at the Harbour Board gate in front of the Ocean Building. It was an official order which they could have chosen to disobey. It comes as no surprise to learn that only a handful did.

At 3pm they gathered at the appointed place and were joined by others who had also obtained passes to depart. For the next hour, women and children, mainly from the hospitals, arrived in ambulances, cars and on foot. At 4.15pm, they were instructed to enter the Taluk Ayer Area and were directed around the dock to the godowns on the Southern Arm where a makeshift flotilla had been created consisting of the *Vyner Brooke*, the *Mata Hari*, the *Giang Bee*, the *Kuala*, and others.

*   *   *

ACROSS the China Sea, Pontianak was taken, and the onslaught on Sumatra and Java began. My mother and the girls, the Elams,** Daphne Large, Richard Sagar, a junior with the Borneo Company who had signed up with the Sarawak Volunteers, and Gordon Myles, the district warden for Sankei, were scheduled to set sail for Australia from Surabaya in East Java three days after my father's departure, which coincidentally was my mother's 30th birthday. On that day Surabaya was bombed, and no ships sailed.

---

*   Boris Hembry reached Colombo via Sumatra and became I.S.L.D (Inter-Services Liaison Department) chief in India.

** Lisa Elam was joined by her husband Edgar who, as an employee of the Sarawak Government, was summoned to Batavia where Rajah Brooke had arrived from Australia to set up a temporary administration in exile.

On 15th February, while they were still waiting to ship out from Java, the news broke that Singapore had fallen. My mother's friend Jean Allen from Penang was among the women who had died while trying to escape. With 250 souls on board, the *Vyner Brooke*, the Sarawak Steamship Company's pride since 1927, got as far as the Banka Strait before it was attacked by nine Japanese fighter planes. It took about twenty minutes to sink, the approximate time of its disappearance identified by the survivors' watches which stopped at twenty minutes to three, the moment they encountered sea-water. The oil from the *Vyner Brooke's* tanks spilled into the sea covering the swimmers who leapt overboard, many of them drowning.[4] Those who managed to swim free, including the captain, chief officer, second engineer and 21 nurses, were later massacred by a small party of Japanese soldiers. Only one nursing sister, Vivien Bullwinkle, although shot through the throat, survived the killings and her subsequent imprisonment.[5]

The *Mata Hari*, having reached the open sea, had the misfortune to sail straight into the middle of the approaching Japanese fleet, and had no option but to surrender.

On its first day at sea, the *Giang Bee*, formerly a Chinese-owned coastal steamer, was blown out of the water with over 100 passengers still on board. Just moments before, Robert Scott, Singapore's director of information, had embarked in a rowing-boat which succeeded in reaching the coast of Sumatra. Seeking refuge in a small village near Palembang, he was later betrayed to the Japanese, arrested five months later, and returned to Singapore.

Jean Allen, and allegedly Jiddy Dawson,* general manager of Guthrie & Co, were among the 700 passengers on the *Kuala*.[6] When it was bombed and it sank off the island of Pompong, some of the women passengers escaped by swimming ashore onto the little islets in the Banka Straits, where they were rescued by the *Tanjong Penang*, an island trading steamer. Moments later the *Tanjong Penang* was in turn destroyed by Admiral Ozawa's fleet.

There were forty-four vessels in the main evacuation fleet of which

---

* Another account is that he was hit by a sniper's bullet when his boat sank in the harbour area.

only a handful got through. Ketchil Ashworth of the Borneo Company lost his life when *Scorpion*, the river gunboat he was commanding, came under fire and sank in the Banka Straits. Sir John Bagnall was among those who boarded *HMS Grasshopper*, another small gunboat, which departed from the Outer Roads after dark, but instead of proceeding to Batavia, as expected, spent the following five hours cruising outside the harbour, mainly between Pulau Samboe and Blakang Mati, and then, much to the astonishment of those on board, returned to the Teluk Ayer wharf to pick up further passengers.[7]

On the quayside, the railway godowns and their large stocks of rubber were blazing furiously and in the darkness, the buildings were no more than twisted steel and flames. While tied up alongside the wharf, a salvo of shells came over and fell into the water fifty yards from *Grasshopper*. Minutes later, a second salvo arrived, this time only twenty five yards away. Having picked up its additional cargo, *Grasshopper* did not wait for a third burst and cast off at full speed.

Shortly after noon, *HMS Dragonfly*, *Grasshopper*'s sister ship which had accompanied them, was attacked and sunk. *Grasshopper* was forced to beach on a nearby island known as Pulau Mas and before he swam ashore, Sir John Bagnall safely embedded the deeds to the Straits Trading Company in his hat. Moments later, nine enemy planes swept overhead machine-gunning the beach.

Having reached the larger Pulua Buoya in a small boat, the party spent the night in a small fishing village and were lucky enough to find a motor launch which took them to the larger island of Sinkap. From here they took ship on a succession of small boats and motor launches, eventually arriving on mainland Sumatra – by which time their numbers had swelled to sixty men and forty women. From Padang, the assembled company set sail on a small steamer, *The Palopo*, arriving in Colombo on 14th March, whereupon Sir John set off to South Africa.

On one of the few ships escaping from Singapore Harbour which remained afloat for the duration of its voyage were Charles's friend Joe Penrice with Cecil Starkey, Mansfield's Scottish accountant, and Dennis Peterkin, married to Joan Black's sister Greta. Like the fugitives on the *Mata Hari*, they had the misfortune to sail straight into the middle of the invading navy, and were ordered to sail to Muntok in Sumatra, where they were sent to Palembang for internment. Cecil Starkey* survived the ordeal, but both Joe and Dennis died in captivity.

Among those who did affect a successful escape unharmed, was F.D. Bisseker, who was much maligned thereafter for having done so by those who felt that he should have stayed behind with the Civil Defence Corps. After the war, his immediate superior, Brigadier Ivan Simson, went to great lengths to emphasise that it was on his express orders, confirmed by the Governor, that Bisseker left. For once he and the Governor had agreed that men such as Bisseker and Sir John Bagnall would be of much more use to the ongoing war effort elsewhere than they would be in captivity. Simson himself had fully intended to leave on a motor launch commanded by Major Goode of the Royal Engineers,** but at the last moment General Percival had personally asked him to stay.[8]

Since his departure, my mother had received only the one letter from my father. She knew that lots of other European men had got out of Singapore before it was taken, but a chance encounter with two of them confirmed her worst fears. They told her that they had seen him the day before they themselves had escaped, and he had said he had no intention of leaving. Writing to her mother, she made a brave attempt to hide her emotions: "I had no feeling of fear," she insisted. "From the moment of Charles's departure to Singapore in early December, a quiet coldness settled over me which only broke down once in the jungle, and when he walked into the hospital in Batavia with Virginia.

"The rest of the time it was as if I hardly thought at all. I just went on to whatever task needed to be confronted. Always running through my mind were the words of Charles's father as my father lay dying. 'Take each day as it comes,' he said. I think that was how I lived from the start of this adventure, just as I have had to since Charles left me to fly back to Singapore."

At long last, the big Dutch KPM*** liner, the *MS Boissevan*, crept

---

* When the war was over, Cecil Starkey, having attended the funerals of all the Mansfield employees imprisoned in Palembang, became known as 'Mansfield's Chief Mourner.'

** Goode took an alternative route to the other ships, and therefore got through to Sumatra with 31 passengers unharmed. The party then crossed to Padang by road.

*** Koninkylke Paketvaart Maatschappij (Royal Packet Navigation Company).

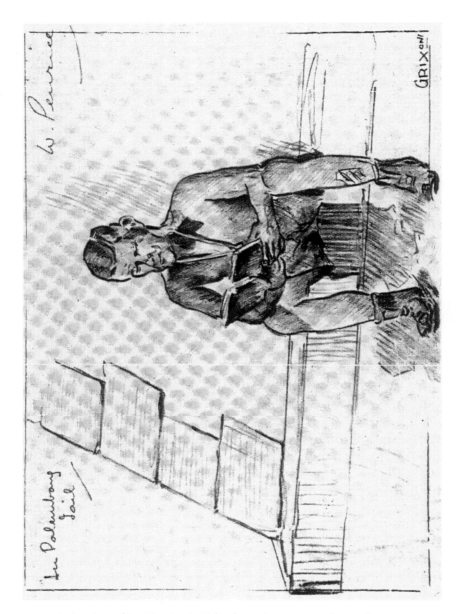

A drawing of Joe Penrice in Palembang Internment Camp, Sumatra

(Martine Family Collection)

into Batavia's Tadjong Priok harbour to take them to Australia. Pat later discovered that it carried all of the Dutch gold reserves, but she and the other passengers were ignorant of this as it raced through the Sunda Straits into the open sea late that night. The voyage, a journey of 2,500 miles, was uneventful as they skirted round New Guinea and Australia's coastline to reach Sydney Harbour. They had been told to expect trouble, but amazingly encountered none; the Japanese were preoccupied with taking Java and Sumatra, and whatever their extended ambitions might be, Australia could wait.

However, my sensible mother wore her clothes day and night for the first part of the trip, and she and the girls carried life belts at all times. The ship was 'bung-full' of Dutch airmen and all kinds of itinerant refugees, but my mother and sisters were among the lucky ones with a cabin to themselves.

My mother was especially grateful for this when she once again became ill. Although neither she nor the ship's doctor had the slightest idea what was wrong, it was later discovered that she was suffering from hook-worm, a parasite she had picked up in the Borneo jungle.

CHAPTER FOURTEEN

The Fall of Singapore

The looting of the big houses and warehouses of our British masters symbolised the end of an era. It is difficult for those born after 1945 to appreciate the full implications of the British defeat, as they have no memory of the colonial system that the Japanese brought crashing down on 15th February 1942.

Lee Kwan Yew, *The Singapore Story.*

THE Japanese took Singapore on Sunday 15th February 1942, a catastrophe which Winston Churchill described as 'the worst disaster and largest capitulation in British history.'[1]

It tolled the death-knell of British imperialism in the Far East, causing passionate debate both at the time and in historical appraisal.

Singapore's defences were centred on a powerful coastal artillery system. Twelve batteries of guns were located on Singapore, Pulau Brani, Blakang Mati and Pulau Tekong. A little to the south-east of Pulau Tekong, on the Malayan mainland, was another six-inch battery at Pengerang.

Singapore was therefore considered invincible from sea attack, but although the guns had all-round, or almost all-round traverse, they were hopelessly placed for any attack from the north. Added to this, the RAF had only a few aircraft, and there were no tanks on the island.

For two months it had been clear that the Japanese army was advancing overland from the north, down the Malay peninsula, many of them riding on bicycles. It defies belief that the British military authorities were so unprepared. Even the Japanese strategists expressed their astonishment.

In his personal diaries, General Tomoyuki Yamashita, Japan's commander-in-chief in Malaya, himself confessed that his 25th Army was outnumbered more than three to one. "My attack on Singapore was a bluff," he wrote. "I knew that if I had to fight for Singapore I would be beaten. That was why the surrender had to be made at once. I was very frightened all the time that the British would discover our numerical weakness and lack of supplies and force me into disastrous street fighting."[2]

In the culture of Japanese militarism, where surrender is tantamount to cowardice, was it any wonder the conquerors were so contemptuous of their captives? Although easy to be wise in retrospect, it has to be concluded that virtually everyone in a position of authority in Singapore, the UK Colonial and War offices in London, even Winston Churchill, was to blame for the ensuing disaster.

"It never occurred to me for a moment that the gorge of the fortress of Singapore, with its splendid moat half a mile wide, was not entirely fortified against an attack from the northward," he wrote to his chiefs of staff – but too late.

To be fair, he had two months earlier written to General Lord Ismay to demand reassurance. "Nothing compares in importance with the fortress. Are you sure we shall have enough troops for a prolonged defence? Consider with Auchinleck and Commonwealth Government moving 1st Australian Division from Palestine to Singapore. Report action."

The reality was that despite the blinkered belief that Britain would stand by Singapore at all costs, Europe took precedence. But that still does not excuse the ensuing fiasco. General Wavell had observed from the beginning that the main objective of the Japanese would be the north-west coast of Singapore. So why did nobody listen to him?

There must have been intelligence reports of General Yamashita massing his forces in Johore, and therefore even when General Percival did eventually blow up the Causeway, it was too late to make a significant difference. Earlier Wavell had asked him, "with some asperity," why no north shore defences had been started, and much to his commander-in-chief's disbelief he had replied that "the construction of defence works would have been bad for the island's morale." [3]

That morale was already undermined. From across the Straits, Japanese guns began a relentless shelling of the Government House area, while their Air Force, meeting virtually no resistance, launched attacks on the Kallang aerodrome and Singapore Docks.

In October 1941, my father's cousin, Mary Hannay, had started a job with A.P.C (Shell) in Singapore, and by December was sharing an apartment in River Valley Road with a group of other women, mostly over thirty, who had left their husbands up-country and taken refuge in Singapore. As the situation worsened, her mother Kate arrived from Ipoh and, since some of the girls in Mary's flat were leaving, Kate Hannay moved in. Sixty-seven year old Harry Hannay Snr reached Singapore with the Ipoh Defence Volunteers, in mid-January, and was quartered in a military camp. Ted and Harry Hannay Jnr were stationed at the Straits Settlements Volunteer Headquarters in Beach Road, opposite Raffles Hotel, and the family joined forces for Christmas dinner. It was to be the last time that they would all be together.[4]

Seeing an 'overseas' job advertised at Fort Canning, General Percival's defence headquarters, Kate persuaded Mary to apply for it and she was selected to join General Wavell's administrative staff in Java. On the 1st February 1942, she was driven to the harbour by Ted in his Singapore Volunteer uniform and, having said good-bye to her parents, she boarded a small Dutch freighter, taking with her one small suitcase which contained her stamp collection and photo albums.

"There were a few alarms – a plane or a submarine sighted which could only have been Japanese, and when that happened, we were told to hide under the awnings or on the lower deck," she recalled. "After two long days we went up river to Palembang and spent all day sweltering under the sun. None of us were allowed off the boat, but we did manage to buy fresh pineapples from the locals and, as a result, we all had sore tongues."

The party reached Batavia the following day and transferred onto a train which took them to Bandoeng, in the mountains, whence they were driven to Lembang by car. "We were billeted in a small house opposite the hotel which General Wavell had turned into his Allied Headquarters. The other girls were mostly employed on coding, but a wretched young corporal took a shine to me as the youngest and I had to work in his little Orderly Office."

In Singapore, Kate Hannay was left on her own in Mary's flat, but made up her mind to stay there so as to be near her husband and sons. However, accommodation was at a premium and a chance encounter in the market place with Ewald and Helen Beck, a couple from Ipoh, led to their moving in with her. With the bombing from Johore at its height, Ewald, who had been in the Ipoh Police Force, was soon called up for defence work, and the two women, having both had a previous involvement with the Ipoh branch of St John's Ambulance Brigade, presented themselves at the Fullerton Building on the waterfront which was in the process of being turned into a military hospital. With Joan Draper from Kuala Lumpur, Raja Musa, an Indian doctor, Ethel Mulvaney, the Canadian wife of an army major, and Katherine de Moubray from Trengganu, they set about transforming the Singapore Club on the first floor into a hospital ward.

During the night of 8th February, 13,000 Japanese soldiers crossed the Straits by landing-craft, followed by a further 10,000 before dawn. Some of them even swam across carrying their rifles and ammunition.

When daylight arrived, there were five, possibly six Japanese divisions landed on the north of Singapore island and preparing to attack along a front of four miles. Yet despite the intelligence that surely must have been available to General Percival at Fort Canning, no Allied troops were dispersed to confront them. By the time the full significance of what was happening had sunk in, the enemy had control of Bukit Timah and Bukit Mandai, and one of the large reservoirs in the catchment area, thus completely cutting off the island's essential water supply. The supply from the mainland had already gone with the blowing up of the Causeway.

At the Volunteer Headquarters, Ted Hannay observed that eleven bombs had dropped into the compound, but nobody had been killed. The shed they hit contained all of the Volunteers' 18-pound shells and .303 rifle ammunition, but none of it had exploded.[5] On the following day, the 10th February, just for his own record, he copied down the text of General Wavell's Orders of the Day:

"It is certain that our troops in Singapore Island heavily outnumber any Japanese who have crossed the Straits. We must destroy them. Our whole fighting reputation is at stake, and the honour of the British Empire. The Americans have held out in the Bataan Peninsula against heavier odds. The Russians are turning back the picked strength of the Germans, and the Chinese with an almost complete lack of modern equipment have held the Japanese for four years.

"It will be disgraceful if we yield our boasted Fortress of Singapore to inferior enemy forces. There must be no thought of sparing troops, or civil population, and no mercy must be shown to weakness in any shape or form. Commanders and Senior Officers must lead their troops, and if necessary, die with them. There must be no question or thought of surrender. Every unit must fight it out to the end, and in close contact

Japanese troops marching along Battery Road past the Hong Kong & Shanghai Bank building 16th February 1942

(photo: Imperial War Museum)

with the enemy. I look to you and to your men to fight to the end, to prove that the fighting spirit that won our Empire exists to enable us to defend it."

As my father and his colleagues, including several groups of volunteers, continued with spoiling missions, shocking news filtered through from the Alexandra Military Hospital. As the Japanese soldiers had approached, Lieutenant Weston of the Royal Army Medical Corps had gone out to meet them carrying a white flag. In a re-enactment of the butchery in Hong Kong, the invaders ignored the flag and the Red Cross signs, and bayoneted Weston to death. Following this, they entered the hospital and massacred the patients and the other R.A.M.C. staff. [6]

In the Fullerton Building, Kate Hannay and the other volunteer nurses became inundated with hundreds of wounded and dying. The women collected all the Singapore Club's vegetable bowls, electroplated makan dishes, tall cut-glass vases and heavy ashtrays and transformed them into hospital utensils. The only water available had to be brought from a well by the local Defence Corps, who at the same time removed the bodies of the dead for burial. [7]

At 5am on 12th February, Ted Hannay received the command "Local Defence Positions." His was in a ruined building looking down Beach Road, towards the aerodrome. He had his rifle and six hand-grenades, of which he was terrified, having never thrown one. Nearby he could hear the rat-tat-tat of machine-guns, the Japanese being only a short distance away, and occasionally something larger than a machine-gun bullet came over, possibly a mortar bomb. Looking out of his window into the pitch black of the night it felt as if he was holding back the entire Japanese advance alone, and to calm himself he chewed several bars of chocolate. When dawn broke, he found, much to his amazement, the road in front of him covered with bren gun carriers and anti-tank guns, from which not a sound had been heard.

The following three days were chaotic with thousands of Allied soldiers of all nationalities pouring into Singapore town, some of them even sleeping in bathrooms and latrines. All of the essential services broke down. There was no electric light and no telephone. It was a challenge even to find enough water to brush one's teeth.[8]

At Fort Canning, General Percival reviewed the situation as he saw it.

Supplies of food and petrol were running out. The water situation was critical, and the hospitals and hotels in Singapore city were packed to capacity. He was considering what to do next when a telegram arrived from Wavell. His instructions were that so long as he was in a position to inflict losses and damages to the enemy and his troops were physically capable of doing so, he must fight on. Should this no longer be possible, he gave Percival discretion to cease resistance.[9]

In Percival's mind there were only two options: either to counter-attack the enemy immediately and regain control of the reservoirs and military food depots, or to capitulate to avoid further bloodshed. Genuinely believing that, having achieved their objective, the Japanese would behave honourably, he chose the latter course. His decision was reported to the Governor who, after Government House had come under shell attack, had installed himself, with his wife, in the Fullerton Building.

On the afternoon of 15th February 1942, a squad of men were seen marching along the Bukit Timah Road and carrying a Union Jack and a white flag of truce. In a comical pastiche, the British officers, led by the tall, skinny figure of their commander, were dressed in khaki shorts, shirts and steel helmets. Old school Singaporeans were horrified that the British Military wore shorts to surrender. Their Japanese escort was attired in full uniform with high boots and appeared to be formidably armed. It was an image that would flash around the world. 'Lo How the Mighty Have Fallen,' read the headlines.

Under normal circumstances the Chinese would have been celebrating on that day. It was the Lunar New Year, their biggest annual festival, but there were no gongs or drums to be heard; the atmosphere of foreboding prevailed.

The terms demanded by General Yamashita were simple. In return for the Japanese undertaking to protect *British* civilians – men, women and children – the British Army must cease hostilities immediately. No copy of the surrender document survives, but that Percival did not insist that *all* civilians should be protected does seem extraordinary. Perhaps, as the archetypal English military man abroad, he assumed that they would be.

Documents, however, meant little to the Japanese who had distanced themselves from the pre-war Geneva Convention which governed the conduct of prisoners of war. Their opponents were all too soon to find out what this entailed.

As for Percival, there are those who remain convinced that he did the right thing. The official view following the war was that 'the disaster to the million Asians in the city, and to the troops, would have been very great had the surrender been delayed by even a few hours.'

What followed was terrible enough.

The ceasefire came at 8.30pm, and it was the silence that particularly struck my father. "It was eerie to a degree," he recalled. "When you'd been running helter-skelter in all directions, with the pandemonium of bangs, and explosions and all sorts of noise all around you, the silence after the surrender was sudden and dramatic."

Half an hour after the surrender, the Rt Reverend John Leonard Wilson, Anglican Bishop of Singapore, took a service at St Andrew's Cathedral which had astonishingly survived the bombardment. It was a sombre interval. For four days, the imposing church had been used as an emergency hospital, and several hundred anxious civilians, largely Asiatic, assembled with the wounded to pray. [10]

That same evening my father and Jack Bennett surveyed Singapore town from the roof of the Mercantile Bank Building, where they were billeted. From that height it was as if they were surrounded by a vast ring of fire, four walls with Singapore city burning in the middle, although as a whole it had not been 'that badly knocked about.'[11] No vast areas of the town were devastated beyond repair. Damage appeared to be local, and Fort Canning was virtually untouched. It was Chinatown that had suffered the most, and would continue to do so.

Fires too were localised, though they gave the impression of being much more widespread than they actually were, especially at night. The impression of a holocaust that was widely circulated by those who had fled from it, did not look nearly so bad in daylight to those who remained.

At the Straits Settlements Volunteers Headquarters, Ted and Harry Hannay Jnr, with their colleagues, held a party. Someone produced a ham, and somebody else, a Dundee cake. At midnight, they solemnly smashed the hundreds of bottles of Scotch whisky and brandy they had been unable to consume. When they had finished, the Sergeant-Major said to them. "Boys, tomorrow the Japanese will come and we do not know what they will do to us. We will face them like men, and have our buttons polished!"[12]

For that night, and the one that followed, Charles and Jack Bennett sheltered in the Mercantile Bank. On the second morning they were summoned to parade in front of the Japanese and as they descended the staircase into the entrance hall, noticed the crowd separate and walk around something, as if there were an obstruction. Lying on the ground was a British Army revolver. It would obviously not be sensible to be seen with one of those in your hands.[13]

Buttons and boots polished, Ted Hannay received a visit from a Japanese officer who, having saluted him, politely informed him that he would like to take over his office. The officer spoke perfect English, and shortly afterwards his soldiers arrived to remove the volunteers' guns and arms. Thereafter, much to Ted's astonishment, the two sides began to fraternise with each other, comparing photographs of wives and girlfriends. In the afternoon, one of the Japanese soldiers arrived at headquarters with a brand new Ford van which he said he had found abandoned. It was full of packets of cigarettes.[14]

That fraternisation of this sort should have been allowed to take place at all was unexpected, but indicates that many of the Japanese soldiers were ordinary conscripts, not all of them the crazed invading force of vicious bullies so commonly depicted. At this stage, neither side knew what would happen next and were doubtless longing to return to their homes. As the enormity of the Imperial Army's achievement became apparent, and thoughts of repatriation faded, the darker side of the Bushido code emerged. The containment of so many prisoners was a massive and thankless task and, in venting their frustration, the Japanese command often as not treated its own soldiers with as much contempt as the prison guards treated their captives.

At the Fullarton Building, Kate Hannay and her friends continued their nursing duties, sleeping in a card room on the floor or on tables, and managing to keep themselves going with an occasional tin of cheese, salmon or bully-beef, and cups of tea. Naturally concerned, Harry Hannay Snr came to see them and Helen Beck promised that no matter what happened, she and Kate would stick together. It suited both of them to do so. When the Japanese did arrive, Helen, who had been born in Nagasaki and grown up in Japan, acted as an interpreter for the military,[15] which, as it transpired, avoided a lot of unnecessary trouble.

In Lembang, Mary Hannay heard of the fall of Singapore . . . At the end of the month, she and the other girls employed at Wavell's headquarters

Ted Hannay	Mary Hannay	Harry Hannay Jnr
(Photo: Kirsty Johns)	*(Martine Family Collection)*	*(Photo: Kirsty Johns)*

were told to be ready to leave. In Batavia they boarded the *SS Orcades* and sailed safely to Colombo, despite a Japanese radio broadcast claiming that the *Orcades* had been sunk. Back in Britain, she took a train to Scotland and to the astonishment of her uncle, Dr Martine – my grandfather – arrived on his doorstep just as he was sitting down to dinner. When she had recovered from the journey, she was conscripted into the Women's Auxiliary Air Force.[16]

The invaders had calculated that there were 500 Europeans, other than soldiers, in Singapore. Instead, they found 4,600. The entire European community was instructed to assemble in the Cricket Club ground and made to stand for a day under a scorching sun. Afterwards they were forced marched first to temporary camps for assessment, then a further eighteen miles to Changi Prison, where they were allocated quarters that had been designed to take 600 criminals.[17]

As my father waited patiently with the other civilians, what thoughts must have passed through his mind? He was forty-two years old and a civilian. Although he had promised to return to Singapore when the authorities had allowed him to take his daughter to Batavia, it is unlikely that anybody would have blamed him had he not. Of course, being the man he was, he would have certainly blamed himself. But to what end? Anything was better than this.

It was a bitter and a dreadful moment of truth, coupled with a quandary that would haunt him for the remainder of his days. In doing the honourable thing, he had become trapped, and by one of the most vicious, co-ordinated fighting machines that has ever existed, his captors a far cry from the baggy-panted, slitty-eyed cartoon characters of popular Western invention.

He had abandoned his wife and two small children in Batavia. He might never see them again. Although he had made arrangements for their escape, he had no idea if they had been successful. Nor had he any way of knowing if they had reached their destination, or how they would survive if they had. Added to this was the fear that their ship might have been sunk en route.

That was not all. For the incoming Allied troops, there was the humiliation of defeat. For men such as my father, it was far worse. He had lived and worked in this country for twenty years and given of his best to it. Now he was obliged to witness this land he had come to know and respect, overrun and decimated, its native population left at the mercy of the invader.

At 2pm on 17th February, the march to Changi began. "It took us many moves to learn just how much we could carry," recorded Ted Hannay. "We all left Singapore town with mountains of kit, food, etc, not to mention some 600 cigarettes that I carried. These were packed around the turn-ups of our shorts (tropical pattern which could be made into short slacks). We walked some twelve miles, and weary ones they were, and then were allowed to camp for the night. On the way out we saw a few damaged cars, still with dead occupants in them, but apart from holes made by shrapnel and bullets, the damage was not so very great.[18]

'My brother and I were detailed to go forward by lorry to prepare the place for our chaps. The journey was extremely slow because of the bottle-necks created by bomb craters, but eventually we reached Changi and found the whole place swarming with people. The only thing to do was to squat down for the night on our groundsheets and sleep out in the open, no hardship in the tropics. The following day some sort of order was made out, and we found ourselves on concrete floors and very closely packed together. We were on the third (top) floor of the Kitchener Barracks, and this had its advantages and disadvantages. It was cool, and the view up the Johore Strait almost to the Naval Base was very beautiful and interesting. Units of the Japanese Navy used to steam past us, quite a lot of them.'

The fundamental disadvantages were that there was no water, no latrines, and every time anyone wanted food or to relieve themselves, six long flights of stairs had to be faced. After a few weeks of inadequate feeding, climbing the stairs became an exhausting task.

With the capture of Singapore, the myth that the British were invincible and the oriental incompetent, was shattered. The forces of the Japanese Emperor were nothing if not determined, resilient, and ruthlessly efficient; not least did this become apparent from the manner in which they subsequently dealt with anyone who challenged or undermined their authority. Under no circumstance were they to be trifled with.

What additionally underlined their determination was that the Japanese soldier had been almost universally brainwashed into considering himself a superior being. They were the chosen ones who had come to cleanse Asia of the vile exploitation of the British and Dutch. The Bushido, the code of the Samurai, made them omnipotent. They were rising up to fulfil the destiny of their forefathers. Death in battle was the guarantee of a glorious after-life.

In this way, an entire nation, although most certainly not an intrinsically bad people, was indoctrinated into the cult of Emperor worship.

Within hours of the surrender, looters who were found breaking into the European residential areas in Holland Road, Tanglin Road, and Bukit Timah Road, were caught and beheaded, their heads stuck on pikes at eight road junctions. Six days later General Yamashita issued a brutal decree designed to punish the Chinese in Singapore who had collected funds in support of China's war effort against the Japanese.

All male Chinese between the ages of 18 and 50 were ordered to assemble at five assembly points. On the orders of Colonel Masanobu Tsuji, the Kempeitai Military Police began house-to-house searches to round up young Chinese men and girls. Hundreds were dragged into the streets, beaten up, raped and killed. Among those who escaped by going into hiding was a young Lee Kwan Yew, the future prime minister of an independent Singapore.

It is estimated that over six thousand Chinese civilians were murdered in what the Kempeitai called their 'Operation Clean Up' and the Chinese called 'Sook Ching', which means 'Operation Wipe Out.'

After the war, the Chinese Chamber of Commerce exhumed the mass graves in Siglap, Punggol and Changi and estimated that in the region of 100,000 Chinese had paid a heavy price for sending financial support to their homeland.[19]

Would it have made a difference had General Percival's surrender terms been more inclusive?

As for the immediate future, there was nothing that anyone could do to change it. For the people of Singapore, European and Asian alike, brutality, starvation and disease, in or out of captivity, were to become the stark reality for three and a half long years.

CHAPTER FIFTEEN

Guests of the Japanese Emperor

O Lovely Dawn when, through the wide-flung casement,
I see the rolling downland, clean and sweet,
And all the spectres of this strange abasement
Are but as shadows passing in the street.

Helen Beck, written in Changi Gaol.

POST-WAR, my father had an endearing and socially challenging habit of saying in conversation to strangers, 'Of course, when I was in jail . . .'

As a child I remember laughing at this, but more often than not squirming with embarrassment at the looks of curiosity he attracted from people we did not know.

Aside from the occasional reference though, and in common with many other prisoners of war I have since met, he never willingly talked about his ordeal. My mother must have had a pretty good idea of what had taken place, but neither my sisters nor I were ever allowed to know just how bad it had been.

For the civilians and military prisoners of war in Singapore between 1942 and 1945, internment was an ongoing battle against hunger, intimidation, loneliness, and depression. The district of Changi occupies a large chunk of the east coast of the island of Singapore, some several thousand acres, and when people said that they were imprisoned in Changi, it did not necessarily mean that they were all incarcerated in the same division of the camp. In February 1941, prisoners were allocated quarters according to their nationality and status. British and a few Dutch military were placed in the Kitchener and India Barracks, both formerly used by the British Army. The Selarang Barracks was turned over to Australian soldiers, and Changi Gaol, designed to hold 600 criminals, was allocated to 3,000 civilians.

Under constant observation, the prisoners from all of these groups erected a barbed wire fence to surround the acres of their not insubstantial encampment. Segregated, and under strict guard, they were nevertheless allowed to take on individual responsibilities for their own administration, but as the war dragged on and tensions between captive and captor inevitably grew worse, freedoms became more limited.

Changi Gaol was a three-storey, H-shaped concrete building with iron

Changi Gaol, Singapore

stairs and metal grilles to prevent escape. Civilian internees were split into four blocks – A, B, C and D. B, C, and D Blocks opened into each other, but the 400 women, and children under the age of nine, were housed in A Block, which was separate and strictly monitored. The Japanese attitude was that since their men were separated from their families, why should prisoners of war, especially civilians, fare any better?

Conditions throughout were overcrowded, three prisoners to a cell and others, of all ages, obliged to sleep in the hallways, senses stupefied by the indignity; a tangled mess of humanity, nerves and sweat. The average age of the internees was 45. The oldest among them was 93.[1]

Many already knew one another well having worked and socialised together in better days. Among them were Malayan civil servants, policemen, rubber planters, miners, technicians, representatives from the many commercial firms, and a group of professors and academics from Raffles College. My father and Harry Hannay Snr found themselves in D Block, where Charles, allocated to share cell no.8, was unanimously elected Shop Representative.

Being well-acquainted with Singapore town, he became one of four prisoners recognised by the Japanese as 'Communications Officers,' which meant that he was allowed out of the camp under escort to buy provisions. On one of his first trips, he asked his Japanese guard for permission to call in on the Singapore Club in Battery Road where he found his aunt Kate Hannay working as a nurse. Imagining that she would soon be repatriated, he gave her messages to pass on to his father in Scotland. Repatriation was very much on his mind, and that of every other European civilian at the time. Surely the Japanese would not want to hold on to them for any longer than was necessary?

My father and his friends miscalculated. While a few prisoners were certainly exchanged from places such as Bangkok, mostly for reasons of disability, the Japanese had come up with a very different plan for Malaya; cheap labour was not something to be readily discarded.

Meanwhile, his captors remained unaware that he spoke any local languages other than Malay. Nor did they realise that he had previously been acquainted with a large number of the Chinese shopkeepers he visited. This was useful, enabling him to negotiate and bring into the gaol all kinds of illicit and desperately needed supplies under the very noses of his escorts. However, he had to be cautious. There was always the risk that he or one of the other Communications Officers might be caught in the act, or that the surplus goods they had brought in would be discovered. To avoid either contingency, a camp committee was set up specifically to disperse merchandise as soon as it arrived.

Otherwise, food, when available, comprised small amounts of rice, salt, sugar, tea and vegetables. Insects were an ever present problem. Someone, somehow, fabricated a blowlamp to deal with them, but the ants were everywhere. No grain of rice escaped their attention. I remember being told by Ralph German,* a schoolmaster at the preparatory school I was sent to in Surrey, himself a Changi Gaol survivor, that he and my father had supplemented their diet with worms and ants for protein. (At the age of eleven, it made me sick to think of it).

Prisoners of war were organised into work parties and given tasks at the docks and other locations for which they were paid a basic pittance. Tented camps were set up and empty buildings requisitioned. Most regarded this as a blessed relief from their previous confined conditions since it enabled them to pick up items from the black market, and snippets of information concerning the progress of the war. Those who did heavy work were generously rewarded with an extra tablespoonful of rice.

Others were assigned to dig, collect wood, teach, nurse, cook, and mend. One of Dr 'Commie' Bain's duties was to plough up his beloved Bukit Golf Course in order to plant cassava.[2] Many discovered talents that they never knew they had. Some manufactured lemonade from lemon-grass. With whatever was available, the prisoners made brooms, brushes and toothpaste. Showers were created from stolen piping; bars of soap from

---

* Ralph German had previously been in the Malayan Civil Service.

palm-oil and potash. Robert Scott made a pocket-knife. Ewald Beck fashioned buttons and a buckle for his wife Helen. With a couple of slats of wood and a scrap of canvas, my father fabricated a small fold-up seat. It survives to this day.

Under such circumstances, the gaol was astonishingly well organised as at the beginning prisoners were allowed to run the blocks for themselves. There was an office, a registry, shops, stores, a smithy, a laundry, and a kitchen. There were gardeners, carpenters, and two magazines.

There was another debatable bonus. When anyone forgot to bow in respect to a guard, their faces were slapped with a hand or the butt of a gun. Those who wore false teeth soon learned to remove them quickly when guards approached. My father, being short-sighted and anxious to preserve his spectacles, stopped wearing them only to discover that his long sight improved rapidly. However, so traumatic was the humiliation to which he was subjected that, on his release, he would go out of his way to avoid having his eyes tested.

Jimmy Kemp, the magnificently corpulent Scottish miner from Kroh, experienced no such catharsis. Almost blind from broken spectacles and cataracts for the duration of his ordeal, he was attempting to create a lather on his shorts when his neighbour in the communal showers shouted to him, "You'd get on better if you used a cake of soap instead of a coconut bar."[3] By the time liberation came, Jimmy had lost over half of his weight and was down to under nine stone.

Before long, a certain resignation set in, but some were fiercely critical of those who had escaped. The prime target was the Penang-based businessman who had been second-in-command of civil defence. 'Doing a Bisseker' soon became a slogan in the camps, meaning someone who had gone but who should have stayed.[4] To be fair, it is hard to blame Bisseker given his stalwart criticism of the lack of government preparedness well in advance of the invasion, not to mention the lack of support he and his colleague Brigadier Simson received from the Governor and his underlings when they tried to do something about it.* If anything, F.D. Bisseker deserves recognition, not ridicule, for his role in the whole desperate affair.

---

* Brigadier Ivan Simson was captured and later sent to the senior officers' POW camp at Mukden in Manchuria with Sir Shenton Thomas and General Percival. In 1970, he published *Singapore: Too Little, Too Late*, a blistering indictment on the way he and Bisseker were treated by the Malay Civil Service.

Working with the Japanese was as impossible as it would have been to work against them, but most of those who experienced the ordeal soon found a way to distance themselves from what was going on around them. My father described it as 'learning to look through the wrong end of a telescope.'

Throughout the long, hot days, and the long, fitful nights, his priority was to think positively; but thoughts gave way to dreams that became nightmares. He succeeded in convincing himself that Pat and the girls must have reached Australia safely, otherwise he would surely have heard. What he did not know was that his captors were deliberately holding back and destroying letters. My mother wrote to him every week through the Red Cross, but her letters did not reach him; nor was he allowed at this time to send letters out.

Fatigue from physical exertion was aggravated by poor sanitation and diet. There was little joy to be found in Changi Gaol and, after a time, people stopped talking to each other. Often there was no point.

Then, after several months, came one of the high points of the whole wretched business. John Haxworth,* a former police officer who had joined the Singapore Immigration Department, approached my father and said, "I think these are yours."

John's wife Anne had finally got a letter through to him with a photograph of their two daughters playing with two other small girls – Virginia and Patricia. Haxworth was able to reassure him that my mother and sisters were safe with his wife and children in Sydney. My father's sense of relief was absolute; now at last there was something worthwhile to live for.

On 2nd March, Kate Hannay, Helen Beck, Joan Draper, and the other volunteer nurses were evicted from the Fullerton Building which the Japanese had decided to transform into government offices.[5] To begin with they were moved to a house at Katong, already badly overcrowded, but Helen at least managed to acquire a mosquito net for each of them, and the women slept side by side until they were relocated to Changi six days later. Helen and Joan were forced to walk the distance, but Kate, being

---

* John Haxworth's younger brother, W.R.M. 'Bucky' Haxworth of the Singapore Police Force, was also a POW in Changi. An accomplished artist, his drawings of prison life were gifted to the Singapore National Archives.

older, was allowed to go by lorry. When the others arrived, she had already got their mattresses laid out and mixed Klim milk to welcome them.

On 17th April, Ted and Harry Hannay Jnr left the Kitchener Barracks and marched into Singapore, this time with their kits carried for them.[6] In the town they were given fresh bread and fruit. The news spread rapidly that the Volunteers were marching through the town and many of the parents of the Eurasian soldiers came along to watch the spectacle on their rickshaws. Ted noticed that many of the women were weeping to see their sons in such a predicament.

Ted and Harry Jnr were quartered in a camp at the bottom of River Valley Road. It was made up of atap roofed huts that had been built for homeless Chinese. One of the Volunteers recalled having been to inspect them as possible family housing for his 'boy', but had turned them down as unfit to live in. The huts were approximately 100 yards long with only three electric lights, soon improved with bulbs of a higher voltage. There was a good water supply, and very soon the occupants had built concrete floored bathhouses with scrounged shower units, which made communal living marginally more bearable.

The Volunteers were put to work on building sixteen large godowns on a piece of waste ground adjoining Jervois Road which had a special significance for Ted since for three and a half years he had lived in a house overlooking the site, the same that had been used by Churchill's envoy, Duff Cooper, as his Singapore office. Ted Hannay remained remarkably stoical. "Although we were working like coolies, it did very few of us any harm," he reflected. "The Japanese in charge were even friendly, the commanding officer, a man called Watnabe, was quite reasonable."

What also helped was that food in Singapore town was still plentiful and for a few weeks, the brothers were permitted to run a stall selling coffee, hot, sweet and milky, which did big business. With the profits they and their fellow prisoners bought extra food to supplement their own rations.

The problem was always how to get hold of money. Since few Europeans ever carried ready cash on an everyday basis, everything being 'signed for', neither Ted nor Harry Jnr had any funds at all with them. At considerable personal risk, Harry Hannay Snr, with the co-operation of their camp commander, managed to smuggle them enough dollars to enable them to start their own shop, which again proved a great success.

They dealt in eggs and sweet potatoes, small 'pokes' of pepper and salt, peanuts, writing pads and, towards the end of the venture, they cornered the market in Vegemite (Australian Marmite). There was also an excellent library, all of it scrounged from private houses and the average price of a book running at 10 cents. All of their available cash would go out in the morning to buy stock, and they would be sold out by midday.

For an all too brief period, life was almost enjoyable, but then came a smuggled message from Harry Hannay Snr with some heartbreaking news: Kate Hannay was dead.

In all of the Far Eastern internment camps, there were four killers – the Japanese soldiers, starvation, despair, and illness: worms, beriberi, impetigo, malaria, or dysentery. A fortnight after her arrival in Changi Gaol, Kate Hannay succumbed to the latter. Helen Beck, her devoted friend from Ipoh, who had become a volunteer in the prison hospital, nursed her until she herself fell victim. Helen recovered, but Kate, who was moved to the Miyako Hospital, died on Easter Eve.

Through Changi's Red Cross* representative Ethel Mulvaney, a Canadian army wife, Helen was allowed to break the news personally to Harry Hannay Snr. He was permitted to attend the burial, and Mrs Mulvaney told him, and repeated it often to her friends, that if ever there was a woman who deserved to have the Union Jack on her coffin, it was Kate Hannay.[7]

Kate's only remaining possessions were kept in a locked Gladstone bag which she had left in the care of Joan Draper. It was handed over to Harry Snr who somehow managed to take it to Charles in his cell. It contained only a few clothes, and some bits of family jewellery. Unsticking the back of his attaché-case, Charles slipped the engagement and wedding-rings into the fold of the lining and sealed it up. The clothes were sent to the women's quarters where some of the inmates were in rags. Miraculously the contents of the attaché-case lining** were never discovered, despite its being rifled by the Japanese guards almost daily.

On the suggestion of Ethel Mulvaney, each of the women prisoners

---

* Strictly speaking there was no official Red Cross in Changi Gaol. The first time the International Red Cross representatives were allowed into the civilian camp was in August 1945.

** In 1946, back in Scotland, Charles was able to hand the rings over to Mary Hannay.

was invited to embroider a patch for a set of quilts for the Red Cross. Helen Beck dedicated her contribution to her friend Kate. The design was a simple St John's Cross worked in black thread on white linen. The inscription read: 'In Memoriam of Kate Hannay of Fullerton Building Feb 15th to March 2nd and also St John's Ambulance, Ipoh, Perak.'*

In August 1942, Major-General Fukei arrived from Tokyo to take overall command of Changi Camp, but soon after he had taken up the post, two British and two Australian soldiers staged an almost successful escape in a rowing-boat. Fukei ordered the men to be shot on the beach, and Lt-Colonel Holmes of the Manchester Regiment, the senior British officer remaining in the barracks, and three other officers, were forced to watch.

General Fukei then demanded that all military prisoners sign a form giving their word of honour not to attempt to escape.[8] When this was unanimously rejected, all of the military prisoners, with the exception of a few hundred hospital patients, were transferred to the Selarang Barracks, where there were no washing facilities, and the majority of the men were obliged to sleep out in the open.

Next Fukei ordered that the sick should also be taken to Selarang, and with disease rampant, Colonel Holmes reluctantly agreed for the no-escape agreement to be signed, but 'under duress' which thereby nullified it. Fortunately it satisfied the Japanese commandant, and the majority of prisoners were allowed to return to their barrack cells or encampments, the remnants dispersed to a range of other camps.

By October 1942, the Singapore Causeway had been rebuilt and the Volunteers were split up. Detachments were sent off to join work gangs in Borneo and Sumatra, the remainder up country to build the Bangkok to Rangoon Railway with picks and shovels, gunpowder and pulleys. In a letter to Wendy, John Grant thanked his lucky stars that he had been fortunate enough to be in hospital with malaria, and therefore considered unfit to travel.[9]

There was a consensus of opinion that the men bound for the railway

---

* Three quilts, each made up of 66 squares, are known to have survived: one is held by the British Red Cross in London, two more are with the Australian War Memorial in Canberra. None of them includes the patch described by Helen Beck, and it is thought that there was a fourth quilt which was either lost or purloined when the women were moved to the Sime Road Camp in May 1944.

Banana Dollars
(Courtesy of the Very Rev Dr William McDonald).

had ample clothes for the excursion, but to everyone's relief a large consignment of Red Cross comforts suddenly arrived and on the day before their departure, each man was given 16 tins of food.[10] That was all very well, and they would need it, but they already had more kit than they could possibly carry.

On 11th October, they set off, but had it not been for the Chinese rickshaw coolies, it would have been impossible to transport everything down to the station. These rickshaw men willingly piled their vehicles high with kit-bags, and stubbornly refused any kind of repayment. Afterwards, they looked on sadly as the men of the Volunteers crowded into goods wagons, thirty-two to a truck.

In Changi Gaol, Harry Hannay Snr and my father heard of Ted and Harry Jnr's departure with concern, but like many of those who were seconded to or indeed had volunteered to join the working parties, the hope was that the conditions up-country would be an improvement.

The camps at Tasao, Wampo, Chunkai and Tamuan, to name only a few, are carved into the annals of human wretchedness. Of the 61,000 Allied prisoners sent to Siam, 12,500 perished. Of the 183,000 Asian workforce, mostly Tamil, 91,000 died.

Sooner or later, everyone contracted dysentery, malaria or pellagra. With rapidly depleting supplies of quinine and other essentials, including food, only the strong survived. Ted Hannay was separated from his brother at

Tasao. Eight months later, he was informed of Harry Jnr's death. By then Ted's weight had dropped from eleven to seven stone. "I used to look at the bones sticking out all over the place and wonder if it was really me," he recalled.

On 27th March 1943, the inhabitants of Changi Gaol were witness to the extraordinary sight of an Anglican Bishop arriving on the top of a lorry piled high with provisions. Upon his head he wore a top hat, and his pockets were stuffed with cash.

My father was always evasive when the name of John Leonard Wilson, Bishop of Singapore, later Bishop of Birmingham, arose, and I have only recently discovered why.

Although the Bishop was certainly a dedicated and deeply well-meaning man, Charles and many of his fellow prisoners felt that a lot of unnecessary trouble was caused by the cleric's extrovert personality, not least his determination to remain in control. Certainly this was the view of other camp inmates, in particular the camp quartermaster when the Bishop refused to distribute the items that were smuggled in for him around the camp in order to avoid their discovery.[11] Although no-one could have foreseen what would later occur, this refusal to conform with normal camp procedure was to lead to untold misery for everyone concerned.

A major upheaval, but one which did not directly affect civilian prisoners at the beginning, took place in May of that year. Although not the most suitable of locations available, the Japanese nevertheless chose Changi as the site for an airfield, and all Allied military prisoners quartered in the northern and eastern parts of the camp were transferred to Selarang Barracks to make way for Japanese engineers and air force personnel. For those who remained behind, daily existence continued its dull routine, at least for the following five months.

CHAPTER SIXTEEN

The Double Tenth

We lived in a world of half-verified information, smuggled news and above all, rumour. The stories that circulated around the camp added to our pervasive anxiety. Always you wanted to believe that the worst could not be possible.

Eric Lomax, *The Railway Man.*

ON 10th October 1943, a date which, following the post-war trial of the instigators, became known in infamy as the "Double Tenth," the internees of Changi Gaol, men and women, were summoned to parade in the prison's main yard. There was no reason to believe that this was anything other than a routine call, but they were soon to be enlightened otherwise.

The first name to be called out was that of Robert Heatlie Scott, Singapore's former director of information.[1] The Kempeitai had arrived to make a search of the cells and, over the following thirteen months, fifty-seven individuals in the camp, and the same number in Singapore town, were arrested and taken to the Kempeitai headquarters in the former YMCA Centre in Stamford Road. Most of those arrested were released after an interrogation of varying degrees of intensity, but some were not so fortunate.

What sparked off the inquisition was an incident which had taken place two weeks earlier. A combined British and Australian commando raiding party had slipped into Keppel Harbour and destroyed seven tankers causing the Japanese to conclude that not only was there a spy network in operation, but that the civilian prisoners must somehow have made radio contact with the outside world.

To a certain degree they were correct. A group of prisoners *had* assembled short-wave receivers, but not to make outgoing broadcasts. That was considered far too dangerous.[2]

However, a camp news committee did exist, made up of Robert Scott; William Stevenson, a Scottish electrical engineer; Lionel Earl; Hugh MacIntyre, an osteopath from New Zealand, and John Long, an accountant with Shell Petroleum, who was also the camp ambulance driver. Scott, owing to his propaganda association, became the prime suspect. Interviewed by Colonel Sumida Hozuro, head of the Kempeitai, he was told that he was 'a super spy,' and that his name was known to 'every schoolboy in Japan.'

All of this was news to Scott who remained defiant. His tormentors told him that he was unworthy of the honour of being called 'the man who had turned the people of East Asia against the Nipponese.' It did not help his case when he told them that they had only themselves to blame through their conduct in Formosa, in Korea, in Manchuria, in China, and now in Malaya. It was to be a long haul for Robert Scott. Following a chance encounter with him years later in Edinburgh, my father remarked that Scott was the first prisoner he had seen when he was taken by the Kempeitai to the YMCA for questioning, and he was the last person he saw when he left.

The orgy of accusations and search of belongings continued until a large sum of money was discovered in the quarters of the Bishop of Singapore.

For a full year after Singapore's surrender, the Bishop, through his calling as head of the Anglican community, was permitted to remain at liberty in his official residence at Bishopbourne. A charismatic man, with a big personality, Leonard Wilson easily struck up a friendship with Lieutenant Ogawa, the incoming Japanese Director of Religion and Education. Ogawa, an Anglican himself, had given permission for the Bishop to visit the various prison camps on the island unaccompanied.[3]

He was even provided with a letter of authorization, and it was this freedom that enabled him to establish an illicit system of communcation between the various camps using the Miyako Hospital (formerly the Tan Tok Seng General Hospital) as a conduit. It was simple enough.

As civilian patients were moved back and forth between the gaol and the hospital, information travelled with them. This enabled the Bishop to set up a fund-raising mechanism in order to send food and medical supplies into the camp. With the money the internees had brought into the gaol, a common fund was established by an elected camp committee. The Japanese sanctioned it on the understanding that loans would be repaid when hostilities ceased. This money enabled inmates to purchase through camp officials the items they required.

With so little prison food and essential medication available, camp funds soon began to run low, and an urgent message was sent via the hospital to the Bishop who forthwith set about borrowing from Anglicans in the town. For a full six months, this extra cash was brought into the camp under the very noses of the Japanese guards using a number of different methods. So long as the Bishop was at liberty, it remained a relatively simple operation.

However, everything changed in September 1942 when Lieutenant Ogawa was posted to Sumatra. Certain Japanese officials had not approved of Ogawa's friendship with the Bishop, and began to take a closer interest in the cleric's activities. When it became obvious to him that his days of freedom were numbered, he made the necessary arrangements to continue the ploy with his Indian secretary, K.T. Alexander.

On the receipt of a message sent through the hospital, Alexander was to go to a pre-arranged rendezvous and borrow money to hand over to Choy Khun Heng and his wife Elizabeth, a Chinese couple who ran the tuck shop attached to the Miyako Hospital. Khun Heng had previously worked in the Borneo Company's accounts department, and had innumerable contacts throughout Singapore town.

Through Ah Tek, a Chinese shopkeeper whose store in nearby Albert Street was one of the approved camp suppliers, the Choys began to filter provisions and money into Changi Gaol. The internees had the use of an ambulance driven by John Long, and three old trucks. One of the truck drivers accredited by the Japanese was my father.

The Bishop's belongings were not the first to be searched, but the money that he had refused to distribute was soon discovered among his effects. The Kempeitai, not unnaturally, wanted to know how it had got there.

Both the Bishop and Long were subjected to appalling treatment, and between them the story of the money's origins slowly emerged, but not before John Long, in a bid to mislead his torturers, had somehow managed to implicate Robert Scott and the other members of the camp news committee along with the Choys. The Kempeitai were clutching at straws and Scott, in fact, had nothing to do with the smuggling.[4] He did not even know the Choys.

Among those taken for questioning at this stage was Cuthbert Stanley, the doctor who had attended the birth of my sister Patricia in Penang General Hospital. Stanley had cleverly made himself an electric clock from various mechanical parts he had salvaged and was accused of having built a transmitter (the electric clock). Unable to stand the pain of being beaten up daily, he attempted suicide by hurling himself from a veranda, but instead broke his pelvis. The Kempeitai continued their torture regardless of his injury until it became pointless. His emaciated body was collected by my father who delivered it to the Kedang Kerbau Hospital in his van. Cuthbert was dead on arrival.[5]

K.T. Alexander and Ah Tek were also rounded up and subsequently died under interrogation. The Choys had bravely made an agreement with each other not to reveal anything and although they were abominably tortured in front of each other, kept their silence.

Little tends to be heard in the West of the gallantry of loyal Malays, Chinese, and Indians trapped in the invasion politics. Irrespective of race, it was the individual heroism of ordinary men and women such as K.T. Alexander, Ah Tek, and the Choys,* the ones that we know about, which serves as an example.

During the inquisition, several of the Asiatics under questioning had petrol poured on their bellies and ignited. Some had their hands tied together and immersed in a bowl of methylated spirit which was then lit. The Japanese were nothing if not thorough in their dealings with their Asian brothers and sisters.

According to his own account,[6] the Bishop was made to kneel on his haunches, his hands tied behind his back and pulled up to a position between his shoulder-blades. Eventually, after hideous pain, he confessed his involvement and where the money had come from.** Unfortunately, his figures did not add up. Ten thousand dollars were unaccounted for, having been used by Long, the ambulance driver, to buy much needed medical supplies.

As one of the four communications officers, it was only a matter of time before my father was arrested and interrogated. Normal practice was

---

* Mr and Mrs Choy survived their internment and torture and were later decorated for bravery by the British Government. In 1953, Elizabeth Choy attended the Coronation celebrations in London. Mr Choy continued to work as a bookkeeper and accountant for the Borneo Company until his death in 1983. At the Singapore Drama Festival in 1986 the theatre company TheatreWorks produced a play, *Not Afraid To Remember*, based on Elizabeth's war experiences.

** Leonard Wilson survived his ordeal. Post-war, he became Dean of Manchester, then Bishop of Birmingham.

nothing less than simple brutality, but it varied depending upon how important the Kempeitai considered their victim to be. Usually, it involved being put in a crowded cage with no bedding, and bright lights left on twenty-four hours a day. Inmates were made to sit straight on the bare floor with their knees up and forbidden to talk or move. If they did so, they were beaten by the sentries.

When the Kempeitai failed to extract the answers for which they were looking, some of their victims were suspended by their wrists on a wall and struck with rods and bamboo sticks. Others had their hands tied behind their backs and were forced to kneel with bars of wood or metal placed behind their knees. Their interrogators would then sit on their backs. In other instances, the prisoner was tied to a table and beaten until he lost consciousness. The punishment of Norman Coulson, a water engineer who *had* made contact with the Chinese underground, was so prolonged, that he was literally beaten to death.

In each cage there was only one pedestal water closet. The water which flushed into the pan was the only supply available and used for all purposes, including drinking. Two European women, Dr Cicely Williams and Dorothy Dixon, her successor as Womens' Block Commandant, and Mrs Freddy Bloom, an American, were detained under exactly the same conditions with the men, all of them accused of dispersing information. When it became clear that they knew little or nothing about radio transmissions, they were reluctantly released.

My father, who was accused of carrying information, counted himself among the more fortunate, being only kicked and punched before being confined to a heat box. This was one of the Kempeitai's favourite tortures where the victim was incarcerated without food or water in a corrugated tin hut exposed to the full glare of the sun, usually for several days.[7] The ultimate sacrifice was made by the ambulance driver John Long.

What proved doubly unfortunate for Long, was that during his trips into town he had innocently, or otherwise, made notes about the shipping anchored in Keppel Harbour.[8] When these were discovered among his belongings, the Kempeitai not unnaturally concluded that along with his having confessed to being a member of the camp news committee, this was the proof they had been looking for. John Long was accused of espionage and beheaded.

Yet even that did not put an end to it. The Kempeitai's obsession with radio sets and spy rings continued. As late as February 1944, Hugh Fraser, the much admired acting Colonial Secretary, was taken for interrogation and five months later died from his treatment. Unable to find conclusive evidence against the indomitable Robert Scott, the Kempeitai eventually sentenced him to six years hard labour. Since by that time he had been overcome with ill-health, he was mercifully confined to hospital instead.*

Of the many internees rounded up over this period, and there were over two hundred, twelve died of sickness directly attributable to the appalling conditions under which they were detained. Of the survivors who were returned to Changi Gaol from Stamford Road, some sooner rather than later required prolonged hospital treatment for extreme emaciation, chronic dysentery, neuritis, sores, ulcers, scabies, beriberi, weak hearts, and injuries to joints and limbs.

As for my father's well-being when he was released from his cage, it was something that he would simply never, ever discuss, not even with my mother. The only comment he occasionally made when the subject was raised was that better men than he had suffered far more than he had. He was grateful just to be alive.

Alive indeed, but in February 1944, his condition prompted him to stand down as shop representative for D Block.[9] A week or so after this, one of the D Block superintendents approached him to enquire if he was familiar with either Lewis Kennedy or Walter Pepys? A sock containing three packets had been hurled over the prison wall addressed to himself and the others, and when he opened his envelope, it contained a wad of dollar bills from Wee Kheng Chiang. This must have entailed an enormous risk for his Chinese friend who was a wanted man in Kuching, but had managed to go into hiding in Singapore. Although my father attempted to repay the loan after the war, Kheng Chiang categorically refused to be reimbursed. "You have paid enough," he told him.

In May 1944, yet another dramatic change took place in the Changi encampment. The Japanese had decided this time to turn the entire

---

* Post-war, Robert Scott served as Commissioner-General in South East Asia and Permanent Secretary at the Ministry of Defence. He was knighted and, in 1963, retired to live near Peebles in Scotland.

prison complex over to the military prisoners from Selarang, added to which were the remnants of the Thailand working parties. All civilian prisoners, male and female, were therefore evacuated to a camp in Sime Road. For the civilians it was a blessing as by now 12,000 prisoners were concentrated in the gaol area, 5,000 in the gaol buildings, and the remainder in atap huts, which they built for themselves in the courtyards using bamboo, barbed wire and palm fronds.

In comparison, the Sime Road Camp's location was a well planned area of hilly land, formerly a rubber estate, east of the racecourse, and south west of Bukit Timah. It had been occupied by Allied troops prior to the invasion, and a considerable amount of fighting had taken place in the vicinity. As a result, most of the original lines were burned, as were the many concrete paths between units, but although the concrete on which the huts stood was bomb damaged, the surviving lines had been roughly rebuilt with poor atap roofs. Such conditions were considered an immense improvement on the gaol,[10] especially when the prisoners were told that they would have to grow most of their own food. This, generally speaking, suited them down to the ground – literally.

Rising to the challenge, land was rapidly cleared, areas dug up for planting, and a beginning made on growing sweet potatoes, two kinds of spinach, papaya chiefly, mint, onions, tomatoes, and several kinds of beans.[11]

It proved a godsend, but was still not enough to feed the number of the starving. Latterly the daily cropping of 400 to 600 leaves from these vegetables became a major industry providing for the three areas – north, south, and central – into which the camp was divided for feeding, but food still had to be imported from Singapore town, where the prices were fantastic.

Food was not the only commodity that cost 'an arm and a leg.' A Swiss neutral agent in Singapore from time to time sent in cigarettes and tobacco, which were paid for out of the camp fund into which everybody was asked to contribute. To be able to afford his rations, Harry Hannay Snr was obliged to sell his gold watch and a gold cigarette case he had been given by a group of Chinese tin miners of Ipoh when he returned to Scotland in 1929.

At one stage, food supplies were so low that the committee approved the introduction of a snail farm, and only the collapse of Japan prevented this from becoming the camp's staple diet.

In October 1944, John Grant was given a job with the Medical Group Police, more of a night watchman than anything else. To Wendy he wrote: "I get a bit of extra food in consequence, and walk up and down between 8pm and midnight. The time passes quite quickly as I think of where and when and also how I can retire after this is all over. My present choice is near Fort Augustus where we can get a bus to Inverness. I have stood in a queue in the canteen for an hour without luck to buy a coconut costing 80 cents. Prices have gone mad. I am paid $9.50 a month. Sugar costs $6 a pound, and peanuts, $50."[12]

Early the following year, he was sent to join 200 men at Kranji on the north of Singapore island bringing back memories of a pre-war Sunday afternoon when he and Wendy had enjoyed a picnic by the sea. To get there, he was driven through the residential districts which did not look that much different from the way they had looked then, except that the front lawns were overgrown with vegetables. "For a Christmas present, the Nipps have given us 2oz per head of very ripe gorgonzola," he enthused. "Lord knows where it came from, but it is certainly very acceptable!"

Following this unexpected treat, he vowed that he would never again complain about plain food or the simple way of life. "On the subject of food, local salted sprats, which they are pleased to call whitebait, now cost $11 a pound, but are seldom obtainable," he noted. "They continue to give us rice and a little salted fish which, together with the vegetables which we mostly grow ourselves, keeps us going. Actually, I'm feeling much better here than at Changi."

On 1st July 1945, John wrote to Wendy: "I said *Rabbits* very loud this morning, and I hope that it brings a present in the form of freedom this half year. Our rations have been cut another 20 grammes, which doesn't help, but it is not going to get us down."

CHAPTER SEVENTEEN

Sydney and the Witches of Westminster

From a far off place called Singapore,
And a strange place named Kuching
There came three witches to Westminster
Tis of these queer ladies I sing.

Pat Martine, *The Witches of Westminster.* *

MY mother and the girls reached Sydney in the first week of March 1942, but the initial relief of arriving there unharmed was replaced by anxiety. There was not a word from my father. The best hope they had was that he was by now a prisoner of war.

He had told them to go to Sydney, and my mother decided that this was where they must stay because if there was any chance at all of his having escaped, it was here that he would come to look for them. Besides, they were not alone. There were all of the other women who had escaped from Sarawak, and many of them in the same predicament.

Among them was Daphne Large, whose husband had last been seen in Pontianak when he, Teddy Edwards, and Shot Spurway volunteered for a posting to the Dutch Border. When my mother finally succumbed to the sickness and vomiting which had added to her misery from the moment of their arrival in Batavia, it was Daphne who stepped in to take care of Virginia and Patricia.

My mother was admitted to the Prince Albert Hospital and when the specialists began searching for 'tropicals' in her system, they found, much to her disgust, 'hook-worm'.

Such parasites were virtually unknown in 1942, but the consensus of opinion was that it must have entered through the soles of her feet when she removed her shoes on the way to Sanggau. Within days of penetrating

---

* The poem is quoted in full at the close of this Chapter.

Having arrived safely in Sydney, Australia. Pat captioned this photograph 'the refugees.'

(Martine Family Collection)

the skin, the intruder had travelled up her bloodstream to make its home in her stomach where it caused a variety of side effects such as inflammation and nausea.

Although of little consolation, the specialists clucked over her and congratulated her on pioneering a treatment that would in future be used to cure countless Australian jungle fighters similarly afflicted. That certainly made her feel better. Lying helpless in a 100-bed hospital ward, she soon found herself going 'crackers' with too much time on her hands to think. Normally the most patient of beings, there was always a limit to my mother's tolerance.

Then, as if to add insult to injury, 'some sweet soul' stole the clothes she had bought for herself on reaching Sydney. They were, in fact, the only clothes that she now owned. It was for her the last straw so far as hospitals were concerned. She discharged herself, but not before her doctor had prescribed a drug for her to use at home and promised to treat her personally as an out-patient. In many ways, this was better for everyone since the hospital beds were by now filling up rapidly with casualties returning from the Pacific campaign.

So Pat left the Prince Albert Hospital 'minus her clothes and still with her worms,' as the nurse so wittily put it, but it was at this stage she realised that she had other, more pressing problems.

Top of the list was money. She still had some of the cash Charles had given her in Batavia, and funds from their Singapore bank account had been successfully transferred to both Sydney and London, but she knew perfectly well that they would not last long. What proved particularly alarming was that, following enquiries through an agent, the Borneo

Company back in London negated all responsibility for her situation. While the majority of Far East trading companies were going out of their way to help their beleaguered employees and their families, the Borneo Company appeared to be in a state of shock, stunned at the overnight disappearance of virtually all of its assets. To her utter dismay, Head Office told her it could do nothing to help, although she might be able to claim compensation when the war was over.[1]

The only course of action open to her was to suppress her pride and cable home in desperation to her mother and brother a request for help. Fortunately back in England, her brother Alec was well established in the oil business and had the necessary international connections to transfer funds through a sophisticated system of share dividends. With help from their sister Jess, he made Pat a loan which she vowed to repay.

Even so it was tight. A very long way from home, with two very young children to feed, and barely enough money to pay the bills, the situation was a challenge, especially for someone in ill-health who had never previously had to worry about making ends meet. To make it worse, Sydney was expensive. Everyone else appeared to have cars, furniture, wirelesses and new clothes. For the remainder of her life, thrift became Pat's byword. She would only ever spend money on essentials. She rarely spent money on herself unless she considered it absolutely necessary.

To avoid dwelling upon their plight, she kept herself occupied with practical things, teaching herself to knit, darn and sew. Exhausted at the end of the day, her bed became the best place in the world and sleep the greatest comfort.

At the start, all of the Sarawak group had booked into a cheap hotel while they sorted themselves out. Some moved on, some attempted to return home to England, but Pat, Daphne, the Elams, Gordon Myles and Richard Sagar were fortunate enough to be offered an available block of flats called 'Westminster' in Edgecliffe Road, Woollahra, in which to see out the war. Terrified of a Japanese invasion from the Pacific Ocean, all of the previous well-heeled occupants had moved inland leaving a caretaker in charge. They were thus available at a low rental.

Built during the 1930s, the Westminster block was modern, the rooms clean and well furnished, and east facing bow windows commanded superb views over the city towards the harbour. To the rear was a concrete area

Pat, Lisa Elam and Anne Haxworth with Gillian Haxworth, Virginia Martine,
Hillary Haxworth, Patricia Martine and Susan Elam

(Martine Family Collection)

for washing lines; to the front a small lawn which dropped down to the pavement. With a large park nearby, Edgecliffe Road was and remains one of Sydney's most popular residential areas.

In all there were twelve flats, on three floors, with Mrs Narr, the caretaker, and her daughter Laney, living at the back of the building. My mother and sisters had a double. In another were Edgar and Lisa Elam with their baby, Susan. Soon afterwards, Edgar Elam, no longer employed by the Sarawak Government, joined the Australian Air Force and was posted to Ballarat, then Hamilton, but his wife and daughter stayed on in Sydney where their son Bruce was born later.

Brenda Burnham, whose husband was still believed to be fighting somewhere in Malaya, rented a flat on her own. Another flat was shared by 'Uncle Gordon (Myles)', disabled from a childhood attack of polio, and 'Uncle' Sagar, who like Edgar Elam, also enlisted in the Australian Air Force.

Then there was 'Aunty' Peggy Sinclair* and her mother from Shanghai, and Anne Haxworth, whose husband was also interned in Changi Gaol. Anne, with her daughters Gillian and Hillary, had been evacuated from Singapore to Perth, but had come to Sydney where Anne's brother was living.

For the mothers it was a fortunate arrangement since Anne's eldest daughter Gillian was a year older than Virginia, and Hillary in between her and Patricia. The youngest of the group was Susan Elam.

Soon familiar faces began to re-appear, among them Winky, the Sarawak police constable last seen in Batavia. Having been sent on various missions, he had not been allowed to return to Borneo, which was thought too dangerous. Still employed by the Sarawak Government, he and another soldier had escaped the continuing Japanese invasion in a small boat. Living on ship's biscuits and sardines for eleven days, they had crossed from Tjilatjap in South Java to Geraldton, 300 miles north of Freemantle, in northern Australia.[2]

Winky had been instructed to deliver $2 million of Sarawak currency to Rajah Brooke, now in Melbourne, and it was the conclusion of a curious chain of events. When Pearl Harbor was attacked, Vyner was on holiday in Brisbane accompanied by Gerard MacBryan. He and MacBryan had

---

* Peggy Sinclair was a singer and actress and after the war played a nurse opposite Ron Randell in the film *Smithy*.

immediately flown to Bandoeng, in Java, where Major General H. Ter Poorten, Commander-in-Chief of the Dutch East Indies, had his head-quarters, close to those of General Wavell at Lembang. They arrived to discover that Kuching had fallen two days earlier.

Rajah was convinced that he could rally his Dyaks into a resistance movement and therefore despatched MacBryan to Pontianak to collect funds from the Sarawak state bank account. But when MacBryan arrived there on New Year's Eve, there followed a bizarre debacle in which he was arrested as a Japanese spy. He was returned to Batavia under military guard and immediately sent off to Singapore for examination by the British authorities.[3]

Quite what this was all about remains a mystery since there are no surviving records to provide any explanation. In Singapore, MacBryan was put under close arrest in Changi Gaol until he succeeded in contacting the lawyer Dato Sir Roland Braddell,* who rapidly persuaded the Governor to release him on the grounds that there was no evidence against him.

It can only be assumed that this extraordinary incident had something to do with MacBryan's unpopularity with members of the Sarawak Service. It may also have had something to do with his attempt to draw on the Sarawak state funds which had by then been transferred to the bank in Pontianak, presumably the same $2 million that Winky was later told to deliver to the Rajah in person.[4]

At this juncture Vyner Brooke seems to have gone into a deep depression, hardly surprising under the circumstances. Having returned to Australia he disbanded the Sarawak office of government-in-exile he had established and, from Melbourne, instructed that all Sarawak affairs would in future be handled by a Commission in London presided over by his brother Bertram.[5]

When Winky arrived in Melbourne, therefore, he discovered that he no longer had a job. Writing to his mother in Kent, he told her that Rajah had at least given him lunch. For somebody who had arrived in Sarawak as a young man so full of hope and ambition only three years earlier, it was not much of a pay-off.

---

* Dato (in Malaya, Dato, also Datuk, was a chivalrous title conferred by the federal government) Sir Roland St John Braddell, born 1880, was Singapore's foremost barrister, founder president in 1930 of the Singapore Rotary Club. He also became a member of the Singapore Legislative Council.

Winky was now determined to get back into the fray. Taking the train to Sydney, he booked into Ushers Hotel where he found the Australians extraordinarily hospitable, but the prices terrific.

"Sydney is a wizard place," he told his mother. "Grand beaches, a lovely harbour and nice shops and offices. The spirit and morale is good here, but there is still too much complacency and not enough effort."

Winky, along with all of the other Europeans from Sarawak, had lost everything he owned – cars, furniture, wireless, bank accounts, clothes. Among the missing possessions he regretted most were his cigarette case and signet-ring, his photos, the prayer-book his parents had given him in 1919, letters from his mother and sisters, his sword, uniform, some Burma silver, Bali heads, and a lot of stuff he had been intending to take home to England as presents. All the same, he remained convinced that the Allies would ultimately win the war. "Lack of support from the air made it hopeless," he said. "We have been blooded and we now know their mettle. None of us are afraid."

If Winky was afraid, he would be the last one to admit it. With the Sarawak Constabulary disbanded, he applied to join the Australian Cavalry Division. Instead he was recruited into the Royal Australian Naval Volunteer Reserve. Although not exactly what he had had in mind, he accepted the posting with enthusiasm. "With arms and planes we can beat them," he wrote enthusiastically to his mother.

Adversity brings people from all kinds of background together, and before long the occupants of the Westminster block of flats had become a small community, sharing the work of looking after each other's children, and helping one another with shopping and housework. It was a far call from the luxurious colonial lifestyle of Singapore and Penang or the debatable leisure of Kuching, but Pat and the girls soon got used to it. In all of the apartments the occupants did their own cleaning, and my mother was delighted to discover that she had inherited her own mother's skill in the kitchen without ever having had a cookery lesson.

Between my mother and Lisa and Anne, a strong bond was struck, and they comforted each other through the long and testing months, providing support whenever one or other of them needed cheering up. On the wall of her kitchen Pat pinned a large map of the Pacific Ocean and daily listened to the wireless, following the movements of Allied and Japanese troops. Whenever an Allied victory was announced, she marked the location with a red dot.

On some days there was good news; on others, bad. Jokingly the three women started to call themselves the 'Witches of Westminster,' each determined to put the world to rights. Yet the more optimistic they became, the more they realised that the war was not going to end in a matter of weeks or even months. Although nobody doubted that the Allies would ultimately triumph, there was no certainty about anything. The Japanese forces were not that far away and very definitely had their sights set on Australia.

This was highlighted by an incident which took place only six weeks after the family's arrival at Edgecliffe Road. On 21st May 1942, Virginia was gazing out of the windows towards the bay when, all of a sudden, there were explosions, and Australian fighter planes soared through the sky. She called to the others excitedly, and they came and watched as, in the distance, the Australian air force strafed and sank two Japanese two-man submarines which had furtively penetrated into Sydney Harbour.

Although neither my mother nor Jean Hembry knew the whereabouts of the other at the time, Jean had also reached Sydney. That same day she and little John had departed for England on the troopship *Strathallan*, which mostly carried widows from Hong Kong. As the boom protecting Sydney Harbour was raised to allow the *Strathallan* to sail out into the Pacific, the Japanese submarines had slipped in.

The year 1942 crawled past bringing little of cheer, but with the arrival of the funds sent by her brother and sister, Pat managed to work out a budget to keep them going. Australian fruit was cheap and plentiful. Virginia was putting on weight, and Patricia had begun to drink milk again, having rejected it ever since her jungle experience.

My mother resigned herself to patience, there being no other option. She worried constantly about my father and every night before she closed her eyes to try and sleep, she prayed for his release. She knew that he was physically strong, but just could not imagine the psychological and emotional strain of being cooped up in a jail.

Then reassurance of a sort came with the news that Kenneth Simpson, also over forty, had been repatriated from Bangkok on medical grounds. Kenneth wrote to her from a hospital bed in London to say that he had been told that all people in uniform were being treated as military prisoners (i.e. volunteers and suchlike as well as the forces) and the rest as civilian internees. "Of the military, those under forty apparently have to work but for those over forty this is optional. Whether or not this applies to the civilians I do not know, but imagine it would not be the case. For a time at any rate. Internees concerned with Oriental services are going about their normal business. The treatment of people is said to vary according to the Commandant of the locality: the only first hand information I have is that people in Taiping are being well treated."

At Lourenço Marques*, in neutral Portuguese East Africa, Kenneth had seen thousands of tons of food stuffs being loaded onto the Japanese steamers which had taken him there to be handed over. He was told that these were destined for Singapore and Hong Kong, but if this was the case, they certainly never arrived.

Perhaps it was as well for my mother and Anne Haxworth not to know the conditions their husbands were having to endure. Nobody outside of the occupied territories did. The Japanese newspapers showed set-up photographs of happy, smiling captives. Even in Tokyo, the Japanese public was unaware of the cruelty being inflicted on their behalf and in their name.

The American author Agnes Newton Keith and her husband, a forestry expert in Sandakan, North Borneo, were both incarcerated in the Batu Lintang Camp in Kuching. As famous in Japan as elsewhere for her book *Land Below the Wind,* she was ordered to put on her best dress and to pose with an easel and drawing-board beside the camp pig pond with a group of children. The photographs appeared in *Domei News* under the heading 'Artist at Play – following chosen profession, encouraged by Japanese protectors in Kuching Internment Camp.' Similarly a group of Australian officers were taken to the commandant's pool and photographed wearing Japanese-supplied bathing suits. They were given empty coffee cups and told to smile and wave before being returned to the camp without even being allowed a dip in the pool. Nobody in the outside world had any idea of the degradation to which Allied prisoners of war were being subjected.

So for the time being, safe in Australia, life for the Witches of Westminster settled down to a daily routine which centred almost

---

*   Now Maputo in Mozambique.

exclusively on their children. Pat's mother, wondering if she would ever see her daughter again, wrote from England to ask for a photograph, so my mother decided to splash out and have her portrait taken which she could also send to my father. The pictures turned out well, making her look wonderfully glamorous, Hollywood-style, and she was amazed at how little the photographer charged her for them. On passing the shop window a fortnight later she discovered why. He was selling enlarged prints of her as pin-up pictures to the Australian troops. She did not know whether to be outraged or flattered. Pat never did fully appreciate just how good-looking she was.

In one of the letters that did eventually get through to her husband – only one page was allowed by the censors – she comments on how grown-up Virginia was becoming. "It is school holiday time and she makes the beds every second day and helps out with the washing up. Sometimes she plays amah and puts Patricia to bed as her baby."

Virginia was also losing her top teeth, and becoming rather too bright, in her mother's estimation. Richard (Sagar) having joined the air force, Gordon (Myles) had taken to having his weekend meals with them, and one Saturday Virginia was made to help with the washing-up. Gordon had handed a rather dirty plate back to her with the remark that if she wanted to do a job, she should do it properly. The seven-year-old replied that she had not wanted to do it in the first place!

Pat was also concerned about Ah Cheow, last heard of in Singapore. "I often wonder if he got back to Ah Soh," she told Charles in her letter. "She must be so lost without him."

Aside from surviving, and feeling relatively secure in Sydney, my mother was only too aware that what was taking place throughout that summer and autumn of 1942 was not cheerful. At Bataan in the Philippines, General MacArthur's American and Filipino troops withdrew to avoid encirclement. Although they put up a tremendous stand against Japanese forces five times their strength for three months, they were finally overrun.

However, it was not all doom and gloom. In the Coral Sea, the Japanese advance southward was abruptly halted by the American Air Force. On Midway Island in the Pacific Ocean, the Japanese fleet sent to demolish the US base was soundly thrashed, proving a turning point in the Pacific war. There followed a successful American attack on Japanese held Guadalcanal in the British Solomon Islands.

Virginia, Pat and Patricia. Three photographs that did eventually reach
Charles in Changi Gaol. Each has an official Japanese stamp on the back

(Martine Family Collection)

Writing to her mother again, Pat remained stoical. "I still wake
sometimes in the night believing it is all a dream and quite impossible. I
wish sometimes that I had got Charles out of the East before it all began,
and yet after what has happened I don't feel that there is much use in
trying to arrange one's life. When I think of all our savings and treasures
'gone with the wind', living for the day seems the only way."

In March 1943, there arrived a more personal glimmer of hope. My
mother was notified by the Colonial Office that a Japanese controlled
radio broadcast from Singapore had been picked up. A Japanese
announcer had relayed the following message: 'T.C. Martine, a civilian
internee somewhere in Malaya, is very thrilled receiving photographs. Am
well and longing for our reunion.'

My father was alive. Towards the end of the same month, Pat was told
that Lieutenant John Wink, stationed at *HMAS Moreton*, the Australian
Royal Navy base in Brisbane, was missing, presumed killed in action.

Two months earlier, Winky and F.A. 'Sailor' Moore, another former
Sarawak Government officer, had set off on a secret reconnaissance mission
in an Australian submarine. They had landed near Miri, but were not heard
from again. The obvious conclusions had therefore to be drawn.[6]

Scraping together the little money she could spare, her mother decided
to enrol Virginia at Annesley School, Bowral, where Anne Haxworth was
sending Gillian. Virginia loved it; Gillian liked it less. The school had its

own cows and sheds, and some of the day-girls came to classes on horse-back, others in a pony and trap.

Annesley School worked well for a couple of years, but then Gillian decided to run away and, having made her way to the railway station, was halfway to Sydney before she was caught. Virginia thought she was terribly brave, but the outcome was that both girls were removed to Askan School at Woollahra, much nearer home and, to Pat's relief, much less expensive.

To her own mother, Peggy Macquisten, in England, she wrote once again to emphasise that she had made up her mind to stay on in Australia indefinitely because when Charles was released, he would know where to find them. Australia would also provide a far better place for him to recover than the UK, where things were bound to be very difficult until the country was back on its feet again. Also, the children were settled. Much to her amusement, they were even learning the language, using expressions such as 'Sticky Beak' and 'Tall Poppies.'

As long as the money held out, Pat felt that she could adequately provide a home for all of them in the shape of a very easily run flat which boasted not only a refrigerator, but constant hot water.

Then, at last there came a dramatic improvement in the international situation. It began on 6th June 1944, when Allied forces under General Eisenhower landed in France. In early 1945, the Germans came under attack on two fronts; the Russians entered Berlin, Adolf Hitler and Joseph Goebbels, his Minister of Propaganda, committed suicide. On 7th May, Germany unconditionally surrendered.

About the same time, Admiral Lord Louis Mountbatten was appointed Commander-in-Chief for South East Asia. With the collapse of its Western partners, Japan soon became increasingly beleaguered. The dots on my mother's map of the Pacific Ocean began to look as if the war might at last, just possibly, be moving towards an end.

*　　*　　*

THE WITCHES OF WESTMINSTER

Pat Martine

(this poem became something of a cri de cœur in the Haxworth, Elam and Martine families)

From a Far-off place called Singapore
And a strange place named Kuching
There came three witches to Westminster
'Tis of these queer ladies I sing.

The First one changed to a Koala Bear
The Second to a Kangaroo
The Third a Kookaburra became
So their fate may end in a zoo.

Now the Witch who changed to a Koala Bear (1)
Was, by nature, fairly serene –
But her husband kept on coming and going,
    you see
'Till the lady got so she could scream.

As last she said, with a sorrowful air,
"A witch no more I can be –
This worry and planning is just TOO much
I truly am 'up a gum tree'.

That being so I may as well change
A Koala Bear then I'll become
And with Susa I'll climb to the top of my tree
And patiently wait, chewing gum!"

The second Witch thought as a Kangaroo (2)
She could easier make the change
From here; to Bowrel, or 'down on the Farm'
As jumping would then be her range.

The cost of her travelling would thus be nil –
Her 'young' in her pocket would then go,
Her FEET as a Kanga – would do quite well,
And her tail the luggage could tow!

The third Witch, a one-time silent wench (3)
A-gossiping one she became –
And having no longer control of her tongue
Decided to cover her shame –

'The gift of silence no longer mine,
I will change too,' said she.
'Kookaburras talk, blether, and laugh all day
    long.
I think, to be one would suit me.'

A Koko she thus became one day,
And wherever she now appears
Among those who know her very well,
Their work will be Days in Arrears.

But withal; these witches, mad as they were –
NO problem could 'floor' them for long,
For one of the Witches was sure to solve
Where t'other, or all three, had gone wrong.

. . . to be continued (perhaps!)

(1) Lisa. (2) Pat. (3) Anne.

CHAPTER EIGHTEEN

V J Day

If this account, being published, comes to the hand of any Japanese, let him read with understanding, pay his debt to humanity with sorrow, and determine never to let such things happen again. Then we shall indeed be friends.

Ken Attiwill, *The Rising Sunset.*

SOUTH East Asia was in chaos, but such was the psyche of an entire nation that Japan's war could have gone on indefinitely. Something overwhelming had to be done to stop it.

In Changi Gaol, the common riposte of the guards was 'Japanese are superior people. War cannot finish until British completely beaten. War finish one hundred years.' When the war did finish, exactly three and a half years to the day that Singapore fell, it took most of the Japanese troops and almost all of the prisoners, in Singapore, Malaya, Borneo, the Dutch East Indies and Thailand, by surprise.

The collapse of Germany in May 1945 had left Japan isolated, but the Emperor's military refused to admit to it. At an Imperial Conference held on the 8th June, the Nipponese Army and Navy leaders pledged their determination to carry on with their war regardless, but soon after there followed an unprecedented intervention from Emperor Hirohito himself, demanding that Japan's Supreme War Council find a way to conclude the hostilities. His action was not popular, and there were widespread expectations of a military coup, on top of which the Potsdam Declaration in mid-July, and the Allies' demand for an unconditional surrender, played directly into the militarists' hands.

Surrender meant slavery. It meant the obliteration of the Japanese race. Japan must fight on to the bitter end.

On 6th August, the first bomb dropped on Hiroshima, and wiped out the entire centre of the city. Under pressure from the militarists, this momentous catastrophe was completely ignored by the Japanese media. It was, the Emperor's generals agreed among themselves, something they could sustain.

Next, the Russian Army crossed the border into Manchuria. Three days later the second atom bomb fell on Nagasaki.

Still, the Japanese military commanders stood their ground, but this time the Emperor had had enough. When a meeting of the Imperial War Council reached stalemate, with three votes for the war continuing and three votes against, the Emperor ruled in favour of the Potsdam Declaration. Six days later Japan formally surrendered to the Allies at ceremonies in Hanoi, Ahotu (Taipei), and Seoul.

At the Sime Road Camp, my father noticed that one of the guards was uncharacteristically weeping. That worried him, as it could have meant almost anything. Soon after, one of the radio operators picked up a confused report about surrender negotiations taking place. The word spread rapidly through the camp, but almost at once gave way to concern that things could quickly turn nasty. There were reports that the Japanese were strengthening their defensive positions, and nobody knew for certain what they would do next.

In fact, in Sandakan, Brunei and North Borneo, prisoners in groups of fifty were marched out to dig their own graves, then shot and pushed into them.

Although the actual Japanese surrender was agreed on 15th August 1945, it was not officially confirmed to the prisoners of war in Singapore until two days later. Soon all of the working parties had returned from their various projects, and by the end of the month over 17,000 men were concentrated around the Changi encampment.

An apposite observation is to be found in the papers of Rowland Oakley of the Chinese Secretariat, Malayan Civil Service.[1] 'They wear no shirts, their bodies are almost as brown as the Malays. A few have hats. Most of them worked in the sun without.

'We have become so slowly accustomed to the decline and fall of Malayan society that we think this strange sight nothing very unusual, but could Sir John Bagnall or Mr Bisseker be here they would have difficulty in recognising their former business friends in this collection of tramp-like – no that is an insult to a tramp – coolies.'

On 28th came the first Allied leaflet drop, ordering Japanese soldiers to lay down their arms. On 30th, some stores, accompanied by medical officers, were parachuted in, and five days later troops of the 5th Indian Division appeared.

The end of captivity, when it arrived, came quickly, and without bloodshed. At the Sime Road Camp, a young Eurasian boy delivered the news riding his bicycle twice around the high barbed wire fence that encircled the camp, singing a song to the effect that the Japanese had surrendered. At 12 noon, Tokyo time, the Union Jack was hoisted on a flag staff next to the main gate. Less than half an hour's notice was given, so only a small proportion of the internees turned up.[2]

However, the ceremony, attended by Lady Thomas*, was nonetheless poignant with the camp band accompanying the singing of one verse only of *God Save the King, Land of Hope and Glory*, and *There will always be an England*. Harry Hannay and Charles, both looking thin, stood near the flagstaff and could see and hear everything. There were no speeches, just a word or two to direct the proceedings. There was just a little wind at the right moment to blow the flag well clear, just after it was hoisted.

When the gates of the Sime Road Camp were eventually thrown open, one of the first visitors to arrive was Wee Kheng Chiang, my father's Chinese banker friend, who brought with him paper bags containing hard-boiled eggs. Having rounded up his two other friends, Lewis Kennedy and Walter Pepys, Kheng Chiang took them to a flat down beyond the docks at Tanjong Pagar, where the three of them were given the first civilised meal they had had in four years.

For Charles, gaunt and recovering from his latest bout of jaundice, there was little that he wanted to celebrate other than his personal freedom. His thoughts were on those who had not made it, and he was disgusted by a decision taken by the Churches that no suicides were to be buried in consecrated ground. Accordingly, he had volunteered to help inter those who had not been able to stand it any more.

Nor was it of any redeeming consolation to be later told by certain worthy individuals that as internment camps went, Changi was not so bad. In justification of this, it has been pointed out that of the 87,000 POWs who passed through Singapore, only 850 actually died there. No

---

*   Sir Shenton Thomas, Governor of the Straits Settlements, was transferred from Changi Prison to Japan in August 1942, and moved around various camps thereafter, finally being placed at Hsian in Manchuria where he remained until the surrender. Lady Thomas remained at Changi and, following the Japanese surrender, made a moving radio broadcast to the people of Singapore.

doubt the statistics are accurate enough, but what should not be overlooked is the significant numbers who were held there, even for a short period, and then went on to die in camps elsewhere. Many of them had been my father's close personal friends.

The loss of his kindly, gentle aunt, Kate Hannay, and his cousin, Harry Hannay Jnr, dying alone of dysentery at the age of 27 in some God-forsaken, mosquito infested swamp called Tasao affected my father the most. As the head count of his Borneo company colleagues lost in Singapore and Malaya began to grow, he had yet to discover the roll-call of dead in Sarawak.

What incensed him almost more than anything else was the sheer waste and futility of it all. He felt only pity for the individual Japanese soldiers who were being picked up around him and formed into work gangs. Now it was their turn to be humiliated. Many of them, the most senior, would be called to account for war crimes, but he saw no satisfaction in vengeance. The death sentences imposed and carried out following the trial of Colonel Sumida Hozuro and the key Kempeitai involved in the Double Tenth investigation[3] brought little consolation. Nor did the suicides of General Tojo and Prince Konoye, or the execution of General Yamashita.

News of the Japanese surrender reached John Grant at the Karanjio camp a few days earlier than the inmates of Sime Road. "We don't know as yet what is going to happen," he wrote triumphantly to Wendy. "In fact, the Nipps are not supposed to know that we know." [4]

For John, liberation came just in time. "I'm down to 8 stone," he recorded. "The daily ration has been 9oz of rice and maize, ½ oz of fish, 3ozs green spinach, a spoonful of oil, and half a spoonful of sugar. Fortunately I built up a small reserve by selling things. It is awful how food has become our one interest in life. I hope to goodness I haven't become eccentric."

At the Nakom Patom Camp, 32 kilometres from Bangkok, Ted Hannay and his companions heard the news from a Korean inmate, known as 'Jungle Jim'.[5] They had not known whether or not to believe him, but the following day, Lt-Colonel Coates, the camp's Senior Medical Officer, gave the order that everyone was to have 'nasi goring' (fried rice) and a fried egg for supper. It was obvious that something big was about to happen as eggs, bought locally, cost 3d each, and there were 4,000 men in the camp.

At 6.30pm, just after supper, they were informed that Colonel Coates was going to speak from the stage. Everybody who was able to made their way to that part of the camp did so, and they were told that Colonel Yamagita, the camp commander, had informed the Colonel that an armistice had been signed.

As if by a conjuring trick, British, American and Dutch flags suddenly appeared from their hiding-places, and everybody joined in singing the three National Anthems – *God Save The King, The Stars and Stripes,* and *Het Whilemus.* It was a wonderful, unforgettable sound, recalled Ted, although he and many of the other men were so overcome with emotion that the words they sang were pretty unintelligible. The mood was one of sombre thanksgiving rather than 'hectic whoopee.'

Just how fortunate they were became apparent a few days later when some paratroopers informed him that the 28th of August had been designated D-Day in Siam. The Japanese had anticipated a rebellion of Siamese, coupled with Allied landings from sea-borne craft, and orders had been issued that should such an uprising occur, all prisoners of war were to be shot.

In Sydney, my mother at last received word from my father. He told her that he would be coming to Sydney as soon as possible, but there were difficulties. Everyone wanted to get home or to go somewhere, and the red tape was chaotic. As it turned out, nobody was going anywhere for at least six weeks.

My father's first action on leaving Wee Kheng Chiang's flat had been to go straight to Belvedere, where he found a large Mercedes car with the ignition on, purring on the doorstep. On approaching, he encountered three senior Japanese officers in uniform who looked equally startled to see him.

"The war is over. This is my house," he snapped at them and, pushing past, went inside, half expecting them to follow. Instead, he heard the car engine roar into life as the Mercedes sped off.

Afterwards he wished he had thought to remove the keys, but under the circumstance it was perhaps just as well that he had not.

John Grant similarly returned to his house in Orange Grove Road only to find that its contents had been stripped from top to bottom. The only item left in place was the set of stag's antlers, a Royal, which hung over the fireplace.[6]

Informed that Long Chaney, the Boy, was already out looking for him, he decided to call in on Loke Choon Sing, a Chinese friend who was a paint contractor, where he was fêted with beer and Scotch. John rapidly concluded that a lot of the Chinese must have cunningly turned their money into goods as all of a sudden, as if from nowhere, it seemed, Choon Sing produced bars of Lux soap, towels and toothpaste. It was almost as if he was running a general store.

Back at the house in Orange Grove Road, John found Long Chaney had returned in tears. On hearing that the tuan was back, he had rushed out to buy a pineapple and some fruit. In the following days, despite his protests, John was showered with welcome home presents – shirts, tinned food, butter and cheese.

"Having been on the verge of starvation a few weeks ago, it is all rather farcical," he wrote to Wendy.

Unable to get a passage to Australia, Charles spent the following six weeks involved in mopping-up operations, rallying local Borneo Company staff, opening up the workshops and recovering plant, spare parts, and stores. One extraordinary incident involved a telegram from Kuantan from Nona Baker, the sister of Vincent Baker, tuan besar of Pahang Consolidated in Sungei Lembing, to inform him that she was alive, and asking for his help.

Knowing nothing of her circumstances, he alerted the military to her existence and later learned that she and Vincent had spent the entire war period living deep in the jungle, latterly with a group of Chinese Communist guerillas, who had looked after them with great kindness. Vincent Baker had died of a combination of malnutrition and dysentery. Nona, to whom the Chinese had given the native name of Pai Naa, 'White Nona,' had survived, although she had been reduced to wearing nothing much more than a loin-cloth. When she was located by Colonel Frederick Spencer Chapman's Force 136 soldiers, clothes had to be sent from the Kuala Lumpur convent to enable her return to civilisation.[7]

Some months later, my parents heard that their old friends Mac and Dorothy McLellan had returned to Alden in Penang where they were amazed to find all of their belongings intact. As soon as they had left, their Malay houseboy had removed all of their valuables, including the family silver, and buried everything in the garden before himself going into hiding. When the Japanese eventually departed, he dug up the silver, and put everything back where it belonged. Naturally, he was given his old job back.

One of the greatest conundrums surrounding the fall of the British Empire in its totality is that, wherever it collapsed, those who sought to bring about its demise immediately set about copying everything they had set out to destroy. In South East Asia, a management takeover took place with basic re-branding.

Overnight, the British Raj became the Japanese Raj, with its own currency, known as *duit pesang* or 'Banana Dollars,' because of their banana tree motif. Singapore was renamed Syonanto (Syo is the current Japanese dynasty), and the Pacific and Indian oceans were lumped together as the 'Sea of Greater East Asia.' In Singapore town, the statue of Sir Stamford Raffles was removed, and one of the conquering General Yamashita erected in its place. The Tanglin Club became a Japanese Officer's Mess, and Singapore's two main department stores, Robinsons and John Little, were turned over exclusively to Japanese customers. Books in English were destroyed, and just to make sure that there was no doubt as to who was in charge, clocks were put forward in line with Tokyo Time.

At the beginning of October, on a trip to the Bank of New South Wales in Sydney, Pat ran into John Noakes, Sarawak's former Secretary of Defence, who had been released from the Batu Lintang Camp in Kuching. As a New Zealander, Noakes had been flown out earlier than the other Sarawak prisoners of war, and had already been in Australia for a full week. "He looks very well and fit, although rather yellow," she commented in a letter to my father who was still waiting for a passage from Singapore. "The only thing was his eyes. They had the look of a man who had seen too much suffering and they were sad with a faraway look. But that is a look we have all got used to in the men who have 'had it' in this war."

At this stage she knew nothing of my father's condition, and the card he sent her on 26th August said simply: "All over dearest. I am down to nine stone, but surprisingly well and consider myself fortunate. I hope the daughters have not forgotten me. Please airmail the old man and tell him I am only permitted to send one card. Bless you for bearing up so well. All my love, Charles."

The weeks passed and finally word came that a series of Red Cross ships had been allocated to take passengers from Singapore to Sydney. Receiving notification of this, but no other details, Pat and Anne Haxworth scoured the daily passenger lists published in the pages of the Sydney newspapers.

Pat and Charles re-united in Australia
(Martine Family Collection)

Then at last, the names appeared in black and white. Charles Martine and John Haxworth were on their way on a ship called *The Highland Chieftain.*

In Sydney Harbour, on a steaming hot October morning, the two women waited anxiously for their husbands to arrive. They had set off from Edgecliffe Road almost at dawn, with Virginia left in charge of Patricia, and Gillian in charge of Hillary. Both women expected the worst: long white beards and grey hair with no teeth at all, and perhaps that rather blinded them at first to the real appearance of their husbands.

John Haxworth had undergone an operation for a mastoid, and had had his appendix removed, both without anaesthetic. This alone had almost killed him. Internees' wives were advised by the authorities that children should be kept out of sight for a week or two until their fathers became acclimatised. Anne had therefore arranged for Gillian and Hillary to stay with friends at Rose Bay, but after a couple of days John asked to see them.

"We came out of the drive of Askan School and saw this emaciated figure at the bottom of the hill," said Gillian. "I shouted to Hillary that Daddy was here, and I rushed forward to hug him. He was so frail he almost fell over."[*]

My own father was, in fact, just over 8 stone in weight when he stepped ashore. At one stage, after his ordeal in the cage, he had been below 7, but had managed to fatten himself up considerably in the six weeks following his release. So what he must have looked like when he came out of Changi is best not imagined. The child Virginia, by then, weighed 7 stone 6½ lbs.

What my mother soon realised, not having seen him for almost four years, and hardly having heard from him at all over that period, was that he was 'very buttoned-up, and in on himself.' For Virginia, the homecoming was equally tense. In the hallway of the flat in Edgecliffe Road she was introduced to a tall figure wearing dark glasses. "This is your father," she was told by her mother. Virginia felt very shy.

To get to know each other once again, and importantly, to recuperate and generally to heal the wounds, the family set off on a fortnight's

---

[*] John and Anne Haxworth returned to Singapore where John was appointed Controller of Immigration. In 1953, he retired and the family returned to England.

MV Dominion Monarch
(Martine Family Collection)

holiday to Cronulla, a beach resort south of Sydney, where, slowly, Charles began to look better and less haunted. Four months later, having tidied up all the necessary documentation surrounding the girls schooling and the Edgecliffe Road apartment, the four of them set off for Britain on the *MV Dominion Monarch*,* a repatriation troopship which carried much needed food supplies from New Zealand.

Also on board were Caroline and Michael Hopkins, and David and Derek Robinson, four very brave small children who together with their parents had survived the horrors of Kuching's Batu Lintang internment camp. During those desperate days, Moireen Robinson had passed the time by telling her boys stories of England: of horses and buses, of railway stations and zoos. Following Kuching's liberation, the Australian troops had thrown a tea-party for all of the children, held on board a corvette warship. From this there were joy-rides in a speedboat up and down the

---

* The 26,500 ton *MV Dominion Monarch*, owned by the Shaw Savill Line, was designed as a First Class only passenger liner serving South Africa, New Zealand and Australia. The ship had only just begun her career when the Second World War broke out and she was taken for troopship duties. She was broken up in 1961.

Sarawak River. Suddenly Derek Robinson had turned to his mother and said, "Mummy, is this England?"[8]

Accompanied by 5,000 soldiers picked up in Bombay, the *Dominion Monarch*'s passengers reached the end of that voyage. Even the tiny brass band assembled on the quay to serenade their arrival and the grey drizzle of a Portsmouth morning were of little consequence compared to the sense of relief that enveloped them all.

CHAPTER NINETEEN

Return to Bukit Mata

So strong was the link between the State of Sarawak and the Borneo Company in the early days that Sarawak and the Borneo Company were almost synonymous terms.

Charles Vyner Brooke, 3rd Rajah of Sarawak.

IT was a Borneo Company employee who saved Kuching from becoming a blood-bath. Prior to the invasion, Lau Chai Lim was the Nestle account salesman in the company's Kuching offices. During the occupation period, he went into hiding with his family, and on hearing on the radio that Allied forces were approaching, he appraised the situation. A contingent of Japanese soldiers was still in the town, so Lau and his son Lau Kok Wah crossed the river. Having smuggled themselves into Fort Margherita with comparative ease, they ran up both the Union Jack and the old flag of Sarawak.

On seeing this, the startled Japanese in the town assumed that they were surrounded, and took off into the jungle. When the Australian 9th Division arrived, Kuching was liberated without a shot being fired.[1]

Without their knowing it, the European and Eurasian prisoners of war in Kuching's Batu Lintang Camp, men, women and children, had been reprieved; as part of their retreat plan, Japanese command had issued instructions to Colonel Tatsuji Suga, the camp commandant, that the fittest prisoners were to be employed as a fatigue party and liquidated on arrival at their destination. Those left behind in the camp, the older men and the children, were to be shot. The women were to be locked in their huts which were then to be set on fire. To his eternal credit, Colonel Suga had ignored the order.*

On the site of the Borneo Company bungalow at Pasir Nai, the Baleh Dyaks made their own statement by attacking and taking the heads of a large party of fleeing Japanese soldiers caught loading their stores into

---

* Suga suffered his personal measure of tragedy. His entire family in Japan were wiped out by the Hiroshima bomb. Following his capture, he committed suicide.

Lau Chai Lim, hero of the liberation of Kuching. He is wearing the Order of the Star of Sarawak
(Martine Family Collection)

prahus. There followed carnage at Kapit and lesser incidents at a string of other Japanese holdings, but the influence of Temenggong Koh and his deputy Penghulu Jugah ensured that the violence was kept in check. In later years Koh would always insist that it was the Ibans who freed Sarawak from Japanese occupation.

With the Rajah's government devastated, the countryside of Sarawak was in chaos. Only two months earlier, Cyril Le Gros Clark, Sarawak's chief secretary, and Donald MacDonald, Manager of the Sarawak Rubber Estates, had been taken to Jesselton in North Borneo and murdered in some lonely woods beside Keningau airport.[2] Aware that their reign of terror was coming to an end, the Japanese authorities had not wanted anyone of influence to survive who might later give evidence against them.

Three and a half years of Japanese occupation had destroyed the economies of Sarawak, the Straits Settlements, and the Federated States, and taken a heavy toll of the civilian population, in some cases sinking below subsistence level. One of the most remarkable feats of post-war regeneration in South East Asia was the efficiency with which pre-war British enterprises reinstated themselves.

In mainland Malaya and Singapore, rehabilitation was spurred on by effective military support but, as my father was quick to observe, the British Raj was bursting with important-sounding functionaries – governors, high commissioners, and special envoys – many of whom appeared not to know what they were there for.

In all probability, their presence was intended simply to be of reassurance to the indigenous population, but it was too late. In the aftermath of what many Malays saw as Britain's greatest betrayal – its abandonment of South East Asia under the Japanese onslaught – communism proliferated throughout the peninsula. My father's view, shared by others, was that a different attitude towards the Chinese guerilla units which had so effectively harried the Japanese throughout the war might well have averted such troubles. Or maybe not. The Government's pre-invasion reluctance to allow Asiatics to take up arms to defend themselves had already done the damage.[3]

Meantime, those commercial concerns which had survived four years without trading wasted little time in starting up again. Operating from a large Edwardian country house in Surrey, Sir John Hay, the 'Rubber

Baron' of Guthrie & Company, was appointed Chairman of the Joint Committee on Eastern Affairs, a conglomerate which included the Eastern Exchange Banks Association, the Rubber Trade Association of London, the British Association of Straits Merchants, the Malayan Chamber of Mines, and the Tin Producers Association.

Sir John Bagnall, now almost sixty, returned to Singapore with his brother-in-law Fergie in October 1945 to discover that civilian conditions were punitive. Since all of the transport on the island was at the exclusive disposal of the Military, they found themselves having to walk the three miles to and from the Straits Trading Company office in Ocean Building and Woodside, Bagnall's house in Grange Road. "We had no records, no transport, and worst of all, no tin smelter," observed Fergie.

The re-establishment of Mansfield & Co, however, was no haphazard affair, plans having already been set in motion by Sir John Hobhouse and Sir Charles Wurtzburg. In the early stages, the handling of commercial vessels came under the aegis of the Ministry of Transport assisted by organisations known collectively as 'Malayan Agents Shipping Association,' or 'M.A.S.A.,' and the Coastal Control Unit (C.C.U.). M.A.S.A. dealt with ocean-going vessels while C.C.U. was responsible for small coastal steamers. The thinking behind this was that with a lack of staff and a shortage of office accommodation, it would be quite impossible for pre-war shipping agents immediately to resuscitate themselves.

With Mac McLellan as Chairman of both Mansfield & Company, and the Straits Steamship Company, supported by other members of Mansfield's pre-war staff who had escaped internment, a concerted effort was made to restore normality as soon as possible. However, the difficulty of setting up an organisation in a country which had been occupied by an enemy and was now governed by a Military Administration were all too obvious. Fortunately, Ocean Building was still standing, but as the Japanese had removed all of the internal steel guides and wire cables, no lifts were working.

Reunited in Batavia after Kilner's jungle escape, the Black family had, via Australia, succeeded in returning to England where, following the destruction of Alfred Holt's India Buildings in Liverpool during the Blitz, Mansfield & Company had set up headquarters in Taunton, Somerset. Kilner spent the war dealing with the company's affairs in the Far East, and returned to Sarawak in 1945 when peace was established. With all of the Sarawak Steamship Company's ships either sunk or requisitioned by the navy, and their office still in the hands of the military, Kilner and his four Chinese directors, one of whom was Ong Tiang Swee, sat down for their first board meeting on 13th December 1945. Without any reference to the intervening years, the minutes of 4th December 1941 were read and confirmed without a murmur.

The Blacks did not remain long in Kuching. On behalf of Mansfield & Company, Kilner was appointed chief executive of the fledgling Malayan Airways based in Singapore. Following Malaysian independence, this company's name was changed to Singapore Airlines, and as such it continues today.

Slowly, with much hard work, a semblance of normality was achieved. It was men such as Sir John Hay and Sir John Bagnall, working with Mac McLellan,* Fergie Fergusson, and Kilner Black,** the next generation of tuan besars and their Chinese and Malayan colleagues and counterparts, who put the commerce of Singapore back on its feet again. In 1946, Sir John Bagnall stood down as chief executive of the Straits Trading Company, and was succeeded by his brother-in-law Fergie. The following year, he retired to live in South Africa. In 1953, Fergie too was knighted for dedicated service to the Government of Singapore, as a member of the Legislative Council and the (inner core) Executive Council.

A full year before hostilities came to an end, senior members of the Borneo Company in London had been co-opted into rehabilitation units set up by the British Government. A month after the declaration of peace in Siam, the company was heading a mission for the production of rice. On 31st December 1945, Alec Malcolm, the Borneo Company's general manager in London, arrived in Singapore to assess the damage.

---

*   Mac and Dorothy McLellan returned to Scotland in 1953. From 1960 until 1965, Mac served as Sheriff-Substitute and Provost of Dunblane. He died in 1977, and Dorothy in 2004.

**   Kilner Black retired from Mansfields in 1951. Following a last tour of the Far East, culminating in Hong Kong, he and Joan returned to England where they settled in Devon and kept a small motor-boat on the River Exe, and then the River Dart. Kil had almost reached the age of 90 when he died in 1988. Joan still lives in Devon, a sprightly 97-year-old.

Despite open warfare between the Netherlands and Indonesia, South East Asia was again becoming a seller's market, with banks falling over themselves to provide investment funds. Once more there were great opportunities for those prepared to take the initiative, and Malcolm, among others, recognised the signs. For example, there was Siam, where huge quantities of teak had been expropriated, but where the Borneo Company still enjoyed useful concessions.

A cable was received in London from Nicholas Ponnudurai, the Borneo Company's Chief Clerk in Penang to say: "I wonder if you will recognise me now as I have gone grey, haggard and not my former self."[4]

After the coercion he had endured, this was understandable, but Ponnodurai gallantly had wasted no time in rallying the company's Penang interests, acquiring temporary premises in Logan Road and rounding up former employees. Hours before the fall of the island, he had removed all of the company ledgers and buried them in a tin box in his back yard. L.J. Fernandez, his counterpart in Ipoh, had done the same. Within a matter of weeks, Borneo Motors was operational again, sharing premises opposite the E&O Hotel with its former rival Wearne Brothers. Within months, the two companies were re-equipping Malaya's road transport network.

In the offices and godowns of Kuching, Sibu and Miri, all of the stock, furnishings and plant had vanished.[5] Throughout Sarawak, the rubber had overgrown and gone back to the wild. Twenty-one members of the Borneo Company's European staff in South East Asia had lost their lives, either in fighting, or as prisoners of war. That figure did not include the many Malays, Chinese and Siamese caught and killed while attempting to help their colleagues.

Throughout South East Asia, however, the Japanese had from the start been anxious to affect a live and let live policy towards the indigenous population: the Malays, the Ibans and the Chinese. The Malays were largely allowed to carry on with their jobs in government or encouraged to plant rice, but the Chinese were an obvious problem. It was common knowledge that large sums of money had been sent through the China Relief Distress Fund to support Chiang Kai Shek, the Chinese leader, in his continuing campaign against Japan. Examples had to be made, hence the early Sook Ching massacre in Singapore, and the token public execution of seven men accused of stealing petrol in Sarawak.

News travelled fast and to all intents and purposes produced the desired effect. It was decreed afterwards that so long as the ethnic classes of the occupied regions demonstrated their loyalty and respect towards their overlords, they would be left alone. Happily, this did not deter Ong Tiang Swee, and his fellow merchant Tan Bak Lim, from smuggling loans of money into Batu Lintang to enable prisoners to purchase much needed medical supplies. Passive non-co-operation became the Chinese way. There was no point in unnecessary confrontation.

In Sarawak, a squad of soldiers came to search the house of Ong Kwan Hin for Europeans, but found none and went away. Later on Kwan Hin was nearly killed when his bicycle was in a collision with a car driven by a Japanese officer. When he recovered consciousness in hospital he asked what had become of his bike. 'Oh, towkey, we thought you were already dead, so don't ask about your bike.'[6]

Throughout the occupation, the Chinese community in Sarawak maintained a dignified and cunning indifference, manufacturing and marketing soap from coconut-oil, distilling liquor from sweet potatoes, and carrying on their way of life as best they could. When liberation came, there were three joyful days of celebration.

For some time, the exact fate of Peter Cobbold, the Borneo Company's manager in Sibu, remained a mystery, although there was no shortage of speculation. In December 1941, Cobbold and Batty Miles, the Borneo Company's forestry expert, had been among a group of twenty-four (including two children) which had set off from Sibu with Andrew McPherson, Sarawak's Secretary for Native Affairs, and his pregnant wife.

Their plan was to follow the Bintulu River and escape across the Dutch Border, stopping off at Pasir Naik, Marrit, and Balaga, the highest and last settlement on the Rejang River. It was an arduous trip. In the course of the journey, the party had slept in longhouses, crossed the river thirty-six times, often knee-deep, sometimes up to their armpits, until finally reaching Long Nawang at an altitude of 2,500 feet.

Not all of the party completed the journey. After 12 days, Batty Miles decided to turn back and was taken prisoner. As a civilian, he was allowed to carry on with his forestry work, but his captors soon changed their minds and imprisoned him at Batu Lintang.[7]

This information comes from a report written by W. McKerracher, the Borneo Company's sawmill manager at Salim, who escaped to Batavia after a hazardous 18 day trek to Long Eranand and the lucky discovery of the Dutch Controller's launch which took him to an aerodrome. His account reveals that several of those who did reach the remote hill station of Long Nawang[8] in Dutch Borneo came down with malaria and, since they were well stocked with food and medicine, chose to stay put.

Although Peter Cobbold was making plans to return to Sibu, his sunburn had turned septic and so he too decided to remain at Long Nawang until his condition improved. Just about the time of McKerracher's departure, the party was joined by Donald Hudden, District Officer at Marudi, whose sister Kathleen was married to Anthony Brooke, the Rajah's nephew. Hudden was accompanied by a group of Dutch airmen whose bomber, based in Surabaya, had been shot down. In April, two American missionaries and forty Dutch and Indonesian soldiers arrived to join them.

Truth will out, and from Japanese, Dutch, and native sources, evidence has since emerged that Donald Hudden, who set off for Long Berang in the hope of persuading a Kayan friend to hide him, was murdered by two Ibans who bore him a grudge. On August 20th 1942, the occupants of Long Nawang were taken by surprise by a 'punitive expedition' of Japanese marines, and every one of them was brutally executed, including the women and children.[9] The story soon went the rounds that the children under five had been forced to climb trees and when they fell with exhaustion, were bayoneted.[10]

By the time the facts were confirmed, it proved impossible to track down those responsible for the crime. Since all of those murdered were well known to the European community in Sarawak, their death, especially those of the McPhersons and the Bomphreys, the wife and two sons of the Manager of the Island Trading Company in Selalang, had a particularly depressing effect upon those who yearned to return to the old way of life.

What remained of their old way of life was fast slipping away from them. In Sarawak, it was not so much an upsurge of the communism now sweeping the Malayan peninsula that became prevalent, but Rajahism.

The war had been a desperate period for Vyner Brooke. He blamed the British Government for not fulfilling its treaty obligations and for not defending his country. He blamed himself for not being in Sarawak when the crunch came. Too old to be an effective guerilla leader, he had retreated to England and placed his brother Bertram in charge of a provisional government in exile while he banished himself into a solitary retreat.

When peace was declared, his state of mind was much the same. He knew that vast amounts of capital would be needed for Sarawak to recover. Most probably the necessary sums could be raised on the international money markets, but not without making commercial concessions. It was a daunting prospect for an old man. Vyner was tired. He wanted out.

In February 1946, entirely without warning, he issued a proclamation through Gerard MacBryan to announce that in their own self-interest, the people of Sarawak should accept the King of Great Britain as their ruler. "There shall be no Rajah in Sarawak after me,"[11] he decreed.

Bertram Brooke first heard the news on a BBC radio broadcast. Bertram's son, Anthony, whom Vyner had intermittently appointed his successor, was equally shocked. His immediate reaction was that it was illegal, it was unconstitutional and undemocratic. Anthony vowed to fight "tooth and nail any proposal that Sarawak shall become a Crown Colony before the people of Sarawak have been consulted under their own constitution." Others accused MacBryan of manipulation and treachery. Nobody believed that Rajah could have acted alone in such a decision.

In London, questions were asked in the House of Commons, and Vyner went on the defensive. Writing to *The Times* newspaper, he complained that "members of parliament should not discuss subjects regarding which they know little or nothing: Eastern affairs take a lifetime to understand and such discussions merely prolong the sittings of the House for no useful purpose."

Thus spoke the old autocrat. "All is peace in Sarawak. The natives have confidence in myself and my private secretary, whom I have known for 26 years. The time has come when my private secretary's enemies should substantiate their charges in public or hold their tongues."[12]

Once again, Rajah was coming to the defence of Gerard MacBryan, but within two months, his controversial private secretary had resigned. The following year, having paid a brief visit to Sarawak formally to divorce Sa'erah – who during the occupation had taken up with a senior Japanese naval officer – MacBryan took off to South Africa with his third wife, Frances, whom he had met in England during the war. His story thereafter remains equally unorthodox and obscure, embracing an attempt to sue

Anthony Brooke for libel, a succession of lunatic asylums, and the Ranee's assertion that he was found dead in a cheap hotel in Hong Kong where he had been living like a vagrant.[13]

In April 1946, the 3rd and last White Rajah and Ranee of Sarawak returned to Kuching in a flying boat from Singapore. Although they presented to the public a united face, it was obvious that the relationship was strained. In Singapore, before setting off, they had occupied separate rooms in Raffles Hotel, and Wee Kheng Chiang, a favourite with both, found himself acting as a go-between on Sarawak affairs.[14]

On their arrival in the Sarawak River, they were received with a 21-gun salute and an overwhelming display of affection. There were speeches of welcome, and the presentation of a sword from the 84-year-old Datu Patinggi, who bitterly opposed cession. A memorandum from the Malay National Union leaders and Melanau village headmen was handed over. It pleaded for Rajah to pass over his responsibilities to Anthony Brooke.

Even the Ranee, whose motives in retrospect are extremely hard to analyse, professed herself astonished at the widespread hostility shown towards cession.[15] Wherever she and Vyner travelled, Sarawak flags were waved and handfuls of yellow rice thrown over official cars. This prompted Christopher Dawson, the career diplomat who had been selected to head a colonial government in Kuching should cession be passed, to comment that there must have been something in the past to account for such an overt display of goodwill.

There followed a visit from two British members of parliament, David Rees-Williams, the Labour member for South Croydon, and David Gammans, Conservative member for Hornsey, constituting an official commission of inquiry. In their official report they observed that almost everyone in Sarawak appeared totally confused by what was going on. Only the Chinese community wholeheartedly supported Cession on the basis that British rule would improve their trade opportunities. But even Ong Tiang Swee, meeting with Bertram Brooke a week before the Council Negri proceedings, appears to have had reservations about the way in which such an important change was being introduced.

On 8th May, there was a vote in the Negri Council on the Cession Bill. The motion was carried by 18 votes to 16, there being a native majority against it of 13 votes to 12. The votes of the Europeans therefore decided the outcome. Six voted for cession and three against, with one abstention. On July 1st 1946, an under-secretary of the now defunct Sarawak Government read out the decree which ended the absolute rule of the Brooke Family in Sarawak.

Only a few Chinese and no Dyaks attended the hand-over ceremony. The Rajah, who had by then returned to England, sent a message saying that he had every confidence that Sarawak would benefit from the move. King George welcomed a new country into the brotherhood of the Commonwealth, announcing on behalf of his Government that 'Sarawak would be brought to a higher stage of social and economic development than has hitherto been possible.'

Sir Charles Vyner Brooke,
3rd Rajah of Sarawak
(Martine Family Collection

For just over a hundred years one family alone had dominated this land of the Orient; mangrove swamps, tidal rivers, exotic wildlife and impenetrable forest. In the benign autocracy which the Brookes imposed over the divers tribes and races over which they ruled, they were in certain ways well ahead of their time.

Contrary to rumour, Sir Charles Vyner Brooke was not bribed with a sum of £1 million for the sale of his country. What he in fact received was £100,000 under the terms of a Trust fund established by his father in 1912.*[16] With only the income from this to support himself, the Ranee, and at least two of his daughters, it left him infinitely worse off financially than might reasonably have been expected.

However, living in London toward the end of his life, he often reflected that he had been the luckiest man in the world to have been Rajah of Sarawak.[17]

---

* A surplus sum was set aside for the Sarawak Fund which later became the Sarawak Foundation.

CHAPTER TWENTY

Aneberg

There may be others who will appear after my time with soft and smiling countenances to deprive you of what I solemnly and truly consider to be your right and that is the land. It is your inheritance on which your flesh and blood exists, the source of your self-existence which, if once lost, no amount of money could ever recover.

Charles Johnson Brooke, 2nd Rajah of Sarawak.

I T was to the British Protectorate of Sarawak that my parents returned in the summer of 1946, leaving my sisters behind in Scotland enrolled as boarders at a school in Edinburgh. The girls now had the nearby support of a grandfather, and uncles and aunts, but it still proved a challenging emotional wrench for both them and my mother.

For a while, though, the family had basked in the affection of supportive friends and relatives, but post-war Britain, with its rationing coupons, was a grey, unappealing landscape. More importantly, there were financial considerations to be taken on board. There were debts to be paid. Everything that my parents owned was invested in Sarawak, or at least anything that was retrievable.

In the Borneo Company, a major reconstruction took place. In London, Sir Adam Ritchie remained Chairman. Alec Malcolm, with the company for forty-three years, was appointed Managing Director, and Margaret MacKay, Sir Adam's equally long serving secretary, co-ordinated contact with all of the Far Eastern managers.

Jack Bennett sailed home to join his family in England where he chose to remain. Kenneth Simpson, having recovered his health as much as he was ever likely to do, returned to manage the Singapore office; Red Reddish was back with Borneo Motors as managing director.* Richard Sagar set off for Kuching with his new wife Eileen to deputize for my

---

* Red Reddish was awarded the Military Cross for his role with Force 136. He returned to England in 1954 and lived in Sussex. He died in 1996.

father until his return. Batty Miles was back in his beloved Rejang forests. Charles Horn, who had spent the war in Batu Lintang Camp, replaced Peter Cobbold as manager at Sibu.

Having returned to Scotland, John Grant was reunited with his wife and two sons on the platform of Nairn Station. The Glenmoriston Estate, near Inverness, had been inherited by John's cousin Hamish Grant, and John was asked to manage it on his behalf. As their father had hoped, Ian and Peter Grant were indeed brought up as 'Highlanders'.* [1]

For Ted Hannay, and his father, Harry, it was a more painful transition. Still mourning the death of his wife and younger son, Harry Hannay returned to his house in Ipoh where, before reviving his mining consultancy, he was appointed His Majesty's Custodian of Enemy Property for Perak.[2]** Ted Hannay had loved his pre-war job with Borneo Motors in Singapore but was not reinstated, the reason given that he had not been originally recruited in the UK. He felt immensely let down by this, but despite everything he had been through, later returned to the Far East to work for several years with the British Malayan Petroleum Company (later Shell) in Borneo. Both of his daughters were born there,*** and in later years he 'actually purchased several Japanese-made cars, proving, perhaps, that living is too important to bear grudges.'

In Scotland, Mary Hannay had heard of her mother's death from a postcard dated December 1944, two and a half years after the event. She was later notified that her brother Ted had died and it was not until August 1945, when she received a letter written by him from a base camp in Bangkok, that she realised there had been a mistake. It was her younger brother Harry who was dead.

After VE Day, Mary was posted to a records centre at RAF Innsworth, near Gloucester, but only remembered doing *Daily Express* crosswords and visiting towns such as Cheltenham and Gloucester on her days off. When notified that Ted was coming home, she applied for a compassionate posting to the south of Scotland and, before being herself demobbed, she was able

---

* In his retirement, John became an accomplished watercolour painter. He died in 1978.
** Harry Hannay remained at his home in Ipoh until his death in 1961.
*** Ted Hannay married in 1948 and worked for a spell in Nigeria before joining Shell and being posted to Borneo. He died in 2000.

to help him recuperate while staying with old family friends in Newton Stewart.*

In Kuching, Aneberg, the principal Borneo Company residence on Bukit Mata hill, was a wreck, and during the occupation, BMK, my parent's house, had been turned into a military brothel. 'Comfort Women' were a perk of the Japanese army, and BMK was allocated exclusively for the use of regular soldiers, including the guards at Batu Lintang POW camp. It was mostly imported Javanese girls who provided the services, but some local women of a higher class were recruited for senior officers at the Chan family's mansion on Tabuan Road.[3]

One of my father's particular concerns when considering a return to Kuching was that BMK would be uninhabitable. He remembered only too well my mother's initial reaction when she had first set eyes on it. Six years on, he definitely did not want a repeat performance, so the first condition he made when the Borneo Company offered him his old job back, was that he wanted a 'spit-new' house built on the site of the old Aneberg.

It was agreed, and BMK was converted into flats, one of which he and my mother were to occupy. Under the supervision of William Tan, the local builder, who later went on to own extensive properties and a cinema in Kuching, a rather more spacious and modern two-storey bungalow took shape on a promontory on the adjacent side of Bukit Mata. In keeping with Borneo Company tradition, it too was named Aneberg.

My mother was not at all enthused about returning to Sarawak, but having reclaimed her husband, she was in no hurry to lose him again. Besides, it was the life to which she had naively agreed when they married and it never occurred to her that there was an option.

What made it especially hard for both of them, however, was the fact that virtually nothing among their old possessions remained. Most of the looting had taken place immediately before the Japanese arrival on Christmas Day 1941, and what was left was plundered when hostilities came to an end. Even my father's kilt, and all of my mother's clothes had been taken. The porcelain my father had lovingly collected since his twenties had vanished.

Throughout my childhood, it never occurred to me just how hard

---

* In 1950, Mary Hannay married Alexander Wilkinson and now lives in New Zealand.

Charles Martine on the steps of Aneberg, Kuching 1949
(Martine Family Collection)

such losses must have been, on top of everything else that my parents endured. All of their wedding photographs were gone, and there was not one picture of either of my sisters pre-1941 until a long-forgotten portrait, taken in Kuching's Chinese 'Paris Studio,' miraculously surfaced. A few days after they had returned, they were presented with a large, colour-tinted copy in a gilt frame. For five years the negatives had lain hidden in the photographer's darkroom.

In the months that followed, they would be invited out to dine with friends and would find themselves eating with their own cutlery, somehow retrieved, pooled, and dispersed through His Majesty's Custodian of Enemy Property for Sarawak to whoever needed or wanted it most. In pride of place in my home today is a suite of leather chairs recovered quite by accident on an unscheduled visit to a rubber plantation several miles up one of Sarawak's many rivers. Charles had pulled back a tarpaulin out of curiosity to see what was underneath it, and there they were, scuffed and mildewed, but otherwise intact.

The financial compensation allocated by the Borneo War Damages Commission was a fixed £4,800, related to property but not to contents. The generally accepted idea was that everyone would get by somehow. Some received assistance from the companies they worked for; others did not.

Charles Martine with Borneo Company colleagues on a visit up-river
(Martine Family Collection)

The photograph of Virginia and Patricia taken in the Summer of 1941 by Kuching's 'Paris Studio.' The negative had remained in the photographer's darkroom throughout the war, and miraculously surfaced in 1945
(Martine Family Collection)

Charles Martine inspecting one of the
Borneo Company's pepper gardens in
Upper Sarawak

(Martine Family Collection)

On a personal level, freedom came at a heavy emotional cost. Only someone whose personal belongings and treasures have been similarly violated could possibly understand the full extent of what it meant to them. My mother never again felt the same way about owning possessions. "They are just things," she would say dismissively.

Ah Cheow had also survived, having kept his head down in Singapore, and was now happily reunited with his wife Ah Soh and their child. Virginia's amah, Ah See, having moved in with her family in Chinatown, sent a message to ask if her services were required. She was told that before long they would be, and, shortly afterwards, the household at Aneberg was joined by Zinudin, a second houseboy.

Post-war, the Borneo Company's import business trebled with its agency business flourishing as never before. The company's old interests in pepper, the produce export trade and shipping were revived. Roads in Sarawak pre-war had been virtually non-existent. With the exception of primitive road links to Serian and Bau, everyone and everything travelled on the waterways. Now all of that was changing, but, immediately post-war, it was air travel which was to revolutionize communication. It did not take long for the Borneo Company to open up a bookings office and a thriving passenger agency.

The company no longer enjoyed the exclusive mineral rights granted at the time of the company's birth, but that was of no great concern since extensive surveys now indicated that the commercial potential was negligible. Timber, next to rubber, was the most lucrative investment.

Pre-war, elephants had been imported from Siam, and it was clear that the climate suited them. Unfortunately, wartime losses had made them an endangered species in certain territories, causing not only Siam, but India and Burma to prohibit their export. Looking closer to home, therefore, the Borneo Company bought five beasts aged between 11 and 17 in England from Chipperfield's Circus, and shipped them on the upper deck of the P&O liner *Soudan*, along with 500 bales of hay, three cases of rum, and ten pounds of Epsom Salts. Fifty-two days after leaving Southampton, the elephants were disembarked at Sarikei and soon afterwards set to work ninety miles up the Rejang.[4]

In Singapore, the Rt Hon Malcolm MacDonald, on-and-off Secretary for the Colonies during the late 1930s, was installed as Commissioner General for South East Asia and Governor-General of Malaya and British Borneo. The son of Ramsay MacDonald, Britain's first Labour Prime Minister, he was an astute and clever man, underestimated by those who whispered that he would never have got where he had without the right connections. There may have been an element of truth in this, but MacDonald's steadying hand in a volatile region proved significant. In

Off-loading elephants from Chipperfield's Circus
(Martine Family Collection)

Charles Martine with
Malcolm MacDonald,
Governor General of
Malaya and British Borneo
(Martine Family Collection)

addition, he did make a genuine effort to get to know the people of the territories he controlled, even so far as to visit Temenggong Koh at Kapit.*

On the Sarawak Government front, Gordon Aikman was back from his convalescence in Australia as acting Chief Secretary. Shot Spurway was installed as Conservator of Forest, and Teddy Edwards became Director of Public Works. However, it was a very different kind of administration from that of the Rajah since it was now presided over by an incoming British Governor, Sir Charles Arden-Clarke, a former Resident Commissioner in Basutoland.

It was inevitable that the debacle of cession should leave its legacy. In England, Anthony Brooke felt increasingly bitter at the way he had been treated by his uncle and announced to the *Observer* newspaper that he was seeking a judicial decree to establish the illegality of Sarawak's cession. In Sarawak itself, the Malay National Union, the Pegerakan Pemuda Malayu (Malay Youth Movement), and other anti-cession parties were spoiling for a fight. Four days before he died in November, the ailing Datu Patinggi asked not to see the Rajah, but Bertram Brooke, to say goodbye. At his funeral, patriotic feeling among the 4,000 mourners reached fever pitch.[5]

It was at this point that Anthony Brooke announced that he was planning a return to Sarawak. After a hastily convened meeting with the Commissioner General, Arden-Clarke decided to refuse him entry on the basis that his presence would only inflame the situation.** This, as might

---

* The visit is included in MacDonald's book *Borneo People*, published in 1956.

** The ban remained in place until Sarawak became part of the Federation of Malaysia in 1963. Anthony Brooke was able to return for a nostalgic visit in 1965. In 1975, with his second wife, he co-founded Operation Peace Through Unity and today lives in New Zealand.

Pat Martine presenting the Geiki Silver Cup at the Sarawak Races
(Martine Family Collection)

have been expected caused a furore among Anthony Brooke's supporters, but high-minded and a hardliner, Arden-Clarke was determined to get the message across that the British Government was in no mind to countenance a rethink over cession.

The protests and petitions continued regardless, reaching a climax with a series of walk-outs by Malay government employees. The colonial government's attitude at this time seems to have been that so long as such demonstrations remained relatively peaceable, they would eventually run out of steam. It was yet another miscalculation that would have tragic consequences.

CHAPTER TWENTY-ONE

Sedition

Came here to Kuching which lies on the equator, sweats and swelters on the equator, and which so far as my money goes can continue to do so for ever without me again.

Agnes Newton Keith, *Three Came Home.*

THERE is the memory of a small boy and his amah standing on the lawn in front of a white house perched high above the Sarawak River; I remember them waving to the captain of the *Rajah Brooke*, the Sarawak Steamship Company's successor to the pre-war *Vyner Brooke*. It was a moment of great excitement.

Since the sinking of the *Vyner Brooke* in the Banka Strait, off southern Sumatra, in 1942, it had become a priority for the Sarawak Steamship Company to provide a replacement. The *TSMV Rajah Brooke* was therefore specially built in Scotland and launched by Joan Black in 1948. When this elegant vessel sailed up the Sarawak River on her maiden voyage, the Ibans and other Dyak tribes turned out in force, many assuming that the Rajah himself must be on board. Once the ship docked, they swarmed all over it,

MV Rajah Brooke, launched by Joan Black in 1948
(Martine Family Collection)

examining life-boats, cabins, even the dining-room silver, but were greatly saddened to discover that there was no Rajah.

Much the same arrangement as the captain of the *Vyner Brooke* had had with my sister Virginia ten years earlier, the captain of the *Rajah*

Brooke and I too had a special understanding. As the boat slid elegantly past on the muddy water below Aneberg, I can almost feel the thrill of hearing the ship's horn in response to my shouts.

I was born in Kuching on Boxing Day 1946, at the end of a year of massive rebuilding which involved not just the physical reconstruction of a bruised country, but the re-establishment of trust, not made at all easy by the rumblings of the anti-cession movement. As a child, of course, I understood none of this.

Although I was christened into the Christian Faith as a Presbyterian, which does not usually require godparents, Kenneth Simpson* and Richard Sagar accepted the responsibility for keeping an eye on my spiritual well-being, since the ceremonial took place in an Anglican church. Following this, such personal recall as I have focuses on my mother, my amah, and baby green turtles, dozens of them, clumsily flopping about in a bowl. They were on temporary loan from the extrovert Tom Harrison, curator of the Sarawak Museum. It was, indeed, a world full of wonders.

Although I was far too young to appreciate it at the time, Tom Harrison too was a bit of a wonder. Not only had he parachuted into the heart of Borneo in 1945 to set up a Dyak resistance movement, he was a wonder with animals. Throughout the late '40s, '50s and '60s, countless articles and publications poured forth from this talented man until he met his tragic end in a car crash in 1976. I only knew him as a heavy figure with dark, floppy hair who often visited Aneberg. The baby turtles originated from the three Turtle Islands, which were under his protection, and I was being involved in an experiment to discover details of their diet, growth, swimming skills and fertility. Having reached a certain size, they were returned to the open sea.[1] In the short term, they brought untold delight to one small boy.

There are other flash-backs too. The same small boy fishing with rod and line from the pier in front of the Borneo Company office, or splashing in a paddling pool with two other children, Tuppy and Penny Aikman, the son and daughter of Gordon Aikman, the immeasurably important Chief Secretary, and his wife Sheila.

---

* Kenneth Simpson, a life-long bachelor, retired from the Far East in 1960. He went to live in Tunbridge Wells, and died in 1973.

Charles Martine (seated centre) with Tom Harrison
(standing fourth from right) on the Turtle Islands
(Martine Family Collection)

Gordon Aikman was a corpulent man with an off-colour sense of humour which entertained my parents. He too had endured considerable deprivation as a prisoner of war in Sarawak's Zaida, Padungan, and Batu Lintang camps and, while recuperating immediately afterwards in Australia, had met Sheila by chance on a train journey.

Tuppy was the same age as myself; Penny a year younger. Obscurely I have memories of the three of us dancing wildly to a 78 rpm record of Cole Porter's *When they begin the Beguine,* played on a wind-up gramophone in the nursery.

By this stage, my parents were comfortable ensconced in Aneberg, and life had more or less returned to the way it had been pre-war, except that my father had even more obligations with which to preoccupy himself. He had been invited to become a member of the Negri Council, with an active role in the Finance Committee.

After Cession, the character of the Negri Council changed, although

Pat Martine, Wee Kheng Chiang, Sheila Aikman,
Charles Martine and Gordon Aikman
(Martine Family Collection)

the traditional form was by no means overthrown. One obvious development was that the number of white government officers began to decline, while the representation from the other races was broadened. Instead of meeting every three years, the Council started to meet three times a year.[2]

In a young colony, where democracy was barely understood, Charles Martine rapidly found himself the spokesman of the 'unofficial' members of the Council, those not in government employ, and thus taking up the causes of the wider community. Where politics are only in their infancy, some form of opposition was necessary to voice the feelings of the people at large, and through speaking his mind, he unwittingly found himself laying the foundations of 'Her Majesty's Opposition.'[3]

Horse racing was as popular in Kuching as it was throughout Malaya, and consequently brought together the country's various ethnic groups – Malays, Dyaks, Chinese and Europeans – for a common and highly enjoyable pursuit. Rajah James had started the first races in 1893, but in the absence of horses, then unknown in Sarawak, buffaloes were raced. This changed in 1924 when a high-ranking government official imported a batch of ponies from Sabah, and the Sarawak Turf Club was founded by, among others, Ong Tiang Swee. Pre-1941 and post-1945, races took place regularly at Pedungan,* with the Borneo Company managing the Turf Club's finances.[4]

Another of the great social occasions in Kuching was the annual Sarawak Regatta, held originally at New Year, then late February. Regattas were held on the Sarawak River as early as 1872, and it became the custom under Brooke rule for the European community to be invited to the Astana for breakfast before the start of the first race. Such importance did Rajah Charles attach to this that he would send his yacht *Maimunah* to his outstations to round up his Residents.

The Regatta was, and remains, a fantastic spectacle with traditional longboat and dragon boat races competing with other more bizarre activities such as climbing greasy poles, pillow-fights and catching ducks on the water. Later on, racing-boats from the Samarahan district and as far afield as Sibu were brought in, and since much of it took place on the water below and around the river bend from Aneberg, I can still see the vivid colours and remember the excitement.

In late November 1949, a new Governor arrived at the Astana, and my mother was delighted. He was Duncan Stewart from Achara in Argyll, whose mother had been a staunch supporter of her father, Fred Macquisten, during his election campaigns in the 1920s and 1930s. Duncan, whom she had last met in her early twenties, had in between served in Nigeria, the Bahamas, and Palestine and, at the age of 45, became Governor and Commander-in-Chief of the 'little State of Sarawak,' as it was so patronisingly referred to by both *The Times* and *Scotsman* newspapers.

Tragically, Duncan Stewart did not get much of a chance to prove himself in the 'little state of Sarawak.' Sixteen days into his office, he travelled 75 miles up the Rejang River to visit Sibu, and the entire population of the region turned out to welcome him. Smiling, flag-waving school children lined up in rows, but as the Governor walked past

---

* The Sarawak Turf Club moved to its current premises at 8th Mile in 1991.

them, Rosli Bin Bobi, a 19-year-old Malay youth, stepped out of the line and plunged a knife into Stewart's abdomen.[5]

The Governor's response was magnificent, worthy of the British Raj at its finest. With blood from the knife wound oozing through his hands, he carried off the welcoming ceremonies regardless. His audience remained totally unaware that he had been stabbed, although some may have noticed the red stain on his uniform.

It was only after his official duties had been completed that he collapsed and was rushed into Sibu Hospital. He was hastily transported by flying boat to Singapore where he died two days later. Everyone, as one might imagine, was deeply shocked.

Another Malay youth, Moshidi Bin Sedik, aged 25, and various others were soon after arrested, and

His Excellency Duncan Stewart. On an official visit to Sibu shortly after this photograph was taken, Duncan Stewart was mortally stabbed by a Malay youth acting for the Rukun Tiga Belas, an anti-cession group *(Martine Family Collection)*

it was discovered that the assassination was the work of one of the 16 or more anti-cession parties then in existence. This particular group was based in Sibu calling itself Rukun Tiga Belas (Thirteen Elements). The leader was a former customs officer called Awang Rambli, who had on more than one occasion confronted Sir Charles Arden-Clarke, the previous governor. Arden-Clarke's tactics, derived from his time in Africa, were not best suited to understanding the Malay psyche. In the context of Sarawak, he had openly admitted to my father that he 'had no previous experience of having to deal with really intelligent and serious thinking people.'

There was nothing personal about the assassination of Duncan Stewart. It was unreservedly an anti-cession, anti-British protest, and the authorities were pleased to discover that no communist influences had been at work.

Council Negri – 21st November 1949. Charles Martine is standing in the back row, fourth from the right. Shot Spurway is in the second row, fifth from the left. In the front row, seated on the right hand side is Temenggong Koh, the Iban leader. Fourth from the left is the Council President, Christopher Dawson, seated next to the Governor of Sarawak, His Excellency Duncan Stewart. On the Governor's left are the Chief Justice, Arthur Grattan-Bellew; the Datu Bandar, and Ong Hap Leong, son of Ong Tiang Swee

(Martine Family Collection)

Of course, this was of little consolation to Duncan Stewart or his family. Following a service at St Andrew's Cathedral in Singapore, he was buried in the island's Bidabari Cemetery. Fifty-two years later, his remains were exhumed and brought home to Scotland for reburial at Duror, close to the Stewarts' ancestral Scottish home in Appin.

With Stewart's death, Sarawak reached another watershed. When news of the murder reached the Ibans of the Rejang, they descended upon Sibu in full warrior regalia to support the Government, just as they would have done in the days of the Brookes. Temenggong Koh and seven of the other

Iban leaders attended the trial, an unpleasant episode where four of the accused were sentenced to hang, and the remaining seven given various terms of imprisonment.[6] Right up until his final moment, Rambli seriously believed that Anthony Brooke would intercede on his behalf and that he would be pardoned.

Meanwhile, an increasingly beleaguered Anthony Brooke was accused by his uncle of promoting a front for subversion. In Anthony Brooke's opinion, Stewart's murder was a direct result of the colonial government's refusal to take the anti-cession movement seriously. However, by this stage, it was independence all the way, not the reinstatement of Brooke rule, that was gathering support.

With the British Army under attack from deep-rooted communist aggression in Malaya, it looked as if Sarawak and North Borneo were in line for similar trouble. It was this inflammatory state of affairs, coupled with my mother's concern for her children – her daughters in Scotland, and my 4-year-old self in Kuching – that forced a decision. This time it was my father's turn to compromise.

While the Far East had been his life, my mother had come to loathe it for what it had done to their lives and what it was now in danger of doing to their relationship. The arrival of her mother, Peggy Macquisten, now 72, for a month's stay at Aneberg, and reports from home on the progress of Virginia and Patricia now at school in Edinburgh compounded those feelings. She wanted to be near them. She did not want them to become strangers.

On a May morning in 1951, she and I, accompanied by Granny Macquisten, said goodbye to Kuching. and sailed to Singapore on the *Rajah Brooke*. After a couple of days – I spending most of my time in bed with 'flu – we went on to Penang where my mother took her mother on a tour of all the old haunts which she and my father had known as newly-weds. "I still think it the only place worth living in the East if one has to live here at all," she wrote defiantly to her sister Jess in England. "Now that the old girl can make the comparison with Kuching, she understands the shock I got when I ended up there."

There was an uncharacteristic bitterness in her tone. She had hated to put pressure on my father, but knew that she could not go on for much longer. For her, the enchantment of the Far East had long since faded.

Aneberg 1949. The author (centre) with, left to right: Zinudin and daughter,
Ah See, Cookie, his wife and children, Hessia and her son, Mutu, and Syce

(Martine Family Collection)

My only recollection of that momentous departure from Kuching is
of my beloved amah, Ah See, weeping on the quayside, and my father,
stiff upper lip, attempting to console the old Chinese lady. My mother
had given Amah a much admired silk dressing-gown as a farewell gift, but
it had only made the separation harder for her. I never saw Amah again,
but I can still recall her blowing her nose on the dressing-gown.

From Penang, we sailed on the *MV Breckonshire* to the King George
Docks in Southampton. There was a fine cabin and a spacious lounge,
and only three other children on board. The passage must have passed
smoothly as I have no further recollection of it.

At the end of May, my father attended the glittering coronation of
Sultan Omar Ali Saifuddin of Brunei. Afterwards he stayed on at Aneberg
for a further six months on his own. Before he handed over his
responsibilities to his colleague Charles Horn, promoted to Kuching from
the Borneo Company's Sibu office, there were farewells to be made.

The Coronation of Sultan Omar Ali Saifuddin of Brunei, May 1951
(Martine Family Collection)

Charles carrying the medals of Ong Tian Swee in the funeral procession of the
Grand Old Man of Sarawak

At 8.30am on a humid, pastel-coloured October morning, he walked with measured step accompanied by the sound of the Sarawak Constabulary Band. Ong Tiang Swee, Teochiew Kapitan China, had died at the age of 87, and it was the greatest funeral the people of Sarawak had ever witnessed.

The parade began at the junction of Rock Road and MacDougall Road, led by a formation of Boy Scouts. Forty Chinese pulled the funeral hearse, which was followed by serried rows of mourners including, at the rear, representatives of the European community, Gordon Aikman, Sarawak's Chief Secretary, and Shot Spurway,* representing His Highness the Rajah. Flags were flown at half-mast on government buildings throughout the colony.

---

*   B.J.C. Spurway was awarded the MBE. Returning to Sarawak as Director of Forestry, he succeeded Gerard MacBryan to become the last pps to Rajah Brooke. He retired to England in 1951 and settled in Hampshire with his second wife, Helen. He died in 1969.

The funeral procession of
Ong Tiang Swee, Kuching
1951

For my father, aside from mourning his old friend, there was an even greater significance. As tuan besar of the Borneo Company, and a symbol of their friendship Tiang Swee's family had bestowed upon him the great honour of carrying, in the front rank of the procession, the old man's medals – the Most Excellent Order of the Star of Sarawak and the Most Excellent Order of the British Empire – displayed on a silk cushion. When Rajah Brooke was told of this afterwards, he commented that it was an "unique honour and gesture towards the European community as a whole."

For seven days there had been feasting and offerings to the spirit. A great table laden with food had stood before the coffin on display at the Ong House, and there were nightly visits from the priest to calm the soul of the departed. Around the table, friends and family gathered together to play Mah Jong into the small hours.

The occasion was made even more poignant for Charles with the realisation that he would shortly be leaving all of this behind him: the vivid colours of the Chinese temples; the innocent beauty of the Dyaks; the curry tiffins; the foaming wash of a motor-launch on the Rejang; the pungent smell of tapped-rubber, the sticky greenness of the rain forests. He had suffered dearly for his devotion to this land and its people, but that was of no great consequence. He was confident in the knowledge that he had given of his best.

Proceeding along Rock Road, the funeral march progressed with great dignity, through Carpenter Street, Ewe Hai Street, Wyang Street, Temple Street, Main Bazaar, Gambier Road, Market Street, Khoo Hun Yeang Street and Mosque Road, arriving in its own time at the Ong family's burial-ground at Batu Kinyang.[7]

It was genuinely the end of an era.

The author and his parents on a trip to Miri
(Martine Family Collection)

Epilogue

Far-called, our navies melt away;
On dune and headland sinks the fire:
Lo, all our pomp of yesterday
Is one with Nineveh and Tyre!

Rudyard Kipling, *Recessional.*

IN my parents' drawing-room in Edinburgh stood a Chinese altar table. It was a wedding gift from their close friend Joe Penrice of Mansfield & Company, who died in the Palembang prisoner of war camp in Sumatra. It had been left behind with Pat's parents in England after the ceremony, and was therefore one of their few possessions to survive the war. On this same table stood a framed reproduction of Margaret Noble's portrait of Sir Charles Vyner Brooke, 3rd Rajah of Sarawak.

By then Charles Martine had retired from the Borneo Company, but regularly, perhaps two or three times a year, he would catch the overnight sleeper to London to visit the ageing potentate in his flat at 13 Albion Street where, living alone, Vyner Brooke was fiercely guarded by his secretary, the ever loyal Evelyn Hussey.

These visits were in connection with the Sarawak Foundation over which the Rajah presided, and on which my father served as a trustee. The Foundation's purpose was to provide opportunities for young Sarawakians, and happily it continues to do so under a rather different administration now based in Sarawak.

The 3rd and last Rajah of Sarawak died in 1963. On 27th May, a memorial service was held in the Chapel of St Michael and St George at St Paul's Cathedral, and with the passing of the grand old man, a door to the Far East closed forever.

Recently, I came across a formal note my father had scribbled about him, designed, he wrote, to set the record straight "as someone who was there." It read: " With his command of local languages, Rajah was always available to his subjects, as witness his walks in the garden behind the Astana at 5pm when all or anybody could make contact with him. To me Rajah was a courteous and kindly man, whose nature was often taken advantage of by Europeans."

That same year, 1963, Sarawak became part of the Federation of Malaysia, and two years later Rajah's nephew Anthony Brooke was welcomed back for a nostalgic visit. In 1983, he again returned to Kuching, this time with his second wife, Gita, for the twentieth anniversary celebrations of Sarawak as an independent state within the Federation.

The past remains as we move through it. Anthony and Gita Brooke settled in New Zealand and became peace activists, founding Operation Peace Through Unity. Following a distinguished career in commerce and politics in England, Simon Mackay, Rajah Vyner Brooke's grandson, was created Baron Tanlaw.

I had yet to be born when most of the events I have written about took place, but through snatches of conversation and family legend, they have become part of my memory like a great stained glass window shattered in a storm. Some of those people I loved.

I was a fortunate child; unlike my sisters, I was not sent away to a boarding school. I never lacked the security of a home. The war was rarely mentioned. I once came across a copy of Kenneth Attiwill's book *Fortress* in the bookcase of an hotel on the Mull of Kintyre and noticed that my father's name was listed in the index. He was standing beside me and when I asked him about it, he looked away. "Nothing of interest," he said.

For the ten years before my parents moved back to Scotland, they lived in an Edwardian house with a large garden and orchard in Surrey. In every way they did their best to compensate their children for the separations of the past, and I who was the least affected, was the main beneficiary; childhood memories of humid, exotic Kuching faded fast to be replaced by the leafy, green smell of rural England.

While researching this history, I was assisted by Harold Smyth, a former Chairman of both Mansfield & Company and the Straits Steamship Company. Smyth had arrived in Singapore to work for Mansfield & Company in 1932 aged 18. Called up in September 1939 for mine-sweeping duty with the Straits Settlements Royal Navy Volunteer Reserve, his ship was sunk in the Palembang River on 15th February 1942, the day Singapore fell.

Harold Smyth was repatriated to England with survivors from the *Repulse* and the *Prince of Wales*, and spent the remainder of the war with the Western Approaches Atlantic Convoy Escort organisation. The fall of Singapore and the loss of so many friends caused him great sorrow, but he nevertheless rejoined the Straits Steamship Company in 1946 and was relocated to Sibu. Having lost his first wife Kathleen and infant daughter in the Comet air disaster near Calcutta in 1956, he married Greta Peterkin, sister of my parents' friend Joan Black and widow of the Dennis Peterkin of Mansfield & Company who had died a prisoner of war in Sumatra.

"We were all so grateful for our own survival and were very conscious of the feelings of relatives and friends of those who had perished and suffered so harshly," Smyth told me. "There was a general reluctance among all of us to speak of our experiences."

Six months after I began my research, the telephone rang. "I hope you don't mind me calling, but we met a couple of years ago at a lunch party," said a male voice. "I was wondering if you were any relation to the Mrs Martine who escaped from Sarawak on Christmas Eve 1941 with my mother-in-law and sister-in-law?"

"What was your mother-in-law's name?" I asked.

"Joan Cargill," he replied.

Unaware of any past connection, he and I had met at a friend's house less than a mile from my home in Edinburgh. He was able to tell me that Kenneth and Joan Cargill, with their daughter Rosemary (his wife was born later), had travelled from Australia to South Africa, and later returned to England. I already knew that the Cargills had not gone back to the Far East when the war ended.

In 2003, I was invited to a meeting of the Perth Probus Club by Brian Kitching, whose father Tom Kitching, Singapore's chief surveyor, died in Changi Gaol in 1944, and whose mother Nora was lost when the *Kuala* was sunk in that desperate evacuation of February 1942. The talk, entitled *Life and Death in Changi Gaol – The Medical Background* was given by Nigel Stanley, son of Cuthbert Stanley, the doctor present at the birth of my sister Patricia in Penang – that same Dr Stanley who died from torture in Changi. Also present was Nick Kemp, whose father was in the Malay Police Force in Kuala Lumpur and, like mine, survived internment. Our fathers, although not close friends as such, must have at least encountered each other during their captivity.*

---

* Contractors engaged by the Singapore Prison authorities began the demolition of Changi Gaol in 2004.

In the aftermath of the bombing of Hiroshima and Nagasaki, the emerging attitude of post-imperial Britain was a loss of concern for the South East Asian protectorates. Rejected was the altruism that inspired the Brooke dynasty. With the Japanese invasion, the Straits Settlements and the Federated Malay States formed the conclusion that they had been let down, and who can blame them?

Everything has moved on. Compared with the photographs in my family album, the waterfront of Kuching is unrecognisable. Where once stood the Borneo Company offices, BMK and Aneberg on Bukit Mata hill, now stands the Kuching Hilton. By the early 1980s, the Dyak longhouse of Temenggong Koh* and his successor, Penghulu Jugah,** at Kapit had been replaced by a huge logging park, with tugs and barges jamming the river.

Singapore is also transformed. Where stood Belvedere, there is the Shangri-La Hotel. Gone are the great British trading companies, swallowed up or replaced by multinationals. In 1967, the Borneo Company merged with the Inchcape Group, and what remains of that enterprise today is far different from that which began it all. In 1981, the Guthrie Group came under Malaysian ownership, and in 1989 was listed on the Kuala Lumpur Stock Exchange as the Kumpulan Guthrie Group. Dunlop & Company and Harrison & Crossfield have passed into Malaysian ownership. Blue Funnel and the Glen Line have disappeared, absorbed like Mansfield & Company into the Keppel Corporation. The Straits Trading Company has been absorbed into the Overseas Chinese Banking Corporation.

For the two years before his retirement from the Borneo Company, Charles Martine was President of the Sarawak Association, acting as host at the occasional dinner or reception. To some extent, this kept him in touch. Afterwards, old friends came to visit him in Edinburgh. In 1970, there was evident pleasure when the Sultan of Brunei invited him to join him in his box at the Edinburgh Military Tattoo. He was not forgotten.

There were calls from historians painstakingly preparing their dissertations on the Far East, but while willing to point them in the right

---

*   Temenggong Koh anak Jubang died in 1956.

** Tun Datuk Patinggi Tan Sri Temenggong Jugah anak Barang attended the Coronation of Queen Elizabeth II in London in 1952. He later became Federal Minister for Sarawak Affairs in the Malaysian Parliament. He died in 1981.

Penghulu Jugah at Kapit
(Martine Family Collection)

direction he remained reticent about being quoted. The excuse was always that one day I would be writing on the subject. During his lifetime there were truths he considered best ignored; things best left unsaid.

Charles and Pat Martine both lived to be 84. In Scotland, the Straits Settlements and Sarawak became for them just a distant dream as they lived out the remainder of their days, a gentle and deliberately inconspicuous couple who valued their privacy.

Appendices

CHAPTER ONE

1 E. Jennings. *Mansfields – Transportation and Distribution in South East Asia.*
2 A. Augustine. *Singapore Treasury.*
3 *Ibid.*
4 *History of the Tanglin Club.*
5 R.C.H. McKie. *This was Singapore.*

CHAPTER TWO

1 *History of the Tanglin Club.*
2 H. Longhurst. *The Borneo Story.*
3 *Ibid.*
4 S. Cunyngham-Brown. *The Traders.*
5 *History of the Tanglin Club.*
6 George L. Peet arrived to work as a reporter on *The Straits Times* in 1923 and retired as editor in 1951.

CHAPTER THREE

1 Lord Strabolgi R.N. *Singapore and After.*
2 R. Lee and A. Augustine. *Penang Treasury.*

CHAPTER FOUR

1 H. Longhurst. *History of the Borneo Company.*
2 L. V. Deller. *Valley of Tin. The Straits Times,* 1961.
3 D. Thatcher and R. Cross. *Pai Naa – The Story of Nona Baker MBE.*
4 E. C. Hannay. Papers left to his daughters Kirsty Johns and Patricia Percival.
5 M. Wilkinson. Papers.

CHAPTER FIVE

1 R. Payne. *The White Rajahs of Sarawak.*
2 R.H.W. Reece. *The Name of Brooke.*
3 C. Allen. *Tales from the South China Seas.*

4   M. Brooke. *Good Morning and Goodnight.*
5   M. MacDonald. *Death of a Mighty Headhunter. Straits Times Annual* 1970.
6   Ong Tiang Swee. *Sarawak Memories. Sarawak Gazette Centenary Souvenir 1851-1941.*

CHAPTER SIX
1   Rutter refers to MacBryan under the name of David Chale, a young district officer in Borneo.
     In his text, he comments that he felt that Chale was somebody who always got what he wanted but seldom knew what he wanted.
2   MacBryan once went naked at a party in South Africa and explained afterwards that he thought he was invisible. R. Payne. *The White Rajahs of Sarawak.*
3   R.H.W. Reece. *The Name of Brooke.*
4   S. Brooke. *Queen of the Headhunters.*
5   Reece. *Ibid.*
6   C. Allen. *Tales from the South China Seas.*
7   Reece. *Ibid.*
8   *Ibid.*
9   Brooke. *Ibid.*
10 M. MacDonald. *Death of a Mighty Headhunter. Straits Times Annual,* 1970.
11 S. Baring Gould and C.A. Bampfylde. *A History of Sarawak under its Two White Rajahs.*
12 Reece. *Ibid.*
13 Brooke. *Ibid.*

CHAPTER SEVEN
1   M. Brooke. *Good Morning and Goodnight.*
2   *Ibid.*
3   C. Allen. *Tales from the South China Seas.*
4   T.C. Martine. Letter to Sir Adam Ritchie, 1941. Borneo Company Archives, Guildhall Library.

CHAPTER EIGHT

1   E. P. Hoyt. *Japan's War.*
2   R.H.W. Reece. *Masa Jepun.*
3   *Sarawak Gazette.* Centenary Number 1841-1941.
4   Reece. *Ibid.*
5   R. Payne. *The White Rajahs of Sarawak.*
6   Ritchie/Martine, 1941. Borneo Company Archive, Guildhall Library.
7   Letter from Kenneth Simpson to Sir Adam Ritchie, 1941. Borneo Company Archives, Guildhall Library.

CHAPTER NINE

1   Lt.-General A.E. Percival. *The War in Malaya.*
2   *British Territories in North Borneo. Wartime Intelligence Report (WIR). No 52*, 28 September 1945. WO 208/105. PRO.
3   Percival. *Ibid.*
4   J.L. Noakes. *Report upon Defence Measures Adopted in Sarawak from June 1941 to the Occupation in December 1941 by Imperial Japanese Forces.* Rhodes House Library, Oxford.
5   B. Montgomery. *Shenton of Singapore.*
6   I. Morrison. *Malayan Postscript.*
7   S. Cunynham-Brown. *The Traders.*
8   H. Longhurst. *The Borneo Story.*
9   Sir Shenton Thomas. *War Diary.* December 22nd 1941.
10 Letter to Sir Adam Ritchie 1945.Borneo Company Archives. Guildhall Library.
11 Thomas. *Ibid.*
12 R. Lee and A. Augustine. *Penang Treasury.*
13 J.A. Grant Letters. Grant Family papers.

CHAPTER TEN

1   Papers of J.S. Wink. Rhodes House Library, Oxford.
2   *Ibid.*
3   J.L. Noakes. *Report upon Defence Measures Adopted in Sarawak from June 1941 to the Occupation in December 1941 by Imperial Japanese Forces.* Rhodes House Library, Oxford.
4   *Ibid.*
5   *Ibid.*

CHAPTER ELEVEN

1 Papers of John S. Wink. Rhodes House Library, Oxford.

CHAPTER TWELVE

1 J.L. Noakes. *Report upon Defence Measures Adopted in Sarawak from June 1941 to the Occupation in December 1941 by Imperial Japanese Forces.* Rhodes House Library, Oxford.
2 *The Times*, January 16th 1942. *Fighting on Sarawak frontier.*
3 L. Warner and J. Sandilands. *Women behind the Wire.*
4 Lt.-General A.E. Percival. *The War in Malaya.*
5 Letters of John Grant. Grant Family papers.
6 B. Montgomery. *Shenton of Singapore.*
7 N. Barber. *Sinister Twilight.*
8 Letters of John Grant. Grant Family papers.
9 *Borneo Times*, 1953. Borneo Company Archives. Guildhall Museum, London.
10 Warner & Sandilands. *Ibid.*

CHAPTER THIRTEEN

1 Sir John Bagnall. *Account of a Journey from Singapore to Colombo.* Papers Sir Ewen Fergusson.
2 H. Longhurst. *The Borneo Story.*
3 Letters of John Grant. Grant Family papers.
4 L. Warner and J. Sandilands. *Women behind the Wire.*
5 V.H.K. Foo and Chai Foh Chin. *Story of the Sarawak Steamship Company.*
6 S. Cunyngham-Brown. *The Traders.*
7 Bagnall. *Ibid.*
8 I. Simson. *Singapore – Too Little, Too Late.*

CHAPTER FOURTEEN

1 B. Montgomery. *Shenton of Singapore.*
2 J. Deane Potter. *A Soldier Must Hang.*
3 N. Barber. *Sinister Twilight.*
4 M. Hannay. Wilkinson papers.
5 E.C. Hannay. Papers left to his daughters Kirsty Johns and Patricia Percival.
6 K. Caffrey. *Out in the Midday Sun.*

7 Letter of Helen Beck. Wilkinson papers.
8 E.C. Hannay. *Ibid.*
9 Montgomery. *Ibid.*
10 K. Attiwill. *Fortress.*
11 E.C. Hannay. *Ibid.*
12 Attiwill. *Ibid.*
13 E.C.Hannay. *Ibid.*
14 Beck. *Ibid.*
15 M. Wilkinson. *Ibid.*
16 H. Longhurst. *The Borneo Story.*
17 E.C. Hannay. *Ibid.*
18 Lee Kwan Yew. *The Singapore Story.*

CHAPTER FIFTEEN
1 R.H. Oakley. *Changi Gaol.* Imperial War Museum.
2 *History of The Tanglin Club.*
3 Prison Diary of Katherine de Moubray. Imperial War Museum.
4 T. Kitching. *Life & Death in Changi.*
5 Letter of Helen Beck. Wilkinson papers.
6 E.C. Hannay. Papers left to his daughters Kirsty Johns and Patricia Percival.
7 Beck. *Ibid.*
8 T. McGowran OBE. *Behind the Bamboo Screen.*
9 Letter of J.A. Grant. Grant Family papers.
10 Hannay. *Ibid.*
11 R. McKay. *John Leonard Wilson, Confessor for the Faith.*

CHAPTER SIXTEEN
1 *Double Tenth Investigation 12/9/45.* Imperial War Museum.
2 R. Scott. *Account of Imprisonment 1942-45.* 8181/Box2/2. National Library of Scotland.
3 R. McKay. *John Leonard Wilson, Confessor for the Faith.*
4 Scott. *Ibid.*
5 D. Tett. *A Postal History of POWs & Civilian Internees in East Asia during the 2nd World War,* Volume 1.
6 McKay. *Ibid.*
7 *Borneo Times,* Vol.2 No.12. 1952.

8   McKay. *Ibid.*
9   Internal Communication, Changi Gaol. 29th February 1944. Martine papers.
10 E.C. Hannay. Papers left to his daughters Kirsty Johns and Patricia Percival.
11 *Ibid.*
12 Letters of J.A.Grant. Grant Family papers.

CHAPTER SEVENTEEN
1   Letter to Mrs F.A. Macquisten. 1943.
2   Papers of J.S. Wink. Rhodes House Library, Oxford.
3   R.H.W. Reece. *The Name of Brooke.*
4   Wink. *Ibid.*
5   Reece. *Ibid.*
6   R.H.W.Reece. *Masa Jepun.*

CHAPTER EIGHTEEN
1   R.H. Oakley. *Changi Jail.* Imperial War Museum, London
2   E.C. Hannay. Papers left to his daughters Kirsty Johns and Patricia Percival.
3   *The Double Tenth Investigation.* Imperial War Museum.
4   Letters of J.A.Grant. Grant Family papers.
5   Hannay. *Ibid.*
6   Grant. *Ibid.*
7   D. Thatcher and R. Cross. *Pai Naa – The Story of Nona Baker MBE.*
8   Robinson Family papers.

CHAPTER NINETEEN
1   H. Longhurst. *The Borneo Story.*
2   F.E. Mostyn. *Report on the Keningau Incident.* Rhodes House Library, Oxford.
3   T.C. Martine. Review of *The Name of Brooke. Scottish Field,* 1982.
4   N. Ponnudurai. Letter to Sir Adam Ritchie, 1945. Borneo Company Archives, Guildhall Museum.
5   Longhurst. *Ibid.*
6   Ong Kwan Hin. *The Vanguard,* 29th August 1972.
7   W. McKerracher. Document 64. Rhodes House Library.

8   In his diary, Tom Harrison, war time guerilla and post-war curator of the Sarawak Museum, describes Long Nawang as a "lost world."

9   In a review of R.H.W. Reece's book *The Name of Brooke* for *Scottish Field* magazine in 1982, Charles regrets that that the author made no mention of the Long Nawang massacre. Sadly he did not live to read Reece's fascinating sequel, *Masa Jepun – Sarawak under the Japanese 1941-1945,* published in 1995. Reece's principle source of information on the massacre is Semut III officer Lieut. F.R. Oldham's report made at Long Nawang in 1945 for the Australian army authorities. A copy is in the National Archives, Washington, RG38 Record of the Chief of Naval Intelligence, Monograph Files, Box 13.

10 R. Payne. *The White Rajahs of Sarawak.*

11 Sir C. Vyner Brooke, Rajah of Sarawak. Proclamation to the People of Sarawak, February 1946.

12 Sir C. Vyner Brooke. Letter to *The Times,* 1946.

13 Wee Kheng Chiang in conversation with Harold Smythe.

14 S. Brooke. *Queen of the Headhunters.*

15 *Ibid.*

16 R.H.W. Reece. *The Name of Brooke.*

17 Payne. *Ibid.*

CHAPTER TWENTY

1   Grant Family papers.

2   Wilkinson papers.

3   R.H.W. Reece. *Masa Jepun.*

4   H. Longhurst. *Borneo Story.*

5   R.H.W. Reece. *The Name of Brooke.*

CHAPTER TWENTY-ONE

1   J. M. Heimann. *The Most Offending Soul Alive.*

2   *Council Negri Centenary 1867-1967.* Borneo Literature Bureau.

3   *Borneo Times,* Vol. 2 No.12. May 1952.

4   Borneo Company Archives. Guildhall Museum.

5   *The Scotsman,* December 1949.

6   R.H.W. Reece. *The Name of Brooke.*

7   Ong Boon Lim. *Ong Tiang Swee of Sarawak.*

Bibliography

Allen, Charles. *Tales From The South China Seas – Images of the British In South East Asia In the Twentieth Century*. André Deutsch Ltd/ BBC. 1983.

Archer, Alex L. *The Way It Was*. United Selangor Press Sdn, Bhd. 1984.

Attiwill, Ken. *Fortress – The Story of the Siege and Fall of Singapore*. Doubleday & Co. 1959.

Attiwill, Ken. *The Rising Sunset*. Robert Hale. 1957.

Augustine, Andreas. *The Singapore Treasury – Secrets of the Garden City*. 1988.

Barber, Noel. *Sinister Twilight – The Fall of Singapore*. Cassell. 1968.

Baring Gould, S., and Bampfylde, C.A. *A History of Sarawak under its Two White Rajahs 1839-1908*. Henry Sotheran & Co. 1909.

Barr, Pat. *Taming the Jungle*. Secker & Warburg. 1977.

Braddon, Russell. *The Naked Island*. Bodley Head 1952/ Michael Joseph 1981.

Brooke, Ranee Margaret. *Good Morning and Goodnight*. Constable. 1934.

Brooke, Sylvia. *Queen of the Headhunters – The autobiography of Sylvia Brooke, wife of the last White Rajah of Sarawak*. Sidgwick & Jackson. 1970.

Caffray, Kate. *Out in the Midday Sun – Singapore 1941-1945*. André Deutsch. 1974.

Cooper, Duff. *Old Men Forget*. Rupert Hart-Davis. 1953.

Crisswell, Colin C. *Rajah Charles Brooke – Monarch of all He Surveyed*. Oxford University Press. 1978.

Crisswell, Colin C. *End of the Brooke Raj in Sarawak*. Kiscadale Publications. 1993.

Cunyngham-Brown, Sjovald. *The Traders*. Newman Neame. 1971.
Farrell, J.G. *The Singapore Grip*. Book Club Associates by arrangement with Weidfenfeld & Nicholson. 1978.

Foo, Vincent H.K. and Chai Foh Chin. *The Story of The Sarawak Steamship Company*. The Sarawak Steamship Company Berhad. 2001.

Gilmour, Andrew. *An Eastern Cadet's Anecdotage*. National Press. 1974.

Gordon, Captain Oliver L. *Fight it Out*. William Kimber. 1957.

Hanson, Eric. *Stranger in the Forest – On foot across Borneo*. Houghton Mifflin. 1988.

Hicklin, R. Hugh. *Lieutenant Okino*. Hutchinson 1968; republished as *Crimson Sun Over Borneo*. 1997.

Holman, Dennis. *The Green Torture*. Robert Hale. 1962.

Hoyt, Edwin P. *Japan's War – The Great Pacific Conflict*. Hutchinson. 1986.

Kathigasu, Sybil. *No Dram of Mercy*. Neville Spearman Ltd 1956. Harborough Publishing/Ace Books. 1957.

Kennedy, Joseph. *British Civilians and the Japanese War*. Macmillan. 1987.

Kitching, Thomas. *Life and Death in Changi – The War and Internment Diary of Thomas Kitching (1942-1944)*. Landmark Books. 2002.

Leasor, James. *Singapore: The Battle That Changed the World*. Hodder & Stoughton. 1968.

Lee, Rebecca, and Augustine, Andreas. *The Penang Treasury*. 1987.

Lee Kwan Yew. *The Singapore Story. Memoirs of Lee Kwan Yew*. Prentice Hall. 1998.

Lee Kwan Yew. *From Third World to First. The Singapore Story 1965-2000. Memoirs of Lee Kwan Yew*. Singapore Press Holdings / Times Editions. 2000.

Lomax, Eric. *The Railway Man*. Vintage. 1996.

Longhurst, Henry. *The Borneo Story – The First 100 Years of the Borneo Company*. Newman Neame. 1956.

MacDonald, Rt Hon Malcolm. *Borneo People*. Alfred Knopf. 1956.

McKay, Ron. *John Leonard Wilson, Confessor for the Faith*. Hodder & Stoughton. 1973.

McKie, R.C.H. *This Was Singapore*. Robert Hale. 1942.

McCormack, Charles. *You'll Die in Singapore*. Robert Hale. 1954.

McCrae, Alister, and Prentice, Alan. *Irrawaddy Flotilla*. James Paxton. 1978.

McGowran, OBE, Tom. *Beyond the Bamboo Screen. Scottish Prisoners of War Under The Japanese*. Cualann Press. 1999.

Montgomery, Brian. *Shenton of Singapore – Governor and Prisoner of War*. Leo Cooper in association with Secker & Warburg. 1984.

Morrison, Alastair. *Fair Land Sarawak – Some recollections of an Expatriate Official*. Studies of South East Asia. 1993.

Morrison, Ian. *Malayan Postscript*. Angus & Robertson. 1943.

Newton Keith, Agnes. *Three Came Home*. Michael Joseph. 1948.

O'Hanlon, Redmond. *Into the Heart of Borneo*. Random House. 1985.

Ooi Keat Gin. *Japanese Empire in the Tropics* (Two Volumes) *Selected Documents and Reports of the Japanese Period in Sarawak, Northwest Borneo, 1941-1945*. Edited and Introduced by Ooi Keat Gin. Ohio University Centre for International Studies. 1998.

Ong Boon Lim. *Ong Tiang Swee of Sarawak*. Malaysian Historical Society. 1990.

Owen, Frank. *The Fall of Singapore*. Michael Joseph. 1960.

Payne, Robert. *The White Rajahs of Sarawak*. Funk & Wagnall's Company, New York. 1960.

Peet, George L. *Rickshaw Reporter*. Eastern Universities Press. 1985.

Percival, CB, DSO, OBE, MC, GOC Malaya 1941-42, Lt.-General A.E. *The War in Malaya*. Eyre & Spottiswoode. 1949.

Potter, John Dean. *A Soldier Must Hang: The Biography of an Oriental General*. Frederick Muller. 1963.

Reece, R.H.W. *Mesa Jepun*. Sarawak Literary Society. 1998.

Reece, R.H.W. *The Name of Brooke – The End of White Rajah Rule in Sarawak*. Oxford University Press. 1983.

Reece, R.H.W. *The White Rajahs of Sarawak – a Borneo Dynasty*. The Roundhouse Group. 2004.

Runciman, Steven. *The White Rajahs*. Cambridge University Press. 1960.

Rutter, Owen. *Triumphant Pilgrimage – An English Muslim's Journey from Sarawak to Mecca*. George G. Harrap & Co. 1937.

Shennan, Margaret. *Out in the Midday Sun*. John Murray. 2000.

Simson, Brigadier Ivan. *Too Little, Too Late*. Leo Cooper. 1970.

Spencer Chapman, F. *The Jungle Is Neutral*. Chatto & Windus. 1949.

Strabolgi, RN, Lord. *Singapore and After – A Study of the Pacific Campaign*. Hutchinson & Co. 1942.

Tett, David. *A Postal History of the Prisoners of War and Civilian Internees in South East Asia During the Second World War*. Volume 1 – *Singapore and Malaya 1942-1945*. BFA Publishing. 2002.

Thatcher, Doris, and Cross, Robert. *Pai Naa – The Story of Nona Baker MBE*. Constable. 1959.

Tsuji, Colonel Masanobu. *Singapore – the Japanese Version*. Constable. 1960.

Warner, Lavinia, and Sandilands, John. *Women Beyond The Wire – A Story of Prisoners of the Japanese 1942-45*. Michael Joseph. 1982.

Index

Page number followed by 'n' refers to the footnote

Cover Design: The Digital Canvas Company

Layout: S. Fairgrieve

Font: Adobe Garamond (11pt)

Copies of this book can be ordered via the Internet:

www.librario.com

or from:

Librario Publishing Ltd
Brough House
Milton Brodie
Kinloss
Moray IV36 2UA
Tel / Fax No 01343 850 617